ART PLUNDER

The fate of works of art
in war, revolution and peace

WILHELM TREUE

METHUEN & CO LTD
36 Essex Street, London WC2

First published as 'Kunstraub' by
Droste Verlag, Düsseldorf
© *1957, Droste Verlag und Druckerei GmbH, Düsseldorf*
This translation © *1960, Methuen & Co Ltd*
Printed in Great Britain by
The Shenval Press, London, Hertford and Harlow
Catalogue number 6187/u

Contents

CONTENTS

Illustrations

Preface

'In principle there is nothing shocking about the migrations of works of art. Do we not frequently see great works, or even whole collections of great value, passing by legacy or purchase from one country to another? What is hateful about it is the intentional humiliation which often accompanies these migrations when they are the result of plunder. Booty invokes Nemesis; it cries out for revenge and insists on reparation too. And such depredations are more than an injury to one generation, a generation that soon passes and soon forgets; they are rather a wound afflicting the historical consciousness of a whole nation. The conquered receives a wound that not only smarts but festers, changing defeat into perpetual resentment. Are the civilized nations irredeemably committed to this?'

This is how a French scholar saw the problem more than sixty years ago, and this is the problem with which the following pages are concerned, or with one side of it at least. The other side is the endeavour of nations, of governments and of individuals to safeguard their artistic possessions from the victorious enemy— among the sand dunes, in the mountains or in some remote corner of the country which may possibly be safe from attack and occupation, or perhaps even abroad, where a refuge may for a time be found from the hazards of war.

Ideas about art plunder and the flight of art in face of danger have altered greatly in the course of centuries, as have ideas about the rights of war. There is no straight path leading from the barbarous to the humane, from lawlessness to law, from the senseless to the sensible; there have been times when art has been respected, protected and prized by the conqueror, and other

9

times when it has been regarded as booty and carried off in triumph as a symbol of the total and not merely the military overthrow of the enemy. The road from the Sack of Rome, with its blind frenzy of destruction or of looting by the needy mercenaries, to the generals of Louis XIV and on to Napoleon and to Hitler is long. One thing it shows is that at all times people have had very various motives behind their attitude to art, and another, that Napoleon, at least, honestly believed that the centre of civilization had shifted to Paris, and that Paris must now be, and continue to be, the home of all the treasures of art which Rome had brought into being or accumulated for thousands of years.

The plundering of works of art and their migration form a part of art history and of the history of our Western culture. Political events and their protagonists are familiar to us, but how little we know of what goes on beneath this political and military layer, at the level of art and culture! That is the theme of this work. What has been the attitude of men to art in war and revolution? Have they taken their works of art with them on their flight or abandoned them? Have they looked on art as something of importance in their lives which they could not do without? And how have the conquerors, the new masters, dealt with works of art? Have public and private possessions of art been respected or treated as loot? Have pictures and sculptures, the monuments of past glories, indissolubly bound up with the traditions of a conquered country, been deliberately plundered in order to exploit victory to the utmost and to turn military defeat into spiritual annihilation?

These are the questions that will confront us again and again, questions that probe the psychology of peoples and rulers and the answers to which touch upon those important and frequently incomprehensible phenomena known as 'hereditary enmities' and 'irreconcilable antagonisms'. These are not always or even principally concerned with loss of lives and territory; very often they turn on the symbolic significance of art. The quadriga of the Brandenburg Gate in Berlin is just as good an example of this as the Sistine Madonna, the Gioconda, the Horses of St Mark's, or the Man in a Gold Helmet in Berlin, to mention only a few. All these works of art in the course of centuries have become not only objects of value in terms of money, but an inseparable part of the spiritual life of whole nations for generations.

1

Art Plunder

in Antiquity and the Middle Ages

The Romans never doubted that the rights of conquest included the right to plunder and carry off art treasures wholesale. Indeed, it was they apparently who originated the idea of the triumph as the rape of the works of art in which a nation gloried, and their display in the triumphal procession upon the conqueror's return to Rome; and Napoleon followed their example. Thus in course of time Rome became a vast museum where the masterpieces of Greece, Egypt and Asia Minor were crowded together.

It began, within the framework of Roman expansion, with the conquest of Veii; then came Praeneste (380 BC), Volsinii (264 BC) with a booty of 2,000 statues, followed by the wholesale pillaging of Syracuse (212 BC), of Tarentum (209 BC) and on to the spoliations of L. Mummius (Corinth 146 BC) and Caius Verres in Asia and Sicily in the first century and to the similar depredations of the Emperors and their cousins and provincial officials, leading up to a colossal accumulation of works of art of all sorts and a corresponding covetousness and collector's passion on the part of the cultured Roman.

According to tradition, the so-called Corinthian bronze, a mixture of ordinary bronze with gold and silver, was discovered by pure chance when Mummius burnt the city of Corinth and caused the loss of untold works of art in the conflagration. For the next two centuries Corinthian bronze was considered the most precious, the choicest and costliest possession the Roman

13

connoisseur and collector could hope to acquire. To own a piece of Corinthian bronze was to be a patrician among art-lovers. Seneca remarks on the fabulous prices they fetched, 'owing to the folly of a small number of persons', and Pliny the Younger wrote as follows to his friend Annius Severus about a bronze he had just acquired:

'I have lately purchased with a legacy that was left me a small statue of Corinthian bronze. It is small indeed, but elegant and lifelike, as far as I can form any judgment, which most certainly in matters of this sort, as perhaps in all others, is extremely defective. However, I do see the beauties of this figure: for, as it is naked, the faults, if there be any, as well as the perfections, are the more observable. It represents an old man, in an erect attitude. The bones, muscles, veins, and the very wrinkles, give the impression of breathing life. The hair is thin and failing, the forehead broad, the face shrivelled, the throat lank, the arms loose and hanging, the breast shrunken, and the belly fallen in, as the whole turn and air of the figure behind is also expressive of old age. It appears to be a true antique, judging from the colour of the metal. In short, it is such a masterpiece as would strike the eye of a connoisseur, and which cannot fail to charm an ordinary observer: and this induced me, who am an absolute novice in this art, to buy it. But I did so, not with any intention of placing it in my own house (for I have nothing of the kind there), but with a design of fixing it in some conspicuous place in my native province; I should like it best in the temple of Jupiter, for it is a gift well worthy of a temple, well worthy of a god.'

Dealers in art, books and antiquities had their own quarter of Rome, near the Villa Publica, and here too works of art were restored, also fabricated, and then disposed of at greatly enhanced prices after an adroit manipulation of the market. There were dealers whose exclusive business it was to import the most select and costly objects from conquered territory for the richest collectors, and others who dealt in 'antiques' to suit the taste of the public at large. Petronius in the *Satyricon* gives a specimen in Trimalchio of the *nouveau riche* connoisseur and art-lover, endeavouring to give himself the right air with the help of art, an easily recognized type of the pretentious parvenu. He once boasted at a large and luxurious dinner-party that he was the only person who possessed genuine bronzes from Corinth. 'You will ask perhaps how that can be. The reason is simple: I buy them from a dealer whose name is Corinthus.'

Since the days of the Republic large numbers of libraries had been transported to Rome from Greece as single units; Lucius Aemilius commandeered the library of Perseus, King of Macedon, and left it to his sons, one of whom was the younger Scipio, the conqueror of Carthage.

Lucullus took possession of an uncommonly large and valuable library in Asia Minor, brought it to Rome and put it at the disposal of the learned. Sulla, who occupied Athens in 86 BC, removed Aristotle's library to his own house in Rome and put two scholars in charge of it, one of whom was Andronicus of Rhodes, student and commentator of the works of Aristotle, and the other Tiro, who invented a short-hand, the *notae Tironianae*, and was employed by Cicero as stenographer at meetings of the Senate and as private secretary. The possession of a library, looted from Greece, Egypt or Asia Minor, was the aim of every rich man at that time who wished to have the reputation of cultivated tastes. Cicero's letters are full of allusions to this craze; and he himself had a library installed in each of the eighteen villas he owned in different parts of Italy. Yet his extravagance does not seem to have been at all exceptional, but typical, rather, of a whole class of society in which genuine enthusiasm set the example to the pretentions of the ignorant.

The Roman passion for the 'antique' was by no means confined to libraries and Corinthian bronzes. Francis H. Taylor writes: 'Young Romans who toured Greece, Africa and Asia Minor were inspired by exactly the same spirit as inspired young English aristocrats when they made the Grand Tour through Italy in the eighteenth century.' In both cases the aim in the first place

15

was literary: they wanted to enrich their classical education by a first-hand acquaintance with the scenes of the classical past. The acquisition of works of art was not so much a proof of their connoisseurship as the sign of having satisfied a newly awakened curiosity; it was also thought to be the necessary though perfunctory preparation for entering social and political life.

The 'old', the 'antique', meant far more to the ruling class of Rome than did contemporary works of art, of whatever excellence. Pliny has recorded that the collections of his day consisted almost entirely of old paintings and Quintilian goes so far as to hold up this enthusiasm for the 'primitives' to ridicule. In the reign of Hadrian there was a passion for pictures and statues of the period of the Diadochi.

Dealers could not very well meet demands of this kind. What were they to do when earthenware lamps by Epictetus, ornaments from Germany and silver vessels from the palace of Philip of Macedon were all in demand; when Caracalla desired to complete his collection of weapons which had belonged to Alexander the Great; and when the demand for works by Lysippus shot up to new heights as soon as it was known that Novius Vindex had been able to acquire one of his statues? They did their best by despatching their agents, commissioning soldiers to loot, and even salvaging wrecks at great cost in order to recover works of art.

At all periods war booty was the best source of supply. In this respect Sulla, the first of the great connoisseurs and collectors, was for a long time the model. In his campaigns he spared neither public nor private property if his covetousness was aroused, and among the treasures he acquired in this way were a Hercules by Lysippus, which had once belonged to Alexander the Great before passing into the hands of Hannibal, and also a small golden Apollo, which he stole from Delphi and took with him on all his campaigns, offering up prayers to it before every battle and covering it with kisses. Naturally his lieutenants, such as Verres and Murena, followed his example. His son-in-law and heir made an extensive collection of gems, principally by the same means, and put them on view at Tusculum. This was the first great

16

exhibition of the kind in Rome and of such importance that only the six collections of cameos and jewels presented by Caesar to the temple of Venus could rival it. Caesar, too, had brought furniture from Sicily and had also acquired paintings from Pausias, which came originally from Sicyon, and gold-embroidered tapestries from Messina. The gardens of Lucullus on the slopes of the Pincian, described for us by Plutarch and occupied now by the Villa Medici, were adorned with statues and other works of art from the ancient centres of civilization, and also with exotic plants and a zoological garden collected and stocked from the remotest parts of the Roman Empire.

A man like Verres, the proconsul, got a notable collection together by purchase and loot. The *cursus honorum* was open to him as the son of a patrician and he finally became governor of Sicily. Nothing in that country which had or might be thought to have artistic value escaped him; he was unscrupulous in his rapacity and also he had the keen eye of a connoisseur from which nothing could be hidden. Cicero in his famous oration *Contra Verrem* demanded reparation for his thefts, in Sicily alone amounting to millions of pounds in modern currency, and besides attacking his character and reputation gave a lively description of his mansion and its furnishings. Its gold and ivory gates came from the temple of Minerva at Syracuse; the entrance hall was hung with hangings commandeered from palaces in Malta and Syracuse; the costly furniture had belonged to a famous courtesan, and the noblest ladies of Sicily had worked for three years on the curtains and cushion covers for the chairs and couches.

Cicero's charges were not confined to Verres; rather, he held him up as an example of the systematic robbery which was stripping the whole Empire for the benefit of the ruling few in Rome.

'Year by year,' he thundered while Tiro took his words down in his shorthand, 'we continue to suffer it, and we are silent when we see that all the money of all the nations has come into the hands of a few men; which we seem to tolerate and permit

B   17

with the more equanimity, because none of these robbers conceals what he is doing; none of them takes the least trouble to keep his covetousness in any obscurity. In our most beautiful and highly decorated city what statue, or what painting, is there which has not been taken and brought away from conquered enemies? But the villas of those men are adorned and filled with numerous and most beautiful spoils of our most faithful allies. Where do you think is the wealth of foreign nations, which they are all now deprived of, when you see Athens, Pergamos, Cyzicus, Miletus, Chios, Samos, all Asia in short, and Achaia, and Greece, and Sicily, now all contained in a few villas? But all these things, as I was saying, your allies abandon and are indifferent to now. They took care by their own services and loyalty not to be deprived of their property by the public authority of the Roman people; though they were unable to resist the covetousness of a few individuals, yet they could in some degree satiate it; but now not only is all their power of resisting taken away, but also all their means of supplying such demands.'

Judging from this, the whole known world was being plundered without mercy and Rome alone being put in possession of everything of beauty or value.

The Romans' practice of removing the works of art from a conquered city to their own capital survived even the rise of Christianity. From one end of the Empire to the other, the victors took whatever excited their cupidity: bronze doors, statues, columns, whatever was movable. And the chief or at least exclusive reason was not the value of the objects in money but as tokens of triumph, as in later times the defeated warrior surrendered his sword, or the Red Indian was scalped by his enemy. No wonder the barbarians turned this right of the conqueror against Rome herself: Alaric plundered the temples, and Genseric, himself a passionate collector and a far from bloodthirsty despoiler, had a ship loaded with bronze statues, so being the first, but by no means the last, to entrust his loot to the sea

18

and to forfeit it to the incalculable caprices of the Mediterranean. His successors in this misfortune make a long list, extending into the nineteenth century.

Athens at first fared better than Rome, but soon the Eastern Emperor took what the barbarians had left either from awe, or from lack of artistic appreciation or of means of transport. The masterpieces of Praxiteles, Myron and Lysippus were removed to Constantinople, and the ancient basilica of St Sophia became the richest museum in the world; for a time it contained four hundred and twenty statues by the greatest masters of Greek art.

An Austrian historian writing in 1850 remarks that in the middle of the third century the Romans tried again and again to buy off the hordes of Visigoths with large sums of money.

'But far from inducing the barbarians to respect the frontiers of the empire, these bribes served only as an incentive to dig deeper into the accumulated wealth of Rome. This led to invasions on a big scale, and we have to imagine those who took part in them armed not only with weapons but with sacks. When filled they were loaded on to trains formed of thousands of wagons. For this reason medieval epics, recalling these trains of booty-laden wagons, speak of treasure loaded on wagons, whereas in the art and literature of classical antiquity it is represented as carried off by hand. Thus these invading hordes roamed unresisted through the provinces of the Empire, commandeering gold and silver and precious stones wherever they went.'

Alaric, who descended on Rome in the years 408, 409 and 410, told the envoys of the Roman People that he would not raise the siege until every single object of gold or silver and all the household utensils of the city had been handed over. He demanded in addition 5,000 pounds of gold and 30,000 pounds of silver, and to produce these huge amounts the Romans had to melt down all the ornaments belonging to the statues of the gods. In this way the Romans and the world lost for ever objects of priceless artistic value.

All the treasures of which the hosts of Alaric had not stripped the Eternal City in 410 fell into the hands of the Vandals not quite fifty years later, in 455: the golden chairs, the jewellery, the utensils, cups and countless other works of art. And they actually succeeded in transporting all of it, with the exception of one ship laden with statues, to Africa, one of the greatest and most important art-removals ever undertaken. But as these works of art excited no admiration and inspired no imitators in their new home, the whole operation was really meaningless. It was a very different matter in later centuries. Consider, to name one example, the stimulus provided in England by the sale and dispersal at auction in 1793 and 1798 of the collection of the Duke of Orleans.

When Genseric, King of the Vandals, set sail from Carthage in 455 with a large fleet and advanced on Rome from Portus, the port of Rome, the whole city was thrown into the utmost confusion. Many of the nobles and others of the population fled in the hope of saving their lives if nothing else. When Maximus, who was governor of Rome, tried to do the same instead of staying to carry out his duty, he was killed by a Burgundian of the Praetorian Guard named Orsus, who threw a stone at him, whereupon the betrayed and leaderless mob dragged his corpse through the city and threw it limb by limb into the Tiber. This was on May 31, 455.

It was not until three days later that Genseric and his host entered Rome, welcomed by Pope Leo I, who had gone as far as the Porta Portuensis to meet him. He was credited with having induced the king to refrain from arson and murder and to be content with plundering the city. It is said that in return he had to present with his own hand all the gold and silver vessels of his church, a not very likely proceeding in view of the time it would have taken.

In any case, the Vandals behaved in Rome as they did in other places, and as conquerors did in those times. Like the Goths under Alaric, they preferred to plunder rather than to see their plunder go up in flames, and the deliberate destruction of houses and monuments would have cost them hard work without any reward. No doubt, too, it would have gone against the feeling of veneration and awe which Rome inspired in the German chiefs of those days and their followers. The city itself was the longed-for goal and at the same time possessed the richest spoil they could lay hands on.

The Vandals and their allies remained for two weeks within the walls of Rome, 'time enough to plunder whatever the Goths had left behind or what had since been replaced'. The well-known and also very reliable account of Procopius, an eye-witness, gives details of the plunder. In the first place, there was the loot from the Emperor's palace, the whole contents of which were transported to Carthage to adorn Genseric's palace there, including, of course, the insignia of the imperial dignity, which added more than all the rest to the prestige of conquest. The temple of Jupiter on the Capitol was stripped not only of its valuables but of half its gilded roof, and from the Capitol too must have come the statues, a shipload of which were sunk at sea and irretrievably lost. Gregorovius, the German historian of Rome, wrote:

'It is possible that on board the same vessel that sailed to Carthage laden with the spoils of Rome, the Lychnuchus of Solomon and the statue of the Capitoline Zeus, symbols of the oldest religions of East and West, may have rested side by side. Procopius expressly mentions one vessel freighted with statues which alone perished at sea, while all the others reached the harbour of Carthage in safety.'

For a notable part of the booty was the vessels of the Temple of Solomon, which Titus had brought to Rome. Gregorovius continues:

'The traveller of the present day still gazes with interest on the remains of the sculpture on the Arch of Titus, and there beholds imperfect representations of the sacred vessels of the Temple of Solomon—the seven-branched Lychnuchus, the Holy Table of Sacrifice, with the two censers, two long trum-

21

pets and an ark. He knows that here are represented the sacred spoils, as described by Flavius Josephus, brought by Titus from Jerusalem to Rome. Vespasian, dividing these spoils, caused the Veil of the Temple and the books of Jewish law to be conveyed to the Palace of the Caesars, the Golden Candlestick and the costly vessels to be deposited in his Temple of Peace. And although this latter building was destroyed by fire under Commodus, time was found to save the Jewish treasures, which, removed to some spot unknown to us, remained hidden for centuries. Among the treasures which Alaric accumulated at Carcassonne were some of the beautiful vessels from Solomon's Temple, which had fallen into his hands in Rome. Other Jewish relics he must, however, have left unheeded, since, together with the spoils acquired from the churches, some of the sacred vessels of the Temple, brought by Titus from Jerusalem, were shipped by Genseric to Carthage.

'The singular errant fate of the ancient treasures of the Temple does not end here. Eighty years later Belisarius discovered them in Carthage, and with the spoils of the Vandals brought them amid solemn rejoicing to Constantinople, where the sight of their sacred vessels stirred the Byzantine Jews with such profound emotion that, sending a deputation to the Emperor, they demanded the restoration of their property. Procopius at least speaks of an enthusiastic Jew in the service of Justinian, who appeared before the Emperor and warned him that he must not retain the mystic vessels in the palace of Byzantium, since nowhere would they find rest save in the place originally prepared for them by Solomon. Their removal from the ancient Temple is said to have been Genseric's motive in conquering the fortress of the Caesars, and again to have impelled the Roman army to capture the palace of the Vandals, where the relics lay concealed. Procopius further relates that, seized by superstitious fears, Justinian commanded the vessels of the Jewish Temple to be conveyed to one of the Christian churches of Jerusalem. Whether this anecdote of a contemporary of Belisarius be wholly or partially true, it

22

proves that, nearly five hundred years after the time of Titus, the recollection of these sacred vessels still survived, and we may suppose that throughout the course of centuries the eyes of the children of Israel had continuously watched over them from one generation to another.

'Thenceforward, all trace of them disappeared. The relics of Solomon's Temple, did they ever reach Jerusalem, may have been lost in the East, a prey to marauding Arabs. At the same period in the time of Justinian, the Armenian bishop Zacharias, who compiled a register of the public works in Rome, asserts that five and twenty bronze statues representing Abraham, Sarah, and the kings of the House of David, which Vespasian had brought with the gates and other monuments of Jerusalem to Rome, were still preserved in the city, and Roman tradition in the Middle Ages boasted that the Lateran basilica still preserved the Sacred Ark of the Covenant, the Tables of the Law, the Golden Candlesticks, the Tabernacle and even the priestly vestments of Aaron.'

Contemporary accounts make no mention, on the other hand, of the plundering of churches, although this would be the first thing to be described and lamented by a man like Procopius and by other chroniclers. The churches, then, must have got off very lightly in the general spoliation, if they did not escape altogether. The lives of the inhabitants were spared with few exceptions. But the booty, all told, that fell to the lot of Genseric and his followers, was immense. It included several thousand armourers and craftsmen, and their systematic removal and resettlement is the first instance we encounter of these compulsory migrations. Eudokia, the widow of the Emperor, her two daughters, some senators and other notabilities were only held for ransom, or as political pawns to give Genseric the advantage in any further dealings with Romans of the Western or Eastern Empire.

Looting by the barbarians, helped and even rivalled by the inhabitants themselves, who showed the way to the cabinets and stores of the rich, had a very important secondary effect in the burying of treasure owing to the constant fear of robbery. 'In those times,' we read in a very vivid account, 'the Roman Empire was seamed with trenches and pitted with holes, and every nook and corner was thronged with objects of value seeking cover.' Genseric regarded all such measures as prejudicial to his rights of plunder and punished them as a crime. Here too an example was set which has persisted into modern times: all down the centuries people have buried their treasure, and they or their dependants have been subjected to all kinds of compulsion and torture to induce them to confess or betray the secret. But often the secret was lost for ever for one reason or another, which explains how it was that bombs in the Second World War sometimes uncovered gold and silverware of the Middle Ages or the Thirty Years War. Even today the labourer's spade or the grab of the excavator occasionally brings to light such testimonies to days gone by, a jar of coins, or a gold cup, or piece of jewellery.

The wish to store valuables in a safe place was not the only motive for these burials; sometimes it was to save objects of religious veneration from desecration by the barbarians. This was clearly the case with the nine marble statues of members of the family of Augustus found at Cervetri in an ancient Etruscan tomb. There are earlier and later examples to suggest that women were often concerned; thus Laban's daughter, Rachel, hid her father's idols, and Theodora, the wife of Theophilus, the icono-clast Emperor, kept secret possession of her holy images. But pious and devotional practices of this kind did not by any means debar them from hiding their jewellery in the same hiding-place. It is even said that monks, who are supposed, as everyone knows, to forgo all personal possessions, have not always been proof against the attraction of precious metals and objects of artistic value; they are said to have buried coins and vessels of gold and silver in the obscurity of their cells and to have found a good use for their hoards when the growth of simony produced a brisk trade in spiritual offices. Legends of buried treasure in dilapidated monastic buildings are explained by these circumstances.

Although many of these burials of treasure took place long

after the fall of the Roman Empire, a large part of the hoards still derived from the days of antiquity. 'For those nations,' we read, 'whose arms had laid the Empire low were not only predatory but acquisitive. They kept and valued from generation to generation the precious things they had owed in the first place to the fortunes of war or had received as gifts.' When King Gelimer fell into the hands of Belisarius in 534, he had to surrender the imperial ornaments which had been robbed by the Vandals ninety-seven years before and were still intact. The golden dish weighing 500 pounds, given by Aetius to Thorismond, King of the West Goths, in 453, was still in the possession of his descendants in 630. In 796 the treasure of the Avar kings, accumulated in the course of centuries, became the booty of Duke Henry of Friuli. Charlemagne, who died in 814, bequeathed three precious paintings of the days of antiquity, and at about the same time a judge was offered a fine antique goblet of equally remote date.

These are only a few of the many examples which prove that, although the works of art of antiquity were pillaged, carried off, and finally destroyed, they were also highly prized and handed down through the centuries by gift or legacy. Weapons were particularly prized, as were gold and silver coins and utensils of precious metal; gems too, including all precious stones, whether cut or uncut. Coins were the treasure of the lower orders, gems the luxury of the more opulent.

The riches of antiquity in precious objects, large and small, were so vast that they are still reflected in the literature of subsequent centuries, shown in paintings, and vouched for by the contents of wills. Even in the nineteenth century large or small caches of ancient treasure were discovered during the construction of roads and railways, the building or demolition of fortifications and the growth of towns.

But such windfalls were frequent in earlier centuries too; Valerius, who was prefect of Thrace under the Emperor Constantius, hearing of a recent find of treasure, unearthed three more silver statues from the same site.

A herdsman once noticed that one of his cows had a wound, and following the track of blood, came on a sword, which he gave to Attila; it was known as the sword of Mars, and Attila henceforth believed that he was invincible.

The Seven Sleepers, who were supposed to have fallen asleep in the reign of Decius, persecutor of the Christians, and to have woken up under Theodosius, on waking sent one of the party for a loaf of bread. When he offered the baker a coin of the time of Decius, it was assumed that he had come on 'buried treasure of the days of the old Emperor'.

Chance has brought buried treasure to light, or given the clue to its discovery on innumerable occasions and in all sorts of ways. Saint Benedict, who died in 543, came upon an ancient pagan image when digging a well, and of course had it destroyed by fire immediately. Many an ancient marble sarcophagus was discovered when a grave was being dug, and the plough has uncovered many statues and works of art, mostly in the neighbourhood of ancient roads. When kings and emperors built new churches, as Ludwig the Pious did in Frankfurt and Ratisbon, their workmen were often rewarded by the discovery of buried gold in the graves they disturbed while demolishing ancient walls and buildings.

Often a clue was concealed in mysterious inscriptions; in the eleventh century, for example, a statue was discovered in Apulia beneath some ruins and round its head, inscribed on a metal fillet, were the words: 'On the first of June I shall have a golden head.' An Arab, who had been taken prisoner by Robert Guiscard, hit upon the astronomic interpretation, and on the morning of the given date he dug where the shadow of the statue's head fell at sunrise. With the treasure he found there, he was able to buy his freedom.

Finds of treasure were so frequent during the whole of the Middle Ages that the Emperor Nicephorus, to mention one instance, took it for granted that any sudden prosperity must be due to that cause; but the great period seems to have begun with the second half of the eleventh century. This was the time of the growth of towns, when the Church, too, was building great numbers of churches and monasteries. As more and more foundations were excavated, more and more treasure was discovered, and so the resources for further building were provided; it often seems, in fact, as if ambitious citizens and pious kings had their buildings financed as they went up. In the liturgies of those times there was a special formula for the sanctification of antique vessels, coins and images; for example, there was an *oratio super vasa in loco antiquo reperta.*

From treasure-finding it was a short step to treasure-hunting, and the familiarity with plunder was so widespread that the thirst for gold infected all classes. Kings dreamed of treasure trove and went in search of it on waking. Princes, temporal and spiritual, showed such ardour in this respect that Fathers of the Church expressed the wish that they might be as zealous to lay up treasure in heaven as to find it under the earth. Covetousness even prevailed over the fear of the other world; and resting-places of the dead, respected for centuries, were ransacked and plundered. Nor did the poisonous gases of the more recently sealed tombs hold up the search for gold: the robbers overcame their dread and descended into the vaults. Some called on subterranean and diabolic powers to aid their search; others tried holy water and prayers, or relied on their own unaided cunning. However, that godless man who attempted to rob the tomb of Saint Helius in the dead of night was held fast in the saint's bony grip until daylight, as a warning to all.

On the other hand, the *Digest* laid it down that the graves of unbelievers were not to be respected, and to ransack them was held to be an act pleasing to God. Ecclesiastics thought themselves not only allowed, but bound to open and deface ancient graves, and did not hesitate to take possession of any godless treasure found there. Covetousness and fanaticism held hands and went with a zeal hitherto unknown in pursuit of treasure. From the fear of robbery or reprisal, the body of Attila, and the treasures he took with him, were buried by night and the prisoners who dug his grave were killed. In the case of Alaric, the Busento was diverted and the richly adorned corpse of the king was buried in the dry bed of the river, after which it was returned to its old course. The Nibelungenlied tells the same story: Hagen confided the treasure of the Nibelungen to the Rhine for ever.

However, the spiritual and temporal courts punished the desecration of graves in search of treasure from an early date. In the eleventh century, at the very height of the mania for treasure-hunting, the confessor was instructed, according to the manuals of confession, to ask: 'Have you desecrated any grave?' And the first Christian Emperor forbade, under pain of severe penalties, in the stern spirit of ancient Roman law, any injury whatever to graves; later, it is true, especially among non-Roman peoples, the punishment was less severe. The violation of ancient pagan graves was in any case regarded as a venial offence, and finally the law was restricted to national and Christian graves. Theoderic, as treasure-hunter, was no respecter of graves and excused his conduct by saying that the living had more need of gold than the dead.

At the height of the Middle Ages a new motive entered in: when the Emperor Frederick II had tombs opened up near Augusta in Sicily, it was not in belated reproof of pagan unbelief, nor in the hope of finding treasure, but, as Raumer was the first to point out, in the hope of making discoveries of antiquarian interest. The time had come for the historian, the student, the collector for museums and all those who felt that the past should be preserved and its beauties brought to light. Cardinal Orsini, in the time of Frederick's grandfather, Frederic Barbarossa, had made a collection of ancient works of art, and from then onwards the clergy began to seek them out with increasing knowledge and discrimination, and to pride themselves on their collections. Sometimes these ancient finds were adapted for use on altars, and so restored to daily use. This meant as a rule that they lost their original form and suffered various changes which might or might not be to their artistic advantage. But the chief thing was that they were no longer melted down or burned for lime, but preserved and admired, and so served as a precious link with the

28

art and traditions of classical antiquity. At first it was only among the few that there was any awareness of artistic beauty, but it soon spread to larger numbers, and was sometimes stronger than the sense of the correct or appropriate; we find, for example, Jupiter Tonans adorning sacred Christian documents, or the god of the Muses on the binding of the Gospels. The mingling of the old and the new, of pagan and Christian, throve on the interest in art and tradition, and its often overweening effect is to be found in fantastic genealogical trees and deceptive analogies which innocently sacrificed truth to a higher cause. A great reconciliation had come about, in which beauty often triumphed over religious fanaticism; the ancient gods were given shelter by their one-time persecutors, and in return they added a new glory to Christian art, awakening in their redeemers and rescuers a sense of beauty and nobility which, treasured among a few, was ready after a century or two to spread to the whole Western world when Humanism and the Renaissance opened up a new era of artistic consciousness.

2

Charlemagne and the Statue
of Theoderic

But let us pause for one more glance into the Dark Ages. Charlemagne had the reputation of taking a great interest in matters of art. Briggs, in his book *Men of Taste*, in which he rather surprisingly brings Rameses II into the same company as John Ruskin and William Morris, lays great stress on the number of artists and scholars, mostly foreigners, whom Charlemagne collected round him; and he adds that the court of Charlemagne might well, as regards literature and art, be compared 'in significance, though not in talent, with the Italian Renaissance'.

Charlemagne certainly liked to adorn his Frankish kingdom, or his court and the places he preferred to reside in, with works of art from the great days of Rome. He had various works of art brought from Rome and other Italian cities, and for the cathedral at Aix, which was to contain his tomb, he requisitioned marble columns from Rome and Ravenna. The walls of Verdun supplied him with stone—not that there was none to be obtained nearer Aix, but he wished only ancient material to be used. In addition he wished to have a bronze equestrian statue, which was said to represent Theoderic but was of a far earlier date, brought from Ravenna and erected in Aix. It is recorded in two poems that Charlemagne brought an equestrian statue of Theoderic and had it set up in front of the Emperor's palace, but nowhere else is there any mention of this, and, moreover, the two accounts differ from one another. If the story were true, it would be, as

30

Hermann Grimm writes, 'an unprecedented apparition in northern lands, necessitating a voyage by sea and transport by land through Gaul, or else the crossing of the Alps, before it occupied its position in front of the palace opposite the cathedral, whence it subsequently vanished!—In all the many legends which cluster round the name of Charlemagne, there is not a word of this equestrian statue.'

It may be briefly mentioned here that the forty-six antique columns brought for his cathedral from Italy and the sarcophagus in which he intended to be buried were carried off to Paris by the French in 1794. They were re-conquered in 1815 and restored, with the exception of sixteen of the grey and pink coloured granite pillars. *Habent sua fata columnae.*

To his brilliant investigation into these events Grimm added some penetrating observations on the separate development of Western and Eastern art in Rome and Byzantium, and concludes as follows: 'But the year 1204 may be taken as the date when our art rose again. It was in that year that the Latins conquered Byzantium and when ship-loads of art treasures were sent to Europe and distributed throughout France, Italy, and all the countries bordering the Rhine. Venice, Genoa, Pisa and the coastal towns of Campania and Sicily had long been familiar with the Byzantine style, but from the beginning of the thirteenth century, both in Italy and further north, large numbers of new towns arose, new also in their civic independence and the means to cultivate and to satisfy their own artistic tastes. Thus Byzantine art and style spread far and wide—' The great art robbery of 1204 and its artistic importance is the subject of the next chapter.

3

The Looting of Constantinople
by the Crusaders

Even with the First Crusade the commercial element had
inevitably begun to play its part. Transport by land and
sea, board and lodging, all had to be paid for. And then
there was the victorious Crusader's booty to be dealt with: infidels
who had either to be retained as slaves or sold off, and loot of all
kinds from domestic utensils to valuables of gold and silver and
precious stones and priceless works of art. Finally, the return
journey had to be paid for; and this was usually more expensive
than the journey out to the Holy Land. It was obvious that he
would be glad to get rid of much of his loot before embarking
and there were always Levantine or European dealers ready to
relieve him of it at their own prices or to make a double profit by
taking booty in exchange for a passage.

In spite of protests and complaints, each Crusade gave a fresh
impulse to these mercenary dealings. It was well known that the
Venetians led the way in regarding a crusade as they would any
other commercial or military expedition and that they had almost
forgotten its religious motive. This was particularly so with the
Crusade which began in 1202 and reached its climax with the
conquest of Constantinople in November 1204 and an orgy of
mercenary looting which was only stopped by an eclipse of the
sun. But the effects upon art and civilization have not been forgotten to this day.

At the outset the Venetians made their usual extortionate
charge for transport, but in this case they insisted also that the

1. The sacred vessels from the Temple of Solomon portrayed on the Arch of Titus in Rome.

2. The Colleoni statue by Verocchio in Venice.

3. The Golden Horses of St Mark's in Venice.

crusading army should on its way to Constantinople first capture Zara, a town on the east coast of the Adriatic and a trade rival of theirs, in spite of its being Christian and also subject to the King of Hungary, who was himself taking part in the Crusade. The leaders of the Crusade held out against this for a long time, but as Venice had the monopoly of eastward sea transport they finally had to give way. On October 8, sixty galleys and large vessels put out to sea, accompanied by about a hundred transports for the horses and a host of wagons and other vehicles. Venice, as friend and foe had to admit, had fulfilled her pledge to the full in the supply and equipment of this magnificent fleet. The Pope forbade the attack on Zara on pain of excommunication, and some of the Crusaders refused to take part in it. But the Venetians had their way notwithstanding, and Zara was captured on November 24; its walls and houses were demolished and the first of the quarrels over booty broke out in pitched battles which went on for nearly a week before peace could be patched up, though scarcely restored.

Meanwhile, winter had come; the Crusaders could not resume their voyage, nor, if they had, could their victualling have been answered for. The Doge therefore offered them the ruins of Zara as their winter quarters. Again they had to bow to the will of the Venetians, who made a further substantial profit without the cost of providing fresh transport. The voyage was continued early in 1203 by way of Corfu and the coast of Greece to the Dardanelles, which they reached on June 10; a week was spent off Abydos before entering the Sea of Marmara. 'The fleet,' says Villehard-ouin, one of the most important chroniclers of the Crusade, 'covered the narrow straits like a carpet.' On June 23 they were at St Stefano, three miles from Constantinople, in sight of the thousands of towers—a mere handful of men in front of the strongest fortress on earth, 'the Mother of Cities'.

The siege need not detain us; the fighting went on month after month, sometimes flaring up, sometimes dwindling to smaller engagements. On August 22 and 23 a fire broke out, which, fanned by a violent wind, completely destroyed the

C   33

southern part of the town from the Golden Horn to the Sea of Marmara. Part of the hippodrome was burned, whole streets were reduced to ashes and even ships in the harbour caught fire. A revolution broke out soon after. Finally, on April 8, 1204, preparations for a decisive attack were completed. The Venetian fleet lined the Galata shore of the Golden Horn for half a mile in readiness for the attack. The land forces, on the other hand, never very numerous, had dwindled in the course of the months, and the attempt to scale the walls, launched on April 9, failed completely. The battle was renewed on the 12th, and on the 13th the 'Latins' took posession of Constantinople almost without resistance. Then began the scenes which concern us here.

Old men, women, and children, carrying crosses and holy images, went to meet the victorious troops, but there was no restraining their lust for blood and plunder; they were Crusaders no longer; they were plunderers such as Europe had never known till that day. Whoever stood in their way was killed. In the city there were also some thousands of Italians, Venetians, Pisans, and others, mostly merchants and their families, who had come to take the besiegers' side during the previous months and had suffered distress, insult and punishment for doing so, and now naturally seized the opportunity of revenge and plunder. They alone were responsible for the deaths of over 2,000, irrespective of age or sex. Palaces and churches echoed with the uproar of the pillagers and the groans and screams of the victims of murder and rape. Anyone who could get permission to leave the city thought himself lucky. Henrich Kretschmayr describes the pitiful procession of half naked, trembling wretches, thrown on the streets after a life of riches and luxury and jeered at not only by their enemies but also by their own country people, who collected at the gates, rejoicing to see the hated town-dwellers reduced to such misery.

By order of the leaders of the Crusade, all booty had to be collected in three of the churches for equitable distribution. Much was concealed and not handed over, and those who were caught doing this paid for it on the gallows. The Venetians were adept at this underhand disposal of loot, but even so the churches were heaped high with valuables of every sort, costly dinner-services, precious stones, rich clothing. The Venetians paid particular attention to the methodical plundering of churches and stripped them of their relics and treasures. Clari, a knight who was there, asserted that the forty richest cities on earth could not equal the riches which Byzantium now lost to her conquerors. All this was now distributed throughout Europe and added unimaginable riches to the legacy of antiquity and the medieval Eastern Empire. Venice benefited chiefly, but the whole of Europe as far as the British Isles and Scandinavia, wherever relations and friends of any crusader were to be found, shared in this amazing windfall.

Every Crusader of any rank found himself in possession of a fortune on April 13, 1204. For years the Venetians were transporting relics and other treasures, one ship-load after another of precious, and in some cases, world-famed works of art. There was the marble ciborium, which now adorns the high altar of St Mark's, and the horses of Lysippus, taken from the Hippodrome, to which the Doge Pietro Ziani, successor of the famous Enrico Dandolo, allotted their familiar place above the west door of St Mark's; this was not to be their last removal: 600 years later they journeyed to Paris and back again, and in 1918 they nearly went to Rome. Innumerable other treasures, including those of St Sophia, were among the plunder. But considering the hundreds of works of art destroyed by the crusaders, it is a mercy that some at least were saved, even at the cost of changing hands.

An eclipse, taken to be a sign of the wrath of God, put an end to the looting on April 16.

Not until then could the losses Constantinople had suffered be estimated. Since the time of Constantine the city had remained unconquered and unconquerable. It had resisted the determined onslaughts of Persians, Arabs, Avars and Bulgarians, only to fall victim to the Crusaders, or rather to the Venetians. 'Never since the creation of the world,' wrote Villehardouin, 'did any city yield up such booty.' And 'even the Saracens are merciful and kind compared with these, who bear the cross of Christ on their shoulders,' was the verdict of another eye-witness.

Gunther of Paris has left an eye-witness account of the Fourth Crusade:

'Those on the ships now surged through the opened gates with shouts of triumph, threatening the terrified inhabitants with their lances, swords, cross-bows, arrows and weapons of every kind, but only for show and without the intention of shedding more blood. They drove the people like sheep in such crowds that the streets, wide though they were, were not wide enough. Our men followed them up so impetuously that they dared not pause for breath or to look round. But in spite of such an opportunity for carnage, only a few were killed; pardons were freely granted, for they had often been admonished by the monks who were with them, Martin and others, to keep their hands clean from blood as far as they could. . . .

'And so the enemy were conquered, scattered in flight, and lamentably barred out of their city; and only then when the gates had been shut was the permission to plunder given. It was forbidden on pain of death to lay hands on anything at all until the occupation of the city was completed. And then they found themselves transformed at a blow from needy strangers into wealthy citizens, possessed of gold and silver, jewels and garments, and houses stocked with all imaginable necessaries and luxuries.'

At first sight, this does not look so bad, not nearly so bad as in fact it was. A hint of the true state of affairs is given in the pages that follow:

'When the conquered city had been given over to plunder according to the rules of war, Abbot Martin, too, began to think of his own share in the loot and, not to go away empty-handed when every one else was enriching himself, he set his own sanctified hands to work. But as it seemed improper to lay his

36

hands on wordly goods, he went after sacred relics, of which he
knew there was plenty to be had. Taking one of his two chaplains with him, he set off for one of the churches of which he
had expectations and which was held in high esteem, because
the mother of the very famous Emperor, Emmanuel, was buried there in a tomb of great renown. This meant little to our
men, but to the Greeks it meant much. A great deal of money
from all the surrounding neighbourhood had been brought
there for safe custody,and also precious relics from neighbour-
ing churches and monasteries, in the vain hope of giving them
a safe refuge, and this was known to our men from information
supplied by some of those whom the Greeks had expelled
before the city was taken. While many pilgrims forced their
way in a body into the church and searched everywhere for
the plunder, Martin, thinking it unworthy to rob churches
of anything but their sacred possessions, looked about for some
more secret nook where he might hope to find what he was
after. There he found an old man of imposing appearance with
a long grey beard, a priest of course, but differing very much
from ours in his outward appearance. The abbot therefore
took him to be a layman. So affecting a fierceness he did not
feel he shouted, "Now, you old infidel, show me the precious
relics you've got here, or you won't be long for this life." The
man was more alarmed by the sound than the words, which he
did not understand; and so, thinking that his Greek would not
be understood either, he tried to placate him in the little
French he knew and to ward off the anger which, in fact, was
assumed. Martin then in broken French tried to make the old
man understand what he wanted. And he, after taking stock
of his air and his dress, came to the conclusion that it was not
so bad when a monk collected relics from pious reverence as
when laymen smashed them with bloodthirsty violence, and
so he showed him an iron-bound chest in which were the
coveted treasures, more desired by Martin than all the
treasures of Greece. He plunged both hands among them and
greedily filled his voluminous skirts, as did his chaplain too,

hiding what he thought were the most precious objects about their persons.

'Hurrying back to the ships, laden in this way, if he met any who knew and esteemed him, and were off to loot on their own account and asked him in joke what he had got there, and whether he too had been after the loot or what was it he was laden with, he answered as jokingly as they had put the question and in his usual jolly way, "Oh, we've done well," and hurried on, not stopping for their "God be thanked" or for any other reason, in his haste to be safely aboard. And there in his neat, clean cabin he stowed away his own share of the holy loot and waited for the noise and tumult to pass over. For three days he devoutly performed the sacred offices and no one knew anything of it except his two chaplains and that old man who had handed over the sacred treasure, and who now, finding him to be a well-meaning and high-minded man, went out of his way to show his friendliness. He found him comfortable quarters, suitable to his dignity, close to a church in which he might officiate.

'And so when the confusion had died down, the abbot, with the aforementioned chaplain, took his secret and himself to the refuge prepared for him, and spent the whole summer there, watching over his holy relics with ceaseless solicitude and revering them with a deep though secret love, and compounding for his villainy by his devotion.'

Very different were the feelings of Pope Innocent III:

'These soldiers of Christ, who should have directed their swords solely against the infidel, have dipped them in Christian blood. They have respected neither faith, nor age, nor sex. Matrons and maids, even those who were dedicated to God, were delivered without mercy to the brutality of the soldiery. And not content with laying hands on the treasure of the state and plundering rich and poor without distinction, they have dared to lay hands on the property of the Church. Soldiers were seen to snatch the vessels of silver from the altars, smash

38

them and quarrel over the pieces; and others to violate sanc-
tuaries and to carry off the ikons, crosses and relics.'

St Sophia was the scene of the worst excesses of these marauding bands. One drunken soldier tore up the sacred books, others
stamped the religious carvings under foot, drank out of the
consecrated cups, parted the robes and vestments among them
and went off to whores and sutlers with the jewels they tore from
the altars. Bronze statues were melted down and turned into
coins.

It is true that the captains of the Crusade tried to enforce
discipline and exacted the sternest penalties for indiscriminate
looting, and not without effect; but it only meant that the
plundering became orderly and systematic instead of chaotic.

So much for the immediate and material consequences of this
colossal theft of art; but let us give a glance at least at the wider
issues. No partner in the Crusade had benefited to anything like
the same extent from the looting of Constantinople as Venice in
her role as merchant and shipper. All the coasts of the eastern
Mediterranean, as far as Asia Minor, were now part of her
mercantile and naval empire. In the Aegean, in the Byzantine
Empire, in Egypt, Venice was now the ruling power. Her
development as a mercantile world power dates from 1204.

And at home in the Adriatic, Venice became, with the capture
of Constantinople, the most distinguished heir of that ancient
imperial city in the civilized world. Byzantine influence now
receded, while in Venice a new, Venetian art tradition was born.
Carrying on the old Byzantine and Asiatic tradition under the
influence of the looted works of art, this new Venetian style
made its influence felt on the whole of Western art, in which,
from the thirteenth century onwards, elements of Byzantine style
are everywhere to be found. This is not to say that European and
national, even provincial and local elements were not stronger
and did not prevail in the long run; but again and again they
reverted to those Byzantine features and profited in colour,
splendour, symbolic meaning and the decorative use of light.

39

Mysticism, even the exotic, was encouraged. Emperors and kings, popes and bishops, and other exalted personages wore from now on ceremonial robes of Byzantine silks, adorned with stolen pearls and jewels. The last remnant, the least piece of woven carpet, the smallest clasp, carried with it an exotic, oriental suggestion which the passing of the centuries could not weaken; it lived and and grew of itself without needing even the acknowledgment of the wearer, the heir, the merchant or the connoisseur.

4

Constantinople under the Turks

lmost exactly two and a half centuries passed by before
foreign troops—this time Turkish—once more stormed
the walls of Constantinople, on May 29, 1453, after overcoming a two months' resistance. Venice, during these 250
years, had reached an unexampled height of prosperity. Contemporary records tell us that her wealth steadily increased and
that ever more and more beautiful palaces were erected along
the canals; the Ca d'Oro is one of the most celebrated surviving
examples. Many of them clearly showed the influence of Moorish,
oriental and Islamic architecture.

The families who lived in them and ruled Venice were for
those times extremely rich, and it is not surprising that they
excelled in the enjoyments and refinements of life, among which
the collection of works of art and antiques played its part.
Merchants who despatched their ships and their agents to all
parts of the world imported all that was costly and rare.

The dealers and agents who shared this passion or lived to
meet its demands were innumerable. Marco Polo, traveller,
trade envoy, scholar and merchant, was the most important of
them all. He visited the Emperor of China in Peking and brought
back hitherto unguessed treasures to his native city. Among the
most valuable were the manuscripts, later in the Falieri Collection, and those that first belonged to Petrarch and were presented
by him to the library of the Doge's palace. All these articles of
travellers' luggage added fuel to the flames. Scarcely a ship
returned to Venice from the east without having art treasures
on board, such as marbles and fragments of inscriptions which had

41

to be deciphered and interpreted, monumental statues and examples of artistic craftsmanship of extreme delicacy and fragility.

Meanwhile, Constantinople, if it had not forgotten 1204, had survived it. Once more it had grown rich in gold and in works of art. And now, at noon on that day in May 1453, Sultan Mohammed rode into the city at the head of his strictly disciplined troops, and solemnly took possession of St Sophia in the name of Islam. It was in all respects, political, economic and cultural, a great success for Islam, and the progressive spirit of the conquerors was shown when they immediately made Constantinople their capital and, in spite of their hostility to the West, granted the Genoese in Galata, who had remained neutral during the siege, their lives and possessions on condition they laid down their arms; their trading rights too were confirmed on payment of the prescribed dues and taxes. The East might aim to win the West for Islam in the long run; but first it meant to strengthen the economic and cultural links with it.

The general line of advance was indicated when Mohammed restored the walls of Adrianople before proceeding to rule his empire from the city, so rich in symbolic significance, which he had just conquered. Many Greeks, too, who had left Constantinople before its walls were stormed, now returned at the Sultan's wish. The peaceful conditions within the city were a further encouragement. They settled in the Fanar Patriarchate on the west bank of the Golden Horn, merchants whose worldwide name rested on their skill in barter between East and West and on the commercial link between the two worlds; but there were also among them craftsmen of small or modest means, who were prized for their artistic skill. While the learned refugees from Constantinople spread over Italy, taking with them their manuscripts and their attainments, seeds of humanism and the Renaissance, a learned diaspora of the greatest importance for almost every European country, Byzantium too had its own quickened artistic life.

This, certainly, had quite different origins; in the West the revival of art and learning was a product of the creative energy of the individual, whereas in the East it was accompanied very often by compulsion, force, robbery, kidnapping or imprisonment. As the relations between Constantinople and the West weakened, there was an infiltration from the East, partly voluntary, partly compulsory, impelled by various motives, and made up of Syrians, Egyptians, Armenians, Persians and finally even Indians and Chinese, drawn by the commercial advantages of the city's unique situation or by the wish to benefit from the pious foundations which Mohammed and his successors established for the promulgation of Islamic learning. Hence Istambul, as it was now, soon became the spiritual centre of Islam.

This led to an entirely new attitude to art, since the religion of Islam forbade the representation of living forms. The lovely and characteristic Byzantine gold mosaics covering the vaulted roofs of the churches were painted over. But Mohammed built new and splendid mosques, tokens of his power and greatness, and to these during the next twenty years were added extensive libraries, where the treasures of Islamic literature were collected.

When Mohammed died on May 3, 1481, during a campaign against Rhodes, the economic, cultural and artistic foundations on which Bayasid and his successors were able to build had been laid. Constantinople now, in artistic matters, turned a different face to the East and to the West. The feeling for the West was friendly; in 1480 Mohammed had had his portrait painted by the Venetian, Gentile Bellini, and in 1506 Bayasid II invited Michelangelo and other Italian artists to Constantinople, as Selim did, too, in 1519. Relations with the East and South, on the other hand, were marked by force and violence, outstanding instances of which were the victorious campaigns against Tabriz in 1514 and those against Syria and Egypt, Damascus and Cairo in 1517. The art as well as the craftsmanship in which these cities were so rich had an immediate influence on Selim, no less so than did the art of the West, and all the more because its strength lay in ceramics where the West was weak. The perfection the art of ceramics had attained in Tabriz excited his envy and emulation, and the result of his stay, from September 5 to

43

13, was the despatch of 700 potters' families to Constantinople, and a great number later on from Damascus and Cairo, as well as other capable craftsmen; in fact, he added the robbery of artists on a vast scale to the robbery of art. The practice of their crafts in Turkey gave a new impulse to Turkish art. An Egyptian manuscript of 1626–27—now in Oxford—tells of the booty and the objects of value which fell into Selim's hands in Cairo in 1517:

> 'And when our lord, the Sultan Selim Khan, left Egypt he took with him a thousand camels laden with gold and silver, besides the rich booty of rarities, weapons, porcelain, copper vessels, clasps, horses, mules and much else. He took the best of everything, and his viziers did the same, so that there was no counting all that was taken.'

Is not this the very picture of the systematic robbery and plunder of all times and all nations, from the Vandals to the Crusaders, the sack of Rome, Napoleon, the capture of Peking in 1860 and on to Hitler and Stalin and all their 'vizirs'? It was then that the magnificent collection of ceramics was made for the Seraglio, a collection which has outlasted the centuries and is unique today for its richness and beauty.

Yet the Turks did not stop at looting and plundering and the carrying off of artists and craftsmen. There is a note in a Turkish sailing handbook of 1521: 'I asked the Portuguese what was the material out of which the Chinese porcelain vessels were made and whether it was really true that they were made out of clay which had been laid up for forty years.' The Portuguese, it is added, told the Turks the secrets of Chinese porcelain as far they themselves knew them.

It was this that first enabled the Sultans to start manufacture on their own. They had the craftsmen, experts only in the faience of Persia and Egypt, it is true; but it was faience of exquisite beauty and now they believed they had the secret of the fine, white, transparent procelain of the Far East. It was only natural that they should aim at domesticating this branch of art or of art manufacture on their own territory. Employing Persian workmen chiefly and following the Persian pattern, influenced of course by what they had learned of Chinese methods, not unknown, after all, to the Persians either, they built factories in and near Constantinople, which were soon noted for the quality as well as the quantity of their output. We read of a whole invasion of Persians, partly compulsory, partly voluntary. Even before the arrival of the master hands from Tabriz, blue and white Ming porcelain imported much earlier from China had been copied at Nicaea (the Turkish Isnik) with variations and modifications due to Persian influence. Now, after 1514, Persian artisans in the Ak-Serail quarter of Constantinople were producing the 'Golden Horn ceramics'. Yet Isnik took the lead after 1514; it was there alone that those tiles were made, the beauty of which became famous throughout the world.

The Persian style, domesticated by enforced migration to Constantinople and its neighbourhood, was already predominant by the middle of the sixteenth century; so it was a natural and historical consequence when the domed sepulchre of Sultan Murad III, who died in 1595, was decorated with the cloud pattern, the Chinese Shi motif. Thus Isnik was a centre where many influences met. Murad gave the following instructions to his Kadi in 1589: 'Because faience tiles are needed for the pavilion recently built in my imperial serail, 1,500 aktscha will be paid to my servant by my palace guard. On receipt I command you to waste not a moment in collecting the faience tile masters, in seeing to the manufacture according to the pattern included with your instructions and in sending them to my threshold of bliss. The matter is urgent. Waste no time.'

This shows what could be expected of Isnik only a few decades after the importation of craftsmen from Tabriz. They knew there how to make Persian, Rhodian or Damascus ware, and from that time on, in consequence of the Ottoman invasions which passed through Tabriz in 1534, 1548 and 1585, there was an unmistakable Turkish influence on Persian art, which reached its peak when Tabriz between 1590 and 1603 finally passed into Turkish hands.

5

The Burgundian Booty

S carcely had the Swiss Confederacy overcome, by the year 1475 in the 'autumn of the Middle Ages', an internal crisis of its own, than it was involved in a war with Charles the Bold of Burgundy, a prince who 'in spite of many blunders would gladly have remained on good neighbourly terms'.

When the Emperor Charles Frederick III declared war on Charles the Bold, the Swiss were in duty bound to play their part. It was immediately made evident that they had become involved in quarrels which were to take them far beyond the life and the sphere of action they had hitherto known. The fighting culminated finally, both from a military and a cultural point of view, in the *Goldschlacht*, or gold-battle, of Grandson on March 2, 1476, a quite extraordinary affair.

The Burgundian army, although it was equipped in profusion with every modern weapon, was a mercenary army without inner cohesion; once thrown back by the Swiss, its Burgundian commanders were unable to halt its disorderly flight either at Wagenburgor on the River Arnon or at the large and splendid camp near Grandson at the southern end of the Neuenburger Lake. The Swiss, who had lost scarcely 200 men, drove the routed foe before them in confusion. The Milanese ambassador, an eye-witness, called it 'the most cowardly affair imaginable' and maintained that the Burgundians had hardly lost a man.

What concerns us is that the luxurious Burgundian camp at Grandson, with all its valuable booty, fell into the hands of the victors; booty, according to the views of war held in those days, not robbery in its criminal sense.

It is true that at the beginning of the Burgundian war special orders were issued by the Swiss military command one day at Lucerne, among them the order that strict discipline was to be maintained and that no foreigner was to be injured either in person or property; but in battle no man was to be taken prisoner if he could by any means be killed. There is much evidence that even before the battle of Grandson, the Swiss foot soldier was set on booty, and the consequence was that he was more concerned with his own profit than with the energetic prosecution of the war. The booty he was after was, certainly, simple enough as a rule—cattle and food, pots and pans and other domestic utensils such as bread-baskets, baby-clothes, glasses, farming implements, clothing and weapons, which of course were always paid for in ready money, acquired as a rule by the sale or surrender of prisoners of war.

Looked at through the eyes of Charles the Bold, what he lost with the over-running of his camp at Grandson was not what art-historians and art-lovers today call 'the Burgundian booty', but his artillery. He rightly judged the results of the battle principally from the military standpoint rather than from that of a man of great possessions. The first conclusive report received on March 4 by the ambassador of the Duke of Milan after his return to Geneva expressly stated: 'But the treasure, the jewellery and silver of the Duke, may have been saved'; and a further report of the same date says: 'The most serious loss is the fine and numerous train of artillery, abandoned and left behind by its crews.' Tents and pavilions only come in later, though it is also mentioned that they were very magnificent and full of costly things. Among the contents of the camp is reckoned the Duke's treasure in jewels and silverware, although it was also said that these were in safe keeping in a castle, with the exception of a few wagon-loads of valuable furniture and some cases of silver. The first descriptions of the booty by the Swiss also put first in the list: 'Over 400 big guns, siege guns and culverins, 800 blunderbusses, 300 barrels of powder, spears, battle-axes, cross-bows and suits of armour beyond counting, and lastly 27 banners and 600 flags.'

But all these accounts were drawn up before the full extent of the catastrophe was known; the whole distance covered by the Burgundians in their flight to Grandson was littered with baggage, and then there was the camp itself. Soldiers and diplomats might think more of the losses in artillery and prestige, but the Swiss foot-soldier, like posterity, was more interested in the valuables found there. This was the booty they fell upon, carried off or, in some cases, handed in for equitable distribution.

The booty was so immense because of the riches and splendour of the Burgundian nobles and Charles's habit of taking all the accompaniments of a brilliant court with him on his campaigns. The ornaments of his private chapel were known in those days for their untold value. There was his reliquary of costly as well as artistic workmanship and its sacred contents; there were the instruments of divine worship, his rosary, each bead of which was a precious stone, his Paternoster of gold with the twelve apostles in enamel, a precious Pacem with a Mount of Olives in mother of pearl, his prayerbook bound in red velvet and embellished with gold and painted illuminations, the heavy gold monstrance.

Yet the booty was even richer in articles of secular use, such as the great dinner-service, used in the Duke's town residences as well as in the field for his numerous banquets. The silverware such as jugs, plates, dishes, goblets and so forth was partly gold gilt, and weighed nearly 5,000 ounces, not counting what escaped the general share-out and was bought on the sly from the common soldiers at the price of ordinary metal utensils such as they took them to be. Charles's golden chair, in which he sat to receive ambassadors, excited particular admiration both for its costly materials and for its artistic worth; it was made of silver heavily gilt and was valued at 1,100 florins. The Duke's hat, worn on ceremonial occasions and thickly adorned with jewels, was later bought for 47,000 gulden by Jacob Fugger. The beautiful diamonds, three in number, the most precious at that time in all Europe for size and transparency, were to become world-famous; there were seven other large diamonds and as many large rubies

4. The treasures of the Grandson booty laid out for distribution
in the Sacristy of St Peter's, Lucerne. From Diebold Schilling's
Lucerne Chronicle.

5. The Golden Seal of Charles the Bold.

6. Raphael's tapestry, the BLINDING OF ELYMAS in the Vatican, which was cut in half during the sack of Rome in 1527.

and the fifteen pearls of inestimable value which adorned the handle of Charles's ceremonial sword. His gold seal weighed a pound and there was also the seal of the Bastard, Anthony of Burgundy, of silver gilt. The Duke's lodging and the tents of his retinue were hung with tapestries woven in coloured wool threaded with gold and silver, representing scenes from classical antiquity, the campaigns of Julius Caesar and from the times of the Emperors and the judicial circuits of Trajan and so forth. There were numbers of rich garments of silk and gold or silver brocade, which were measured out by the yard for sharing out, and in some cases cut up or distributed piece by piece, things they had never before laid hands on and which they sold or exchanged among themselves. Silk and velvet doublets, a contemporary says, were so common that many a poor fellow who could scarcely have afforded one of coarse twill had a silk one, which he had to exchange for a coarse one again when his toil had worn it out. The attempt to check misappropriation of booty was made through public proclamation in the camp, and orders were also forwarded to Neuenburg that all soldiers arriving there were to be searched for booty and made to surrender it for distribution with the common stock. Nevertheless, only the smaller part ever found its way there. Many a one, it was said, and his heirs after him, was made rich and powerful by the booty he secretly appropriated for himself at Grandson. Concern was felt for the evil consequences of this laxity in the discipline of the army and also for the bad influence which the booty of Grandson would have on the simple manners of the Swiss.

The orderly sharing out of these treasures, which aroused such natural cupidity, was much more difficult than dealing with the equally valuable armaments and implements of war. All the artillery was removed from the camp and the battle-field to an open space where 180 of the best pieces were selected for despatch by water to Nydau and the other frontier places. The remainder were divided up on the spot among the auxiliaries, including 800 cross-bows among the small arms and 300 casks of powder. Among the 600 banners and flags there were 27 great

D   49

banners, partly of silk threaded with gold. Only a small number was captured on the field of battle; most were packed away in cases and hide trunks for special occasions, particularly for planting before conquered places, so that the arms displayed on them might bring home the greatness and might of the House of Burgundy, as Philip the Good had already done in front of Ghent, Liège and Dinant to inspire fear in his enemies.

Notable among the hand-weapons were the 4,000 maces loaded with lead and heavy enough to fell an ox, intended principally for the use of the English archers to enable them to smash the helmets of the mounted and armoured enemy whom their arrows had laid low. There were also a great many ordinary battle-axes, halberds, lances and other cut and thrust weapons; fire-arms and muskets; bows and the supposedly poisoned arrows; all packed in huge cases and transported by wagon. In the camp, the seven tents of Philip the Good stood out among the 400 other tents of his court, hung with silk cloth and gay with pennons along the ridge poles. To light them by night they were furnished with beautiful cut globes of crystal. Travelling cases were counted to the number of 400, army wagons 2,000; and there were 3,000 sacks of oats for the horses and 2,000 barrels of herrings to feed the army in Lent. The barrelful of hangman's rope may not have been intended solely for the stringing up of pious Christian folk, as the chronicler thought, but partly at least for the execution of genuine criminals, or perhaps for the tying of forage.

Most of these army supplies and equipment, as with the artillery, were divided up on the spot among the various towns, according to the number of men supplied for the army; but this first share-out did not, as we shall see, prevent the booty of Grandson from being discussed year after year at the meetings of the Confederacy. There were negotiations with foreign cities and princes about particular items. To the enquiry of the city of Cologne about certain documents, relating perhaps to Charles's old quarrel about the archbishopric, Berne replied that nothing had been found, but that there were books and the Burgundian army orders still in their possession.

Countess Margareth of Württemberg, *née* Duchess of Savoy, enquired for the prayerbook of the Duke of Burgundy and was informed by letter that it and other treasures had fallen to the share of the city of Berne and were for sale. If it pleased the gracious princess and the house of Württemberg to send envoys with full powers to deal in the matter, they would be welcomed and shown the book, on which a moderate price would be put. The outcome is not recorded, nor do we know the fate of other books which also formed part of the booty; they had been collected by Charles's father, Philip the Good, and were one of the most valuable libraries of the time.

The victory won at Grandson by the Swiss Confederacy is therefore outstanding for the richness and splendour of the spoils which fell into the Confederates' hands. Charles, like the other princes of the day, made a practice of taking his treasures with him on his campaigns, partly to have his most valuable possessions in his own keeping and partly because of the miraculous powers attributed to these precious and venerated objects. Contemporary chronicles and songs are full of this event and give whole lists of the valuables and goods and equipment found in the camp. Johannes von Müller writes:

'According to Charles's own estimate, over a million gulden of his own property was in the camp; six princes, the flower of the nobility of the Netherlands and Burgundy, the whole military command, all striving to rival one another in brilliance, might account for another million; the magazine and artillery make a third million, which reckoned in the currency of these days may be multiplied by ten. Besides corn, wine, oats, salt meat and fish, there was an ample provision of southern produce and spices, all of which was put up for sale in a thousand booths and sold off by four times the number of hucksters and drabs.

'The four hundred splendid tents hung with silk included seven of particular magnificence which served as Headquarters and the court chapel, with those of the Bastard and

51

the chief among the lords, but Charles's own tent exceeded all and was reputed to be second only to that of the Turkish Sultan. Armorial bearings glittering with gold and set with pearls shone outside, and inside it was hung with silk. There stood his golden chair in which he received foreign embassies, there also his rich and fine ducal hat, and among many swords of the finest damascene steel there shone out his ceremonial sword, with seven large diamonds, as many rubies, and fifteen rare pearls as well as sapphires and jacinths for the adornment of the hilt. The Golden Fleece was there too. In the chapel was Philip the Good's rosary of gold with precious stones for beads, a box set with pearls and rubies containing rare and sacred treasures, another, equally precious, in which relics of the twelve Apostles were hid in richly worked effigies and the wonder-working arm of St Andrew in crystal adorned with gold. The prayerbook bound in red velvet, gilded and illuminated, was found here too. The monstrance in heavy gold was taken from the altar. From the chancery they took the seal of the House of Burgundy, a pound's weight in gold, and the silver one gilded with gold of the Bastard, and made a bonfire of the rent rolls and cadastres. The dining tent was emptied of its gold and silver cups and dishes and plates, its easels stacked with portraits for the admiration of emperors and kings; Roman art contrasted with Belgian industry. Lastly, 400 travelling trunks full of linen and silks the like of which had never been seen. The Swiss soldiers treated them as their own home-weave and disposed of silver plates for a few coppers, thinking they were pewter. Money boxes and coins were distributed by the hatful; the embroidered hangings of the gorgeous tents were measured out and cut up as if they were haberdasher's stuff.

'Three diamonds (this duke was the first who had diamonds cut) have shone in history for their stories as well as in the greatest of crowns for their brilliance. The first, of the size of half a hazel nut, known not only to Christendom but seen earlier in a Mongol diadem, the largest in the world and prized by Charles as highly as one of his provinces, was lost either by himself or one of his escort in the general alarm of their flight. It was found on the road in its case with an equally rare unmounted pearl, by a Swiss, who, thinking it to be glass, threw it under a wagon. On second thoughts he picked it up again and the Pastor of Montagny gave him a gulden for it. He in turn parted with it to the Bernese for three franks. Later, Bartolomaus May, a rich man of Berne, who had many ties of consanguinity and trade with Italy, put a more realistic value on it: he made a gift of it to the Mayor, Wilhelm von Diesbach, letting him have it as a favour for 5,000 gulden. The Genoese bought it for only a little more, but the Milanese Regent, Ludovico Moro Sforza, gave them more than double for it. At the dispersal of the Milanese treasures, Pope Julius gave 20,000 ducats for it, so that the first of diamonds might shine in the triple tiara of the High Priest of Christendom. There was only one rival to it, and it too was found in the camp, in a pendant for the Duke's neck, set between three large rubies, "Three Brothers", and the four superb eastern pearls. This and Charles's hat of ceremony (of Italian shape, round and high, of yellow velvet, embroidered with pearls, with a wreath of sardonyx, rubies, pearls and cut diamonds and a decoration on the crown of precious stones in a gold setting) was bought from the victors by Jacob Fugger, a man as rich in wisdom as in money and honours. After Suliman, the great Osman Padishah, and also Charles V had bid for it in vain, the diamond was bought from Anton Fugger by Henry VIII of England, whose whims were not to be gainsaid, and descended to his eldest child, Queen Mary, and from her came to Philip II, great-great-grandson of its original owner. A third, not the equal of the two already mentioned, yet valued in recent times at 1,800,000 French livres, was sold one day at Lucerne to Diebold Glaser for 15,000 gulden. It was destined to come into the possession of the Kings of Portugal, then among the richest on earth, and at the fall of their dynasty it passed into the crown of the Kings of France.'

The Song of Grandson dedicated to this memorable plunder ends in fine mocking style:

> Duke Charles, we know you hate
> The very name Confederate;
>   Of that you'll have no joy.
> Your arms no battles ever win,
> So why not stop your warlike din?
>   It's you it will annoy.
>
> Your goods are now all up for sale;
> Confederates can tell the tale.
>   Shame, shame upon you!
> But if you've any left in store,
> Come along and bring some more,
>   We'll gladly take it from you.

'The booty of Burgundy,' it has been said, 'calls up a wonderful picture of beautifully painted banners, sumptuous tents, embroidered hangings, unimaginably lovely velvets and silks, shining armour and bronze bombards.' Philippe de Commines in his history describes Wagenburg as one of the finest and most gorgeous camps ever known, and there is no doubt at all that the booty of Grandson was out of all proportion to the military expenditure and the numbers involved on either side. It surpassed the booty of the Fourth Crusade when due account is taken of the shortness of the campaign and the lightness of the losses in comparison with a long sea voyage and a siege lasting many months. The Sack of Rome, which was to shock and outrage the world half a century later, had not yet given a new yardstick for measuring plunder, pillage, murder and bloodshed, not to mention the Thirty Years War.

The question remains, what happened to all this Burgundian booty? The treasure included in this general description, which the Burgundians lost and the Swiss captured at Grandson, had far-reaching effects on culture, art, weapons and armaments, and not least on art-dealers, gold- and silversmiths and the minting of money.

The consequences of such a change of ownership of so much valuable property were surprisingly great and far-reaching. First of all the banners were hung in the churches and the guns turned on the enemy or placed in the arsenal. It was observed further that after the battles of the Burgundian war of the years 1474 to 1477, that is, for our purposes, after the battle of Grandson, an unusual quantity of silver in the form of cups, beakers, dishes, plates and platters were for sale in Switzerland. At first, individual soldiers disposed of them; then a law was passed empowering the authorities to require the surrender on oath of all booty in order that it might be equitably divided; this was to take place in Lucerne and was in fact carried out. We have various authentic descriptions of how this new distribution worked out. At the same time we have in the *Eidgenössische Abschiede* the surely justified assertion that not half the original booty was ever given up again; such a demand was expecting too much of the men and it also destroyed their confidence in the better judgment and justice of their superior officers. In any case, many objects of value which were to hand on the day of the battle of Grandson were not produced for the re-distribution in Lucerne. Many must already have changed hands more than once, so that the last possessor did not feel called upon to give up what he had fairly paid for. A Jew of Neuenburg, for example, bought up a great deal of the booty immediately after the battle, a common practice in those days and one to which no serious objection could be taken.

By far the most imposing valuables of which there is knowledge were brought to St Peter's in Lucerne for distribution. A bust of St Leodegar was made out of the numerous platters and voluntary offerings of silver, so that most of the silver from the Burgundian booty is not in existence today. It is true that Grandson was reputed to be the origin of silver dishes in other places, yet such attributions are as a rule very uncertain. In this connection the goblet of Caspar von Hertenstein at Risch and the

Zwingli goblet in the parish church of Clarus may be mentioned. The gold seal of Charles the Bold and the smaller gilded silver one of the Bastard of Burgundy, which are preserved among the State archives in Lucerne, are without doubt part of the booty of Grandson. Nearly every piece which had no inscription or was of no particular value was melted down.

In the most recent investigation into these questions we read:

'Certainly from that time on silver in the form of coins and utensils became more plentiful. In the households of the rich, silver ousted wood and pewter from the table. A great stimulus was also given to the craft of the goldsmith, which was still flourishing when the discovery of America caused an influx of gold and silver to Europe and lowered the price of the precious metals. War service abroad brought in gold, and soon silver drinking-cups and silver-plated or solid silver spoons were in common use. Forks came in later.'

This shows what a remarkable effect the Burgundian booty had in the comparatively small and geographically self-enclosed area of Switzerland; it produced a noticeable enrichment of the whole country; it caused a distinct and very quickly effective increase of the money in circulation and an economic stimulus for which other countries of Western Europe had to wait until silver flowed in from America. But that was some decades off.

There is fairly accurate information about the wanderings of one or two of Charles's particularly valuable possessions. In 1503, for example, the Emperor Maximilian I deposited as surety with the Fuggers a tapestry representing 'Alexander and the Burgundian Envoys'. More striking is the fate of those celebrated pieces of jewellery, the 'White Rose', the 'Three Brothers', the 'Feather' and the 'Garter'. These unique pieces, together with a diamond of the size of half a hazel nut, belonged to the city of Basel until 1504 and do not appear to have been sent to Lucerne for redistribution. Miniatures on parchment of the size of the originals were shown to Jakob Fugger the Rich and his brothers, Ulrich and Georg, in their negotiations for the purchase of them from the

56

city council; the price paid was 40,200 gulden, the last instalment of which was paid at the end of 1506.

It was well established and widely known that these four pieces of jewellery had belonged to Charles the Bold, although this fact was not mentioned in the contract of sale. Half a century later Georg Fugger's grandson, Johann Jakob the Learned, mentioned in his *True Description of the Hapsburg and Austrian House*, written in 1555, three of the pieces bought in 1504, the 'White Rose', the 'Three Brothers', and the 'Feather'. He illustrated the two first in coloured drawings of the size of the originals, and described them as part of the Grandson booty which his grandfather had acquired by purchase from the Confederates. The 'Three Brothers' was known to have been in the possession of the Burgundian duke, John the Fearless, the grandfather of Charles the Bold, in 1419, and Philippe de Commines expressly states that Charles the Bold had it with him at Grandson. The other three Charles had not inherited, but had been given. The 'Garter' he had received from his brother-in-law, Edward IV, when he was made a member of the Order of the Garter. He was given the 'Feather' and the 'Rose' on the same occasion.

The Fugger brothers bought these four pieces between 1504 and 1506 as a speculation and in the hope of selling them at a profit to the Hapsburgs. Maximilian I had married Mary, the daughter of Charles the Bold, and so Charles's son-in-law might be supposed to be eager to acquire them for himself and his heirs.

Being a good businessman, Anton, Georg's son, first obtained the offer of a high price for the 'Three Brothers' from the Sultan Suliman, who was eager to obtain the largest and finest diamonds and pearls, and then let his refusal be widely known. But the Fuggers had overestimated, if not the will, at least the power of the Hapsburgs to come up to scratch. The Fuggers made several overtures to Charles V and Ferdinand I, who belonged to the next generation, but always without success. At last in 1543 the 'Three Brothers' was sold at a 'good profit' to Henry VIII of England and it remained among the Crown Jewels until 1623 when James I had the stones reset and sent to his son Charles in Madrid. There they appear either to have come into the possession of the Spanish princess whom Charles was unsuccessfully wooing, or to have been given away to someone else. In any case they vanished, as the other three pieces had earlier.

The later history of the 'Garter' and the 'Rose' is not known. Of the 'Feather', it is known that J. J. Fugger had the stones taken out and re-set as rings and other pieces of jewellery which he sold for a thousand gulden to Maximilian II. Thus all that remains of these four pieces of Charles the Bold's jewellery is the four miniatures in Basel.

6

The Sack of Rome

The first quarter of the sixteenth century must impress the historian as being as eventful and as bewildering as any other quarter of a century he might have to deal with. The Reformation and the Peasants' War in Germany stand out among conflicts and leagues, agreements and antagonisms as being the events of the greatest importance; the Reformation, because while striving for reform it disrupted the unity of Christendom and created a new confession with consequences extending far beyond the sphere of religion. It was unable to establish itself without long-drawn-out warfare, which quickly led from religion to politics in much the same way as happened with the Peasants' War. This was the second event of cardinal importance in Germany, the grim and bloody struggle between the powerful landed aristocracy and the peasants, joined and supported by the apprentices and small tradesmen of the towns. It was a conflict between the old corporate freedom and the new, strongly organized dynastic states whose aim was absolutism.

Yet even against a background of such disastrous events, the Sack of Rome impressed those who lived at the time as an event of unique horror. The circumstances out of which it arose were the struggles between the Emperor Charles V and Francis I of France which followed upon the Peace of Madrid of 1525. Even within a year of his victory at Pavia, Charles once more found himself in a tight corner. And Clement VII, who, in an age of critical decisions for the Church, gave himself up to Italian political rivalries and was even prepared to be identified with them, joined the so-called Holy League of Cognac in 1536, with Milan, Venice and France as partners, merely for the sake of trivial territorial gains. Nevertheless, one of the main objects of the league in the eyes of the Papal advisers was to cleanse Italy of foreigners. As none of the Italian states was able to dominate the rest, the country could only choose between being occupied and exploited by the French or the Spanish. The hope that French influence might more easily be confined to Milan than the Spanish was a point in its favour; and if the allies had been united they might have overwhelmed the ill-paid, undisciplined rabble in Lombardy with little trouble. But German mercenaries under Georg von Frundsberg crossed the Alps in winter unopposed and joined up with Bourbon's Spanish troops. They headed south, where they were promised their months' arrears of pay and where there was also good prospect of booty. Booty in the career of a mercenary was reckoned as part of the trade, since his pay was adjusted to the probability, or necessity rather, of adding to it in that way. When pay was long in arrears, with the prospect, too, that next pay day would by no means bring it up-to-date, a city like Rome had reason to fear the worst, if these soldiers could scale its walls and get into its churches and palaces.

Frundsberg, who had tried to keep his men in hand, was carried off by a stroke, and Bourbon took over the command. On May 5, 1527, the army was before the walls of Rome. On the day after the attack was launched Bourbon fell, and on the evening of May 6 the city was at the mercy of a leaderless, plundering mob of Spanish, Italian and German mercenaries. This was the Sack of Rome. The sacking of conquered cities and countries was the old-established right of the conqueror; it meant plundering, killing any who resisted, making prisoners of the rest and selling them as slaves or serfs, raping women of all ages, respecting nunneries as little as palaces, getting drunk, dressing up in fine clothes, and being indemnified for all hardships, dangers and arrears of pay. Officers allowed the men unrestricted liberty, partly because they recognized looting and murder as part of a soldier's life and partly because once inside a town's walls they soon lost the power to enforce discipline. They had to put the best face on it, and there was the advantage that their own opportunities to plunder were equally unlimited.

For the actual events of those tragic weeks we have several eye-witness accounts, and also later ones which had the advantage of being able to combine the contemporary records. One of these is to be found in the last volume of the *History of the City of Rome* by Gregorovius:

'During the early days of May the roads to Civitavecchia and Umbria were thronged with fugitives. "Today," said a letter written on May 4, from Collescipoli near Terni, "there have passed Cardinal Egidius, the bishops of Volterra, Bologna and Pesaro, the court of Cardinal Campeggi, Signor Constantino Greco and Messer Baldassare of Pescia, all of them flying from ruin; so hopeless seems the rescue of the city." Among those who fled shortly before the catastrophe was Filippo Strozzi with his wife Clarice Medici and his children. Just returned from his seven months' imprisonment as hostage in Naples, he embarked on the Tiber on May 4 and hurried by Civitavecchia to Pisa.

'The prophet of evil cried woe to Rome; from the statue of St Peter, on Easter Day, the insane but true prophet of Siena had publicly foretold the fall of the city, and even in prison, where he was thrown by the Swiss Guards, he was not reduced to silence. Prophecies of the ruin of Rome and the Papacy were here and there affixed to the walls. Signs, such as heralded the capture of Rome by Alaric, were not wanting: the fall of houses, fatalities by lightning, meteors and the like. Papal Rome was as steeped in sin as the pagan city in the last days of the Empire, and it was now believed that the time had come when the ancient prophecies were to be fulfilled. The saints of the Minorite order, St Bridget, St Francesca Romana and a hundred others, had for centuries prophesied the destruction of the city by fire, the fall of the church and its final reformation.

61

'Like an avalanche Bourbon's army had burst into the centre of Italy and opened a way to Rome. Neither mountains, rivers, impassable roads, snow, winter rains, gnawing hunger nor the enemy who harassed them on every side had availed to check the march of his troops. They were driven on, said the Lutherans, by the dispensation of God to chastise sinful Rome, over which fate now folded its sinister wings. On May 4 the army encamped at Isola Farnese, the site of ancient Veii, where in former days so many emperors had rested on their way to Rome. No messenger from the Pope or the city appeared, a fact that aroused Bourbon's surprise, for Rome was within a three hours march. No enemy showed himself. Owing to forced marches of incredible rapidity the imperialists were in advance of Rangone's cavalry, and so little concerned was Urbino for the Pope's safety that he was still lingering at the lake of Trasimene when the Constable arrived within sight of the walls of Rome.

'Great was the commotion when on May 3 it was known in the city that the enemy was close to Isola. Many carried their possessions to St Angelo; others to places deemed secure, especially to the houses of Spaniards and Germans. On the morning of the 3rd the Pope created some cardinals for money (40,000 ducats for each hat), a now useless measure. The new dignitaries were Benedetto Accolti and Niccolo Gaddi of Florence, the Genoese Agostino Spinola, Ercole Gonzaga and Marino Grimani of Venice. The same day Renzo repaired to the Capitol, where Aldello de Placitis of Siena was senator. Nearly 3,000 citizens assembled in Aracoeli, and the governor exhorted them to defend Rome and the Pope, who had entrusted them with the care of St Angelo and his own person, for he intended to retire to the palace of San Marco. The Romans resolved to defend them to the last extremity. They were of good courage, for already the infantry in the city numbered 4,000 and it was hoped it might soon amount to 7,000. In the afternoon the Pope rode through the entire city to thank the people and to show his confidence. He was greeted

with loud applause. In the evening Camillo Orsini crossed
the Ponte Molle to gain intelligence; but meanwhile the
panic in Rome increased with every hour. In order to prevent
the depopulation of the city by flight and to check the dis-
couragement of the citizens, on the same May 3 it was
proclaimed that no one should leave the city under penalty
of the loss of his property. Those who like the Florentine
merchants wished only to remove their possessions to boats
on the Tiber, were not even allowed to do this. All the gates
were closed. Only to a few was exit granted. Isabella Gonzaga
herself declared her readiness to remain in Rome, and by letters
informed Bourbon and her son Ferrante of her intention.

'On May 4 the Pope issued a summons for a crusade against
the imperial army, the Lutherans and the Sons of Moors, who
with deadly ferocity were marching against the sacred city. . . .

'The historians of the *Sacco di Roma* have placed in Bourbon's
mouth speeches to his captains and his army such as Brennus,
Alaric or Arnulf might have delivered in sight of Rome; and
in truth the different periods of time seem to close in a strange
circle. From the Janiculum Frundsberg's *landsknechts* gazed
with savage hatred on the Vatican, formerly the goal of the
longings of their ancestors and to them nothing but the awful
seat of Antichrist, as Luther had called the Pope. With justice
their leaders might tell them that there was the great manu-
factory of those artificial politics by which peoples and kings
were perplexed and entangled and driven into bloody wars in
order to give the Pope the dominion of the world. There,
almost within range of their muskets, trembled the enemy of
the Emperor, surrounded by his courtiers; tomorrow, perhaps,
their prisoner or dead. They themselves appeared as the
avengers of the long-prevailing wrong which their fatherland
had suffered at the hands of the Roman priesthood. They
could now carry out the scheme to which Hutten had exhorted
his followers when he called on them to arise with horse and
man to overthrow the Pope, restore the rights of Rome to the
Empire and put an end to the temporal power of the priest-

hood. The cupidity awakened in the Goths by the sight of Rome was probably less than the wild fanaticism, the thirst for revenge and spoil felt by Bourbon's mercenaries; these men of diverse race and character from both the north and south of Europe, who, united by the force of circumstances, had gathered to attack the stronghold of the Papacy. In the year 1527, as in the year 410, Rome was an object of contempt to brave warriors, who told one another that this capital of the world was inhabited solely by slaves, gluttons and hypocrites, was only the lying Sodom and Gomorrah of all sins, was decried in Germany and Spain, yea, throughout the whole world. The city of priests numbered, it is true, barely 90,000 inhabitants; nevertheless, next to Genoa and Venice it was the wealthiest city in Italy. Here stood countless churches, as temples had stood in the times of the Goths, filled with gold and silver images and vessels; here were vast and sumptuous palaces replete with treasures of a luxury that had again become classic. No enemy had sacked this city; in it was preserved the wealth of Christendom, which the insatiable Curia had extorted and devoured. All these treasures, amassed by priests and courtesans, by extortioners and usurers, nay, the property of the entire people, might according to the laws of war fall as spoils into the hands of the conquerors.

'. . . Terrible hours passed until midnight; for until then the imperialists, dreading an attack, stood under arms; the *landsknechts* disposed in formidable bands on the Campo dei Fiori, the Spaniards on the Navona, Ferrante Gonzaga with his cavalry opposite the bridge of St Angelo. Terror of death reigned supreme within the barricaded houses; every beat of drum, every shot fired from St Angelo, every trumpet blast caused thousands to shiver. About midnight the ranks on the Navona dispersed, those on the Campo dei Fiori followed, and 30,000 soldiers rushed with fury to pillage the city.

'The morning of May 7 revealed a sight too terrible for words; streets covered with ruins, with dead and dying; houses and churches in flames, and re-echoing with cries; a hideous tumult of robbery and flight; drunken soldiers laden with spoils or dragging prisoners after them. According to the laws of war of that period not only was a conquered city abandoned to pillage, but its entire population was exposed to the sword of the enemy. No *landsknecht* could have understood that it was inhuman to treat defenceless citizens as prisoners of war. The man who loved his life was obliged to redeem it by purchase. With brutal naïveté the knight Schertlin wrote in his memoirs: "On May 6 we took Rome by storm, put 6,000 men to death, took everything we could find in the churches or on the ground, and burnt a great part of the city."

'Nothing and no one was spared. The houses of Spaniards and Germans were sacked as well as those of the Romans. Hundreds of men of every grade had fled to the palaces belonging to the partisans of the Empire. The Spaniards burst open these buildings, and burnt or sacked them. Such was the fate that befell the palace of the Marquis of Mantua the first night, and that of the Portuguese ambassador, where, if we may believe it, spoil was collected to the value of 500,000 ducats. Cardinal Andrea della Valle sheltered some hundreds in his vast palace, which, on payment of several thousand ducats to Fabrizio Maramaldo, was exempted from sack. As in all such cases, the sum was guaranteed by legal document, the people who sought refuge pledging themselves to pay the owner of the palace in proportion to the value of the property of each.

'More unfortunate was the fate of those palaces which ventured on resistance; these were blown up with gunpowder and a tower on the Capitol thus perished. The Palazzo Lomellina on the Campus Martius attempted defence; the soldiers took it by assault; the owner was shot by musketeers while he was letting himself down by a rope into the courtyard in an endeavour to escape. Churches and convents yielded the richest spoils, not only their own property but the property of the fugitives who had sought refuge within them. They were indiscriminately sacked; neither the "Anima", the national

E   65

church of the Germans, nor St Giacomo on the Piazza Navona, the national church of the Spaniards whither Bourbon's remains had been conveyed, escaped. Santa Maria del Popolo was completely ransacked and the monks massacred. The nunneries of Santa Maria on the Campus Martius, of St Silvestro and of Monte Citorio were the scenes of untold horrors. Wherever an entrance was forced into a convent of the poorer orders and no spoils were found, the intruders revenged themselves with savage brutality.

'We must picture to ourselves the wealth of sacred vessels in order to comprehend the amount of spoil; everything was stolen, destroyed and profaned. The heads of the Apostles in the Lateran, St Andrew's head in St Peter's, that of St John in St Silvestro all shared the same fate. A German soldier affixed to the shaft of his own spear the so-called Sacred Lance-head; the Handkerchief of Veronica passed through a thousand hands and every tavern of Rome. The great Cross of Constantime from St Peter's was dragged through the Borgo and lost. The Germans preserved many relics as memorials, but the most ridiculous trophy was probably the thick cord, twelve feet long, with which Judas had hanged himself. Schertlin took it from St Peter's and carried it to his home. Even the most sacred of chapels, the Sancta Sanctorum, was sacked.

'Not even the Saracens had dealt more outrageously with St Peter's. The Spaniards ransacked the very graves, the grave of St Peter himself, as the Moors had formerly done. The dead Julius was robbed in his coffin, and the remains of Sixtus IV were only protected by the solidity of the bronze monument. Soldiers played dice on the high altar and drank with prostitutes from the chalices. Horses were stabled in the transepts as well as in the Vatican palace. Bulls or manuscripts which had been collected by humanistic Popes were used instead of straw. It was with difficulty that Orange, having made his dwelling in the palace, rescued the Vatican library. The streets were strewn with shreds of documents and registers of the papal chanceries.

'Many archives of convents and palaces were destroyed—an irreparable loss to the history of the city in the Middle Ages; and only by this sack can the present dearth of documents in the archives of the Capitol be explained.

'Several works of art were also lost. Raphael's Flemish tapestries were stolen and sold, and the beautiful painted glass of Guillaume de Marcillat was shattered. Foolish national hatred, however, has undoubtedly attributed to the *landsknechts* many outrages of which they were guiltless. Raphael's frescoes were not even blackened by the smoke of their torches, and the odious accusation brought against the Germans—that of having wantonly destroyed the finest statues—is amply refuted by the survival of the greatest masterpieces of ancient and Renaissance sculpture.'

Some of the famous Raphael tapestries reached France and later enabled the Constable Anne de Montmorency 'De faire sa cour au Pape Julius III'. An inscription on one of them testifies today to this act of generosity: 'Urbe capta partem aulaeorum a praedonibus distractorum conquisitam Anna Mommorancius Gallicae militiae praef. rescadiendam atque Julio III P. M. restituendam curavit 1533.'

In another passage Gregorovius, who based his account on a close study of the sources and scrupulously avoided the least exaggeration, expressed the horror aroused in a liberal-minded scholar of the nineteenth century:

'The Sack of Rome in the barbarous times of Alaric and Genseric was humane in comparison with the horrors inflicted by the army of Charles V. We may recall the triumphal procession of the Christian religion in the midst of the city plundered by the Goths, but we can discover no such act of piety in the year 1527. Here nothing meets the eye but Bacchanalian troops of *landsknechts*, accompanied by half-naked courtesans, riding to the Vatican to drink to the Pope's health or imprisonment. Lutherans, Spaniards and Italians all amused themselves in parodying the sacred ceremonies.

Landsknechts attired as cardinals rode about on asses, a soldier disguised as a pope in their midst, and thus passed and repassed St Angelo, where they shouted that now they would only make Popes and cardinals of pious men obedient to the Emperor, who would wage no further wars. They even proclaimed Luther Pope.'

Page by page the historian compiles the record of murder, rape, arson, loot, desecration; and from this account by Gregorovius as from others the reader of today gains two very definite impressions.

The first is the conviction that never before had such ravages taken place, or even could have taken place, as in Rome in May 1527. It almost seems as if the eye-witnesses had made a point of proving to posterity that all previous disasters and afflictions were nothing in comparison. Certainly, the Goths too had plundered Rome, but how mild they had been in comparison, how unsystematic and clumsy, how unskilled in evil, entering as they did for the first time, and in the innocence of a young race, on the page of history. As for the conduct of the Crusaders in Constantinople in 1204, it was not so much as mentioned; perhaps this was because it occurred in the Eastern capital, and any distance, whether of time or space, detracts from the shock of a catastrophe. Yet the Sack of Rome, terrible as it seemed at the time, had not lost its power to horrify even in the nineteenth century; visitors to Rome and lovers of Italy, whether Catholic or Protestant, still felt those awful days as an almost personal disaster. Not even the miseries of the Thirty Years War were able to efface this impression, nor have the destruction of the castle of Heidelberg and the burning of Moscow left such a memory behind. It needed Nazi and Bolshevik frightfulness to hit mankind as hard and to bite as deep into the common respect for humanity and the reverence for beauty as did the crimes of those mercenaries.

'The crimes of those mercenaries . . .' these words bring us to the second peculiarity to be observed. Which mercenaries were meant? We enter here upon the 'nationalizing' of destruction, murder, and looting. There were only faint indications of this tendency in connection with the taking of Constantinople in 1204, when no nation wished to bear the brunt of the blame of bloodshed and spoliation.

In 1527 contemporaries felt the horror of those days so acutely that they did everything to shield their own nations from being chiefly to blame. What Gregorovius has to say on this cannot be read without emotion, and yet it contains all the implications of national prejudice and even of race-hatred, of that sweeping condemnation of peoples and races which a few decades later was to run to such hideous lengths. Bearing this in mind, let us turn once more and for the last time to his scrutiny of the degrees of guilt involved:

'The Germans, more humane than the Spaniards, were satisfied with moderate ransoms. The avarice and sensuality of the Spaniards were unbounded; they outraged even little girls of ten. In many cases the Germans stabbed these demons. No contrast could be greater than that between the demoralized mercenaries of North and South: the Spaniards short, with black hair and yellow, bearded faces, were cunning and cruel, greedy and avaricious; the Germans tall, strong and fair, their hair cut short and wearing only moustachios, were drunken gluttons and reckless gamblers.'

7

Libraries as Loot

Libraries and manuscripts, as we have already noted, were valued as plunder since ancient times. It might be thought that the Renaissance with its profounder understanding of the universality of knowledge—and of art, too—would have shown more respect for books and manuscripts than did earlier centuries; but here, too, it kept to the tradition of antiquity. An Italian duke might sometimes show a more liberal spirit than his predecessors, but the foreign invader exercised his right of plunder without any restraint.

King Charles VIII of France, above all, looted without mercy in his Italian campaign of 1495. He robbed the cities he took of everything he fancied, whether it was private or public property. The far-famed library of the Kings of Naples was his most valuable acquisition. He presented no fewer than 1,140 volumes to his wife, Anne of Brittany, but the greater part of the Naples manuscripts was sent to the castle of Blois. From there they were later removed to the Bibliothèque Nationale, where, in the middle of the nineteenth century, fifteen Greek and Spanish and 240 Latin manuscripts could mostly be assigned to Naples, though some had originated in other campaigns at other times.

If the government of Naples thought they could hide even part of their precious library in a safe place and wait for happier times, they were very much mistaken. Once a victorious commander or prince set his heart on some particular prize, he was sure to find some way of getting hold of it. And so it was with the library of Naples: what escaped King Charles's clutches at his first grab he made sure of in the peace treaty, so far as it had not

70

fallen to the share of Cardinal Georges d'Amboise, likewise by the terms of peace.

But Charles had other fancies which he could satisfy in Naples: he had large bronzes loaded on galleys, and only his hasty departure saved them from being transported to France. And even what he took with him was scattered to the four winds in the battle of Fornova and lost for ever. The rest of his plunder, which was sent on after him—tapestries, books, paintings, marble and porphyry figures and furniture—arrived at Lyons by easy stages. From there the convoy proceeded to the castle of Amboise where its contents were distributed among the salons and rooms.

King Louis XII of France surpassed, if that was possible, his predecessor's passion for the collection of choice possessions. One of his first raids was directed on the library of Pavia, which the Visconti and Sforza had assembled with great judgment. As there was no complete catalogue of this library at the time of its forcible appropriation, it has not been possible to discover how many books were removed to France on that occasion and later reached the Bibliothèque Nationale.

Louis was also set upon another exploit which was worthy of the despoilers of old Roman times: he was determined to carry off Leonardo's *Last Supper* to France. But as the technique of removing frescoes from walls was unknown at that time, he had finally to forgo this coveted prize and to leave the masterpiece to its gradual decay in Italy.

Those years were so remarkable for raids on art and libraries that a French writer wrote at the end of the nineteenth century: 'At no other period have works of art played a greater part in diplomatic exchanges.' But the enterprises of Göring and Rosenberg, with the object of enriching the Third Reich and themselves by the acquisition of foreign works of art under cover of legal form, were still to come.

The most celebrated library to be looted in the sixteenth century was that of King Matthias Corvinus, who was not only a victorious commander and statesman but also 'a generous protector of art and knowledge'. The spirit of the Renaissance passed

71

rapidly from Italy to Hungary, whose throne was occupied by Matthias, a collateral of the Angevin dynasty of Naples, and, thenceforward, the humanist love of learning and art spread swiftly in the country. Matthias Corvinus had been deeply imbued with the literary and artistic enthusiasms of the Renaissance from his early youth, and after ascending the throne his interest in art and knowledge did not diminish. He passed for one of the most elegant and learned princes of his day, a day when the correspondence of princes was larded with quotations from Latin and Greek authors.

Among all the treasures he collected and all his acts of enlightened patronage, the creation of his library at Ofen, known as the Corvina, stands out and sheds lustre on the name of Matthias Corvinus even to this day. It was his most brilliant contribution to the advancement of knowledge; just as it excited the admiration of his contemporaries, so it still exercises the curiosity of scholars. It is not possible to assign a precise date to its foundation, as Matthias is known to have started collecting books and having copies made soon after his accession. He devoted more and more attention to this during the second half of his reign; copyists were in constant employment at his court and his agents travelled the whole of Europe. Besides this he commissioned Italian copyists, particularly those of Florence, where the copying of manuscripts formed a regular industry. The celebrated Vespasian Bisticci, who was in constant touch with the learned bishops of Hungary, presided over one of these 'factories'.

It was the King's ambition to possess as complete a collection as possible of religious and secular literature, drawn from classical as well as medieval times. Although his library cannot have numbered 50,000 volumes as has been stated, it was certainly one of the largest of its day, and he was not concerned only with the subject, the rarity or the number of his books, but also with their beauty and the splendour of their bindings. He had many of them illuminated by the best masters. His missal, illuminated by the Florentine Attavante de Attavantibus between 1485 and 1487, was his most precious example, rivalling the celebrated

72

prayerbook of Maximilian I; it contained numerous full-page illustrations and no fewer than three portraits of Matthias.

There was much controversy during the nineteenth century concerning the place to be assigned to this library in the history of literature and the advancement of knowledge. It is indisputable that it played a considerable part in making the store of ancient writings accessible. It is known, too, that agents with full powers to buy for the library scoured Greece and Asia Minor and brought back a number of valuable finds, which, but for the royal enthusiasm, would probably have perished in course of time.

The King's death meant the beginning of hard times for the library. His successors, Ladislas II and Ludwig II, 'gave away many of its treasures with heedless generosity to foreigners who were visiting their court'. And so, while other princes of those days were collecting libraries by more or less forcible acquisition, these successors of Matthias were dispersing his, bit by bit, from ignorance or indifference, and inflicting irreparable damage on a unique possession. The Emperor Maximilian I, for example, was able to acquire so many volumes from it that they formed the nucleus of his court library at Vienna.

After the battle of Mohacs in 1526, in which King Ludwig II of Hungary lost his life, his widow, Queen Anna, fled westward, taking a number of valuable books with her. When Ferdinand I was in occupation of the Castle of Ofen from 1528 to 1529, still more of what was left of the library was removed to Vienna; and when the Turks took Ofen in 1541, the Vizir Ibrahim, a friend to art and learning, despatched further portions of it to Constantinople, as well as the bronze statues of Hercules, Diana and Apollo. When they were erected in front of his palace, pious Muslims indignantly accused him of idolatry. In the seventeenth century a number of influential persons, among them a cardinal and Prince Gabriel Bethlen, endeavoured to acquire the remains of the library, but soon after it suffered severe damage by fire. In 1666 Peter Lambeck, librarian of the Vienna Court Library, who had been sent to Ofen by the Emperor's orders, found what had been rescued from the fire stacked up carelessly in cellars and left to decay. He returned with three manuscripts he had been given. Twenty years later Ofen was re-conquered from the Turks and what was left of King Matthias's fine library was scattered in all directions. Part of it fell into the hands of the Elector Maximilian II of Bavaria, part was taken by Count Marsigli, and the Vienna Court Library once again had its share.

European travellers visiting Constantinople during the nineteenth century were occasionally allowed to see and even to acquire some of the books and manuscripts carried off by Ibrahim. But as the whole collection was stored with the holy relics of Islam in the old palace, it was impossible for some time for any European to get at it and form any estimate of its state of preservation. It was not until 1862 that the members of the Hungarian Academy of Sciences obtained permission to inspect the greater portion, of which they were then able to make a rapid and summary catalogue. After this it was known more or less what items from the original library had reached Constantinople. In 1869 the Sultan gave four of these now identified volumes to Franz Joseph, King and Emperor of the Austro-Hungarian Empire, and he presented them to the Hungarian National Museum. Further, in 1877, Sultan Abdul Hamid gave the University of Budapest thirty-five old manuscripts, ten of which could be identified as part of the Corvina Library. Finally, in 1889 the manuscripts which at that time were still in the Seraglio among the other treasures were examined by delegates of the Hungarian Academy of Sciences.

Today, the part which either remained in Hungary or returned there has been miserably reduced by revolution, war, fire, and not least by the renewed looting of the last twenty years. From all of which it appears that Ibrahim, who inflicted such damage on the Corvina as the victorious war-lord and plunderer, was also, as the bibliophile who removed many of its treasures to safer keeping, to some extent its rescuer.

8

The Thirty Years War

The story of the Corvina Library has led us unawares
through the years of the Thirty Years War and even into
the nineteenth century, but this does not absolve us from
giving closer consideration to those three frightful decades of
war, destruction, spoliation and bloodshed in so far as they concern our theme.

The Thirty Years War had so many different manifestations
in its earlier and later years, in the north and south, east and
west, with the Swedes and the Imperialists, in large industrial
towns and among the bare heaths, that even today there is no
agreement about what actually occurred or how many lives it cost.

One of the most frequently discussed questions is whether the
decline of German cultural, civilizing, artistic, technical and
manual achievements had already set in before 1618, and if so,
owing to what causes; or whether this decline was a consequence
of the war. It has even been suggested that the war may in
many respects have acted as a stimulus, contributing to Germany's revival in the eighteenth century after a comparatively
rapid recovery from a state of destitution.

It is remarkable that among all the records of the day and
later accounts scarcely a word is ever said about the looting of
art during the Thirty Years War. Everyone who has concerned
himself with this long struggle knows that there were no
limits to plunder and destruction; everyone laments the irreparable losses inflicted on all parts of Germany; but no one has
discovered of what these losses actually consisted. To do so, it
would be necessary to distinguish between what was carried off

75

to enrich museums or private collections in Sweden, France, Italy or Holland, and what was condemned to total destruction.

The scope of the enquiry must therefore be confined to a few particularly striking and typical examples, of which a fairly detailed account can be given; and the final conclusion may be summed up in advance: the war was terribly destructive in the domain of art as elsewhere; fire, bullets, or the onslaught of ignorant, looting mercenaries annihilated in minutes works of art which had existed for centuries. In addition, countless works of art were sent on their travels owing to theft, robbery, extortion, forced contributions, 'thank-offerings', or however else the change of ownership might be brought about. German churches had to sacrifice treasures they had faithfully guarded for years to enrich Swedish nobles, foreign dynasties and public museums. The north of Germany exchanged its treasures with the south and vice versa. Many a mercenary disposed of his loot to sutlers, who in turn sold it abroad, where it may have survived the succeeding centuries secure from rapine and damage.

To come down to particulars, in illustration of these general conclusions, the names of the leading actors in this disastrous war were Tilly, Wallenstein and Gustavus Adolphus.

Tilly was responsible for protecting the Palatina Library from his own troops and for ensuring that the most valuable part of it could be handed over unharmed to the Vatican Library. As for Wallenstein, he took up his quarters in 1625 and 1626 in the monastery of Halberstadt.

'At his very first appearance in north Germany the new prince made such a display that he far outshone the petty North German princes and even the Electors themselves. Seventy-two houses, and later fifty more, were required for his retinue, which exceeded what in our time would be thought necessary for the ruler of a kingdom or an empire. His own stable, in April 1626, consisted of fifty horses.'

His retinue was not confined to his officers: it included the men who chopped up the fodder and even his washer-women, all of whom had to be fed. When all the attendants upon his officers of lower or higher rank are reckoned in, the burden of having such a tribe billeted on the countryside may be imagined. Many persons of rank also quartered their friends on their unwilling hosts, who were asked for contributions in money as well. If cash were not available, they had to meet the bill with pictures and valuables of all kinds, on which naturally a low estimate was put.

Every citizen was distrained upon for his last penny, and soon not one was able to supply the soldiers with food and drink. This led to outbreaks resulting in more robbing, smashing, burning. Carelessness, ignorance and the pleasure of destruction contributed to the confusion. Much of what vanished was of little worth at the time and has only since acquired a museum value.

In general, it might be said that the greed of the officers differed from the men's only in what aroused their covetousness. They extorted their last possessions from their hosts, many of whom preferred to abandon house and home rather than submit any longer; four hundred inhabitants of Halberstadt did so in the early days of occupation. This threw the whole billeting arrangements into confusion, and the Croats and others as well took their revenge on all the movables and immovables which their owners had left behind. 'Stairs and chests, tables and chairs and even vats were thrown out of the houses and if not worth selling went to keep up the watch fires at the gates or else were simply smashed up. When there was nothing else left, they started on the building itself and tore out the wood-work and timbers for burning.'

When the town complained to Wallenstein of these outrages, he was sorry and surprised and said that such lawlessness must be stopped at once. But all went on as before, and as Wallenstein took whatever he fancied, none of his officers or men needed to fear any curtailment of their own opportunities.

But that is only one modest instance of innumerable similar cases. The billeting of troops always meant the sacrifice of all that had been collected and valued in the households of craftsmen and merchants, gentry and nobles for generation after generation. Besides the gold and silver and precious stones, there were all the objects treasured more for their appearance than for their cost, such as examples of weaving, embroidery and other homely arts, which from the pure lust for destruction were trodden underfoot, torn to shreds and thrown aside. The accounts of such outrages are too familiar to need much amplifying. Christoph Grimmelshausen's novel *Simplicissimus*, in spite of some picturesque exaggeration, comes very near the truth:

'. . . others smashed in stoves and windows as though to announce an unending summer, flattened out copper and pewter vessels for easier transport and stowed them away, and burned the beds, tables, chairs and benches though there was fire-wood in plenty stacked in the yards. They sat the farmer down in front of the fire, bound him hand and foot, and rubbed his bare soles with moistened salt. Our old goat then came and licked it off and tickled him till he nearly burst himself with laughing. It was so funny that I had to keep him company and laugh myself. His laughter made him confess his secrets; he told where his treasures were hidden and you would never have thought a farmer would have been so rich in pearls, gold and trinkets.'

In a war diary there is this entry for November 17, 1620:

'His Highness (Maximilian I of Bavaria) has set off for Munich, but first he warned the Comte de Buquox about the Imperial troops, whose continual plundering, robbing, holding up to ransom, raping of women and girls cause daily complaint . . .'

And from Dresden, January 30, 1621:

'The Fuggers have had a good haul of some hundred thousand ducats in Augsburg some months since, and also the fleet, just arrived from India with such valuable cargo, promises them as good again. And although not only His Royal Highness of Bavaria but many other potentates will be very pressing,

78

they ought dutifully to oblige your Grace with fifty or sixty thousand gulden. Otherwise the Austrians, Martin Zobel and Marx Konrad von Rehlinger, and other men of substance have large sums of Reichstaler and other such currency by them, so that they can hold back during this very risky rise in the value of money, because all currencies of that sort are going up day by day and so gold hoarded in their chests pays them far better than if they put it out at interest. But I do not doubt at all that there is something to be had from them now that, thank God, the situation is so good . . .'

Money was the first essential of the war; troops had to have their pay, and equipment had to be bought. Ernst von Mansfeld explicitly condoned robbery, as is shown by Lieutenant Julius von Weissenbach's report from Zwickau, February 7, 1621: ' . . . (Mansfeld) had it posted up everywhere that for a horse he would give twenty Reichstaler and fifteen gulden a month as pay and that he would make no trouble at all about looting.'

From Prague, August 1619, we learn:

'The fine folk are quartered in the town, but the rest in the suburbs. They have plenty of money, particularly in gold, ducats by the bagful, fine dresses by the yard, gold rings and silverware, silver bowls, cups and candelabra, loot from Silesia and Moravia. Passing through two places they came on weddings, both of men in good position; they fell on the bridegrooms and wedding guests, ravished the women and carried off the brides, looted all the silver and jewellery, stripped the women of their clothes, enough to draw tears from a stone. Now, where they sell clothes off cheap, coats go for seven or eight gulden which cost a hundred taler to make. The small boys and camp-followers' children are drinking out of little silver bowls, as I have seen with my own eyes, and the Lord help any if they come their way—words cannot describe what they're like. The Walloons and Hungarians are nothing beside them. Ride their horses straight into the shops, give them almonds by the hatful and water them with Spanish wine.'

ART PLUNDER

Some places might suffer in this way only once during a number of years; others, on the other hand, were occupied time after time. Ramsla, a small country town, was occupied by the Imperial troops in 1631, twice plundered by the Swedes in 1636, twice by the Imperialists and once by the Saxons in 1637, and by the Swedes in 1638. The chronicler remarks on this: 'I could find it easier to tolerate this spoliation if it was inflicted by foreigners. But it is nearly always Lower Saxons, as their speech shows, fellow-Germans, therefore, and fellow-believers, and our friends moreover . . .' In 1640 Ramsla was plundered once more by the Weimar or French army. 'So now, all my cattle having been driven off by the Swedes, I am so shaken and cleaned out and ruined that in my seventy-sixth year I have nothing but poverty and destitution to look to.'

The same authority says in another place, 'If the men threaten to mutiny, they're taken on to fresh ground and given a few towns to plunder.'

In many places, of course, the loss in works of art and valuables was reduced by their rapid removal to a place of safety as soon as friend or foe approached. For example, the Elector George William of Brandenburg, in 1626 and the following years, instructed his ministers to take his wife and children to safety as soon as danger threatened, and with them the archives, the treasure chest, the heirlooms from his mother's side and other valuables. If time allowed, they were to take shelter in the fortress of Kustrin; otherwise Spandau. But if the danger was great and likely to be long-continued, Prussia alone would suffice. Actually, the treasure or at least part of it seems to have been taken to Kustrin. On January 26, 1626, there was in the inventory there a 'splendid effigy of the Emperor Charles in silver-gilt with gold, in his Emperor's dress, richly adorned with pearls, a crown of pearls and precious stones, and many other precious things'. But as the war went on all these treasures gradually perished; for by 1643 no more is heard of them and in the inventory of 1689 not a single one of the pieces minutely described in 1603, 1605, and in part still in 1626, is extant—one of the many

80

signs that however carefully treasures were packed and sent under escort to safety, there was no means of ensuring their protection from robbery and destruction.

Most of the possessions looted in those years but not destroyed remained in the country and often in the same place, changing ownership rapidly at first. From looter, thief or extortioner, they went from hand to hand, through the platoon commander to the inn-keeper in exchange for drink or a woman, or to the sutler, horse-dealer or armourer. On the other hand, they might simply be thrown away or left behind in billets or lost in a fight; the soldier very seldom kept his booty long. We know, nevertheless, that many valuables did in fact find their way to foreign lands, but this was due not to the common soldier, who lacked the love of art or the love of possessions and also the means of transport, but to the officers, generals, commanders-in-chief, ministers and princes.

A Dutch art-historian, discussing some paintings of Carel van Mander which turned up in Cassel from Sweden in the eighteenth century, asked, 'Is it too rash to conjecture that the Swedes took these works from Kronborg or some other Danish castle when they invaded Denmark in 1659?' This tentative question might be asked many times over in reference to this war and answered in the affirmative, for Germany in particular.

There is no question of course of 'imputing the blame for these forceful expropriations 300 years after the event'. There is another way of looking at it. The war-booty taken to Sweden had a widespread influence on art and culture. It found a new home in public and private collections and was spared the dangers of subsequent wars; it gave pleasure and inspiration to countless people, even to visitors from the country of its former possessors, who, after lamenting the accidents of war and the ways of providence, later came to rejoice that these works of art had been kept safe in Stockholm, or wherever it might be.

How much, and what, the Swedes looted, in particular from Germany, during the Thirty Years War has never been ascertained, and cannot be determined with any accuracy today, even in

F

the case of important works of art. No one in the seventeenth century was concerned, or in the position, to draw up lists, and later, changes of ownership within the country as well as outside by sale, gift, legacy etc., were so frequent as to make it impossible.

Even in the nineteenth century the Swedes were accused of wholesale plunder by historians who could not be accused of pro-German sentiments; and hence they were given sole credit for the plunder of the Thirty Years War, but on the other hand there are plenty of instances which fasten the blame on one man, one party or one regiment.

Granberg, the Swedish art-historian, observes of Gustavus Adolphus that from the age of twenty-one in 1615, at the outset of his career as victorious commander and king, he began sending home the treasures of art he had plundered. In Pleskau, for example, he came upon Russian ikons which delighted him greatly and which he carried off without a thought.

When he took Riga on September 15, 1621, he commandeered the library of the Jesuits there and also pictures and precious ikons, one of which, dating from the fifteenth century, was the copy of a celebrated original of 1155. Much of the booty from Riga was still among Gustavus Adolphus's treasure in Stockholm in 1632.

When he occupied Stargard in Pomerania on August 3, 1626, he took from the Pelplin monastery there books and pictures, including portraits of princes and church dignitaries, to a formidable amount in bulk, though the total value was not great. On the day after, he paid the monastery a visit in person and commandeered the organ, the altar and some more paintings, all of which were sent to Sweden, where they were later identified. In the same year he took a singularly beautiful Polish monument from Frauenburg Cathedral.

In October 1631, the Prince Bishop wrote to the Emperor about the plundering of Würzburg by the Swedes: 'The castle contained old reliquaries, gilded silver busts, canonicals, chalices, church treasures and other such fine work and precious things from my own head foundation and others in the neighbourhood, and also from the monastery, parish and pilgrims' churches.' To this must be added the possessions of the Prince himself. Gustavus Adolphus took his choice from the Prince's silver cabinet, and what gold and silver vessels and pearls and precious stones he fancied, and left the rest to his officers and men. But who can say how much of it all may have remained in Germany?

It was another matter with the Prince Bishop's library, for which Echter von Mespelbrunn had been responsible. Gustavus Adolphus had it packed up and sent to the University of Uppsala, together with the libraries of the University and the Jesuits' College. In this, apart from the loss to Germany, he appears in a sympathetic light as the patron of learning in his own land.

The rich Julius Hospice was the only foundation he left inviolate in spite of its wealth of gold and silver and also of corn and wine. It was his intention to reap this harvest as well, but the Master asked him to read the warning of Bishop Julius, the founder, before he did so. When Gustavus had read the curses he had laid on any who ravaged his pious charity, he drew back in horror: 'I don't want to have that bishop to face in the other world. Let him keep his own.'

We know then what Gustavus carried off from Würzburg in October 1631, but Granberg expressly states that his generals, Nils Brahe, for example, were not behindhand; they too plundered and sent much of their plunder home. The inventory of Queen Christina for the year 1652 includes plunder from Munich and particularly Prague and a whole list of precious works of art from Mainz, of which part had come directly from Gustavus Adolphus and part had been presented to his successor by his generals and other highly placed persons.

Among the Würzburg plunder was a reliquary which appears in a list signed in 1631 by a servant of the royal household named Anders. It is still today the glory of the Stockholm Historical Museum. It contained in 1236 the skull of Saint Elizabeth, who died in 1231, and until the beginning of the sixteenth century was in the keeping of the Teutonic Order at Marburg. It was probably removed from there to Mergentheim and taken for safety to the fortress of Marienburg at Würzburg on the approach of the Swedes. Gustavus Adolphus, a lineal descendant of Saint Elizabeth, captured it there and sent it to Sweden.

The literary treasures of Mainz, still today to be found scattered among many Swedish libraries, constituted, however, one of the finest and best known hauls made by the Swedes.

Gustavus Adolphus appeared before the walls of Mainz on December 10, 1631. Terms of surrender were quickly negotiated and he took up his quarters in the Martinsburg. The plunder which fell into his hands was more than usually splendid and included important collections of books: one had already gone to Rome; now, a few years later, the others crossed the sea to Scandinavia.

Already in the sixteenth century the Margrave Albrecht Achilles of Brandenburg had captured Mainz and collected many precious manuscripts and printed books from the libraries of the monasteries, churches, and presumably also of the university, and sent them to Heidelberg to his book-loving father-in-law, the Elector Palatine. Thus manuscripts from Mainz are to be found in both the Vatican and the Uppsala University libraries. But though the Swedes were not the first nor the only robbers of the manuscripts and archives of Mainz, they may claim to have made a longer and more consistent use of the rights of conquest to improve and enrich their own libraries.

They could, moreover, plead legal justification. The work of Hugo Grotius, *De Jure belli et pacis*, appeared a few years before the capture of Mainz by the Swedes, and it devoted two chapters to the question of the right to include libraries and archives as war-booty. And it must be admitted that the practice of the Swedish King was milder than the theory of the Dutch jurist, since the King usually confined himself to the appropriation of 'ownerless' property, whose owners, that is, had fled at the approach of the Swedish army; sparing, on the other hand, houses and buildings which were occupied or defended. It is said that he had a jurist among his retinue whose special task it was to give an authoritative opinion on doubtful cases of libraries.

'He also had in his entourage men of education, court chaplains and physicians, to whom he entrusted the selection and cataloguing of books to be despatched to Sweden. The libraries of Jesuits were plundered with particular pleasure, partly perhaps because it was thought to be an act pleasing to God, also because it deprived them of serviceable weapons in their war against Protestantism and enabled the Swedish theologians at the same time to disarm the counter-Reformation movement.'

We shall meet many more of these specialists: Napoleon had the celebrated Baron Denon, a connoisseur and sleuth, as talented as he was unscrupulous; Hitler and his 'paladins' were advised by men of a much coarser stamp, who did not confuse robbery and plunder either with art or even any real knowledge of the art market.

As for the Swedes, the principal beneficiary of the legalized plundering by Gustavus Adolphus was the recently founded University Library at Uppsala. Books from Riga, Braunsberg, Frauenburg, Würzburg, and Mainz all found their way there. Towns like Västerås and Strängnäs were also allotted some of the booty from Mainz, but both places lost these benefactions owing to a disaster recalling that which overtook the Roman bronzes destined for Africa in 455: the ship carrying the treasure went to the bottom.

Part of the Mainz libraries found their new home in the library of Axel Oxenstjerna and his descendants, whose possessions were sold in Stockholm in 1732. A great many of the books were bought on that occasion by foreign buyers, particularly Hessians. Sometimes duplicates were sold in Uppsala and in this way valuable examples came into private hands, and turned up in the castles of noble families founded by soldiers who had grown rich in the wars and, following the literary fashion, had bought up costly editions by the yard for display. A well-stocked library gave a patina to brand-new coats of arms, and it was tactfully left unsaid whose ancestor had won these splendidly bound books while fighting for king and country.

To return to Mainz: on the very day of its capitulation, while the King was still in his quarters at Weisenau, he gave his physician, Jacob Robert Honius, and his chaplain, Johannes Matthias, orders respecting the measures to be taken about the libraries:

'We, Gustavus Adolphus, . . . hereby make known that we commission and empower our physician and chaplain, Jacob Robert Honius and M. Johannes Matthias, to collect all libraries and books in private hands, found in the castle and in surrendered colleges, schools, monasteries or in any other houses in Mainz, for the benefit of us and the Crown of Sweden, and to bring them together in some safe place for removal at the first opportunity. We strictly command all officers of whatever rank, as well as common soldiers, horse and foot, to leave all libraries untouched and further to be of service to the above named physician and chaplain and their assistants for the safe custody and disposal of these books, and if any has misappropriated any of the same he is hereby ordered to return them on pain of heavy punishment. And the physician and chaplain are authorized to take possession of them.'

It was obviously not very easy or indeed possible to carry out these instructions during the first days of the occupation. The residences of the clerical and Electoral officers who had taken to flight were looted and stripped of all they contained, including books and whole libraries. Much of the plunder was then sold in the town market for cash, by which means the Swedish soldiers pocketed money, and the inhabitants of Frankfurt and Hanau made many a good bargain at the expense of the unfortunate citizens of Mainz.

The conduct of the Swedes was much the same in Mainz as in other places. They imposed a war-contribution in excess of what the town could pay, and to extort the utmost possible they sequestrated the property of the churches, monasteries and charitable foundations, all of which had to furnish inventories of their possessions. The houses of all clerical functionaries and members of the University as well as of other citizens were strictly searched.

86

Catholics and especially Jesuits came in for the harshest measures. On the very day after his entry, the King had their buildings occupied, strongly guarded, sealed, and their goods and rents sequestrated. Half the contribution, not less than 400,000 taler, fell on the Jesuits. As they were unable or unwilling to produce this sum, in March the Swedish government confiscated all their possessions, including their large and valuable library. They kept possession of this for several years and made use of it for their own purposes—that was all. They did not carry off the books or damage them, as a letter of the Rector of the College of 1644 claims, and when they withdrew in 1635 they left them to their rightful owners.

In Gustavus Adolphus's directive quoted above there was mention of private and public libraries, but the most important of them, the ancient library of the Cathedral, rich in manuscripts and incunabula, was not among them, or at least was not expressly named. Presumably the King was not able to decide on the spot whether it could properly be regarded as war booty or not. Certainly no such scruples had deterred him in Frauenburg, but in south Germany he behaved with greater moderation, in this as in other matters. It took him three months to make up his mind, and meanwhile Doctor Balthasar Henkel answered the question in the affirmative in eighteen propositions; and after this the library was twice plundered. On the first occasion the booty reached Sweden safely, but on the second the ship went down in the Baltic, taking with it other valuable presents from Gustavus Adolphus to Axel Oxenstjerna.

Meanwhile Robert Honius and Matthias had commandeered for the Swedish state larger and smaller portions of at least ten libraries. Books from the Mainz Cathedral Library and also dedication copies with the book-plate of various Electors from the Electoral Library are still to be found today in the University Library of Uppsala.

But as it was not found possible to carry off the entire libraries of Mainz, the not inconsiderable remainder served later as the foundation for the libraries of the Capuchin and Carthusian monasteries.

The smaller collections of private persons, such as councillors, clerics, professors and scholars, suffered severe curtailment also. Any enumeration of all these losses, without regard to the importance of single books or manuscripts, would give a figure which would seem paltry to those familiar with libraries today. Large and important libraries now run to hundreds of thousands, even millions of books. In the time of the Thirty Years War and on into the eighteenth century libraries of a few thousand books contained items of great value and rarity. This has to be borne in mind when one reads that the Mainz University Library lost at least 450 volumes to the Swedes, the Elector's Library seventy-six and three manuscripts. Adding as many more from Mainz, of the whereabout of which nothing is known and which may have vanished in private libraries in Sweden, been destroyed, burnt, given away or sold abroad (to France, for example, and the Vatican Library, among the gifts of Queen Christina), we get a figure of between 1,000 and 1,200 books and manuscripts.

The turn of Munich came on May 16, 1632. Although the inhabitants were promised that their property would be spared in return for a payment of 300,000 taler, the library, the treasure cabinet and the arsenal were looted. Granberg very tactfully hints that Gustavus Adolphus departed from the truth in his later assertion that he knew nothing of these 'forbidden' robberies. The King was living in the castle when works of art were removed from it, some as his personal plunder. And it is well known that he took possession of all the valuable works in the place, and in Augsburg too, and sent them home. The rest was smashed up and destroyed, with the exception, Granberg writes, of some 'hideous things'.

The Elector Maximilian of Bavaria did not let his works of art go without protest. He addressed letter upon letter to Swedish generals and also, after Gustavus Adolphus's death, begged Torstenson to restore them, adding that some of them (there were paintings among them of quite immense size) could not be of great value to the officers who had them in their possession.

88

Maximilian had been informed in a report by one of his servants, dated September 24, 1634, of the extent of his losses. Old paintings and battle pictures in gilt frames and various antiques in gold were listed. Maximilian had pressed his claim in all quarters for the return of these objects, all known to have been removed to Sweden, right on into 1635. Finally he had an answer in which he detected a ray of hope: the booty in the hands of Swedish officers, he was told, might and would be returned to him if General Horn, who was a prisoner of war, were to benefit thereby; if, in other words, he were given his freedom.

A list of the missing objects of the year 1634 points directly to this circumstance:

'The accompanying list shows what paintings were taken from our gallery in Munich and removed to Sweden by the King. It appears that there is no other means of recovery except through the captured Swedish Field-Marshal Horn. Therefore, hand him the list herewith provided and ask him kindly to read it, that the objects mentioned may be returned. And we remain, etc.
Braunaw, 24. 7. 1634.'

This inventory names seventeen works, among them one each by Holbein and Mielich, and three by Cranach. Another German list gives twenty; a Swedish one, on the other hand, only twelve. It is known for certain that not all of them reached Sweden or were not all added to the royal treasure, and it is conceivable that some had been sent back to Germany before 1652, the year when the inventory was drawn up for Christina. If so, no record of any such transaction is extant. All the same, three pictures, which, according to the German list, had been carried off to Sweden, were later found in Munich.

One of the pictures by Holbein was, indeed, removed from Munich, but was inventoried in Lisbon as the property of King John IV of Portugal. It is known that Queen Christina placed no value on that part of the booty of the Thirty Years War which consisted of German paintings, and so she gave away two precious pictures by Dürer from the Prague plunder to Philip IV of Spain without a thought. The others could be identified years later in Stockholm by the Bavarian arms on them.

Granberg in his invaluable contemporary record lists a large number of pictures which arrived in Sweden as plunder. They were not only to be found in the Royal collections or in castles: the French secretary of the Legation, Charles Ogier, saw German booty all over Sweden in 1634 and 1635. He too observed the Bavarian arms on the gilt frames, and with what care and skill these paintings must have been packed to withstand months of travel by land and sea without damage. Ogier was struck by the great quantity of admirable works of art in the houses of merchants and prosperous citizens of Stockholm. He even found a collection of pictures in the house of the organist of the German church in Stockholm which included one from Danzig ascribed to Dürer, the origin of which was unknown. Later Swedish kings are known to have drawn on the booty from the Thirty Years War as a convenient means of repaying private loans to the state. And finally it should not be forgotten that many adventurers or officers sold their plunder to merchants, bankers, shippers or tradesmen, whereafter it would be handed on as heirlooms or legacies, or by sale or auction, coming again and again on the market and changing its ownership, perhaps in Sweden, perhaps in Europe, perhaps beyond the sea.

Standing out from all the German plunder, although formally a gift, was one of Philip Hainhofer's celebrated cabinets. He had been paid 6,000 gulden for this magnificent specimen of the cabinet-maker's art, and the town of Augsburg presented it to Gustavus Adolphus in April 1632, in sign of welcome, knowing doubtless that he would never overlook such a valuable piece of work and that as a gift it might at least make a good impression. It was not, however, until 1644 that it was despatched to Wolgast by a citizen of Augsburg, accompanied by a cabinet-maker who would be able to repair any damage suffered on the journey. It was inherited by Christina, who, however, did not take it with her when she left Sweden, perhaps because of her dislike of German art.

The conquest of Prague was left for 1648, the last year of the war. Until then, as Granberg also makes clear, Christina's hoard was small and only of modest worth. Now, with the plunder reaching Stockholm from Prague, it took a leap forward, particularly because of the artistic value of these acquisitions. The question then arises whether this plunder from Prague was her private property? Was crown property at that time identical with state property? It seems that, either by an oversight or intentionally, this not unimportant question has never until recent times been investigated and given an answer. Yet the verdict to be passed on Christina's subsequent removal of numerous works of art when she left the country depends on it. Did she take them with her when she abdicated as the private possessions of a private person, or was she plundering in her turn?

When the Kleinseite of Prague fell into the hands of the Swedes on July 26, 1648, only three of all the palaces of the town were left unpillaged and the famous library containing the *Codex Argenteus*, the Wulfilas Bible, now the glory of the library of Uppsala University, was among the spoil. Yet the Rudolph collection was untouched.

Never had Swedish officers had such a haul to deal with; it was only on August 5, ten days after the event, that Christina had news of the victory. She at once gave orders that all art treasures in the town should be reserved for the crown. *Songe aussi, je vous prie, de me conserver et m'envoyer la bibliothèque et les raretez qu se trouvent à Prag; vous savez que ce sont les seules choses dont je fais estime.* But the letter was delayed and apparently never reached the hands of the general in command, who was in dread every day of being surprised by the conclusion of peace and so being balked of the plunder.

At last in the early hours of November 6, 1648, it was possible to get the books and art treasures out of Prague, where gutted rooms were left with nothing but smashed furniture and empty frames. The convoy was transported down the Elbe and then by sea. It arrived at the fortress of Domitz by the end of November and had to winter there, because the commander of the fortress would not take the responsibility for sending it on over the wretched roads and then through the ice-floes of the Baltic. Also transport was lacking. But Christina was impatient to see the spoils. On January 20, 1649, she ordered the commandant of Wismar to send for it at once and to be ready to embark it as soon as ever the sea was open. Finally it arrived in good order in Stockholm on April 14, 1649. The celebrated periodical, *Theatrum Europaeum*, was well aware of the importance of this art migration and gave a report of its value without delay.

It was, in fact, soon seen to be stupendous. The inventory of Christina's treasures, drawn up very carelessly and summarily in 1652, contains 570 items, but many include several, in one case as many as eighty, objects, so that at least 780 separate pieces or groups can be enumerated. Of these, not less than 470 came from Prague, twelve, as noted above, from Munich, and a few others probably from Würzburg. Prague was also given as the home of the following:

170 marble statues
100 bronzes
33,000 coins and medals
197 ivories
26 objects of amber
24 objects of coral
660 ornaments of agate and rock crystal
174 pieces of china
1 large service of china
403 objects from India
2 ebony cupboards inlaid with gold and silver
16 valuable clocks
185 pieces of jewellery
Several drawers full of uncut diamonds
317 mathematical and astronomical instruments.

In addition there were the presents from generals and other highly placed persons.

The Sack of Rome had not enriched any prince with such a haul of precious things; the Burgundian booty was less extensive, but perhaps most closely comparable; no doubt the Venetians in 1204 extracted even more at least in money value from Constantinople; but for more recent times and even for the Thirty Years War, now ended, Prague was unique, and remained so until the Second World War.

Christina's art collections and all the books which Gustavus Adolphus had either sent or brought from Germany were a continual cause of the profoundest admiration. In her picture gallery she had forty-seven pictures of the first importance, all from Prague, including ten by Correggio.

Many of these paintings were destined for a roving life. Some of them turned up in London in 1793 and 1798, when part of the collection of the Duke of Orleans was put up to auction. Indeed, the nucleus of the Orleans pictures at the end of the eighteenth century consisted of pictures which had once belonged to Queen Christina. But how had they come into the possession of the Duke of Orleans and why did they then come to London?

The relatively small number of pictures bought by Christina in Rome after her abdication do not concern us; we are concerned with those which came to her from Prague. As it happened, they spent only a short time in Stockholm, until her abdication in 1651. When she became a Catholic, and in consequence took up her residence in Italy, Sweden lost the finest collection of Italian paintings to be found north of the Alps, including works of the Cinquecento by Titian, Tintoretto and Veronese. No fewer than eighty of these finally found their way to England. There were also numerous portraits painted in Stockholm by two of the Queen's court painters round about 1650, the Dutch David Beck and the French Sebastian Bourdon, in which an important period of Swedish history is represented. Nearly all the works of these two painters were lost in the course of time.

Christina's baggage is said to have been valued at the enormous sum of two million Reichstaler. But this would not be accounted for solely by Gustavus Adolphus's German booty, because, besides the Dutch portraits, the Queen took with her many much less recent acquisitions from the royal castles and palaces as her final 'plunder'. But she was to prove the truth of the old proverb about ill-gotten gains; 'She had robbed,' a Frenchman wrote in 1859, 'but she was robbed in her turn, and by those in whom she chiefly trusted. When her long wanderings and her tragic visit to France brought her at last to Rome, she found her hoard visibly diminished, particularly in those objects which at a first glance were the most remarkable.'

In her last years she found a devoted and reliable friend in Cardinal Decio Azzolini, who did his utmost to compose her mind and to arrange her affairs. He ended by being her residuary legatee, and the opportunity of accusing him of legacy-hunting has not been overlooked. It does not appear that the Cardinal was guilty, but in any case he inherited all her possessions. He did not enjoy them long, as his own death followed in the same year. Her pictures then went to a nephew of the Cardinal, the Marquis Pompeo Azzolini, who for a time had held a position at the Queen's small court in Rome. Either from lack of interest or because he needed the money, the Marquis sold them to Prince Livio Odescalchi, a nephew of Pope Innocent XI, and with them all the antique statues and fragments of columns which the Queen had bought after her arrival in Rome; these were bought in 1720 for 12,000 doubloons by Philip V of Spain. The next heir to the pictures was a younger Prince Odescalchi, and he, after long drawn out negotiations, sold them to Philip of Orleans, who added them to his large collection, known as the 'Galerie du Palais Royal'. Towards the close of the eighteenth century they came into the hands of another Philip of Orleans, the famous 'Philippe Egalité'. In 1792, the year before he was guillotined, he was endeavouring by all possible means to raise money for the cause to which he had devoted himself, and with this object, and also to pay his gaming debts, he decided to sell his collection of pictures. Most of his Italian and French paintings went to a banker in Brussels, who sold them in turn to a man who had beaten Philip at billiards. The Flemish, Dutch and German pictures went to an English buyer, including, therefore, all those which had first been German, then Swedish, and finally Italian possessions.

Great as the losses of art inflicted on Germany by the Thirty Years War incontestably were, it would be rash to assert that Germany was stripped bare. Against the enormous drain of valuable works of art must be set the equally enormous subsidies which flowed into the country from England, Holland, Spain, and the Pope, and which were not all spent on the war but served as well to rebuild and refurnish its castles. Moreover plunder often meant only a change of ownership within German territory.

9

The Dispersal of Charles I's Collection

'The Prince of Wales,' Rubens wrote in a letter of January 10, 1625, 'is of all princes the most enthusiastic amateur of painting in the world.' Twenty-four years after his collection was completed it was scattered and destroyed.

A great deal has been written about Charles I as an ardent and successful connoisseur and collector of paintings, and there is no doubt that he had no rival in the first half of the seventeenth century, a time of great collectors and of collections remarkable for their size as well as for their quality. It has been called the age not only of the gourmets but the gourmands among collectors.

It was already evident by 1620 that Charles's zeal as a collector was matched by his understanding of art. When he went to Madrid to woo the sister of Philip IV of Spain, he became acquainted with Spanish art and its great masters, notably Velasquez, who lost no time in making sketches for his portrait. Lope da Vega informs us that during his stay in Spain Charles showed great energy in seeking out whatever could be bought. He paid the highest prices, whether they were for drawings by Leonardo da Vinci or paintings by Correggio. The King of Spain made him a present of a Correggio and of a Titian, and Charles had copies made of works of theirs which he was not able to buy.

Soon after his return to England, he was given a list of all the important pictures in his possession; from this it appears that he had pictures by Holbein, by Titian and Tintoretto.

Charles ascended the throne about four months after the date of Rubens's letter quoted above. He was now able to give free rein to his passion for collecting works of art, and of pictures in the first place. In 1629, for example, he bought works from the Gonzaga collection to the amount of £18,000; in 1623, on the advice of Rubens and with his help, he bought the seven now world-renowned Raphael cartoons, *The Acts of the Apostles*, which had remained in Brussels ever since Leo X had sent them there as designs for tapestries. The masters of that industry had wisely kept them as an assurance for the payment of outstanding fees. Meanwhile Rubens had himself been painting in England and from 1628 to 1629 had carried out his much talked of mission to Madrid on Charles's behalf. In January 1631, Jan Lievens visited the English court, and since 1621 Van Dyck, whom Charles esteemed more highly than any other of his court painters and to whom he once gave £500 worth of ultramarine, had frequently been in England for longer and shorter periods. He was, moreover, allowed a yearly salary of £200. It has been said that Charles's most important service to art was his patronage of contemporary masters in Italy, Flanders, Holland and France, in spite of his preference for the Italians and particularly the Venetians of the sixteenth century. Thus paintings by the contemporary painters Caracci, Guido Reni, Carravaggio and others were added to his rapidly growing collection.

After the execution of Charles I in 1649, Parliament ordered the instant sale of some of the pictures 'for the benefit of Ireland and the North'. This order embraced 'all pictures and statues which were not connected with any kind of superstition', by which was meant the Catholic form of the Christian religion. Pictures representing 'the second person of the Trinity or the Virgin Mary' were to be 'burned forthwith'. It appears, however, that this sentence of destruction, the harshest aspect of the wars of religion in the sphere of art, was not carried out or, if so, only in the case of very few pictures. About two months after the King's death, Parliament ordered that 'the personal possessions of the late King, of the Queen and his heir shall be listed, valued and disposed of, with the exception that such objects as are of interest and use to the state shall be kept'. A committee of the

House was to decide which works of art came into this category. The inventory was quickly made and the sale, with which only those who were not members of Parliament were entrusted, followed soon after.

The question whether the state had the right to confiscate the private property of the King was no more asked and answered in this case than it had been in the opposite sense in the case of Queen Christina's departure abroad. But there was a certain feeling for what was right and proper in the disposal of this booty of a lamentable civil war, since the receipts were allocated first to the covering of debts, next to the settlement of justifiable claims for arrears of salary by officials of the court, and only then to the needs of the state, which for a start allotted £30,000 to the fleet.

The three commissioners, a parliamentary official, a poet and a painter—one whom the King had occasionally employed on making copies—carried out their task very correctly and with great care. They understood the importance and value of the paintings and in most cases obtained a much higher price than the estimate which had been put on them.

No picture was sold by auction; in each case the sale was negotiated with persons who were either buying on their own account or acting as agents for others, many of whom were eminent personages who preferred to keep in the background.

The proceedings continued until 1653 and ended by yielding £118,080 10s. 2d. from the sale of paintings, drawings, furniture, and various other objects. And it must be remembered that in accordance with the terms of the order of Parliament mentioned above, Cromwell reserved for Hampton Court Palace the Raphael and Mantegna cartoons, two pictures by Titian, and other historical scenes and portraits as well as the Gobelin tapestries showing the destruction of the Spanish Armada. It cannot be denied that in his choice of many of the pictures he was influenced by artistic as well as topical considerations.

The buyers were by no means confined to the English; Europe was well represented. The Spanish ambassador acting through obscure agents, a timber merchant, a master tailor and others of the sort, bought pictures for Philip IV. Philip himself, remembering Charles's visit over a quarter of a century before, would obviously feel shy of appearing. His acquisitions were sent by sea to Corunna, and Charles I's ambassador, an elderly man, was given his passport immediately before the arrival of the ship. No fewer than eighteen mules were needed for the transport of this precious booty from the coast to Madrid, paintings by Raphael, Titian, Tintoretto, Andrea del Sarto, Veronese, Dürer and other masters. Many were sent straight on to the Escorial; others remained in Madrid and have not been heard of since the end of the seventeenth or early eighteenth century.

Archduke Leopold William, brother of the Emperor Leopold and art-loving Regent of the Netherlands, who had recently bought the greater part of the Duke of Buckingham's collection in Antwerp, was again in the field. In 1656 he took his enlarged collection to Vienna and in 1662 it descended to his brother, the Emperor. It was he who got up the 'picture lotteries', and in the catalogue of one of them, in April 1670, there appear items from the collection of Charles I. Most of them came into the possession of Cardinal Charles von Lichtenstein and thus into the Prince Bishop's gallery in Kremsier.

Christina of Sweden was also a buyer, chiefly of jewels and medallions. Cardinal Mazarin, advised by David Teniers, who had the title of Chamberlain and had made small copies in colour of more than two hundred pictures, bought pictures, statues, Gobelin tapestries and stuffs. Eberhard Jabach, too, a celebrated banker of Cologne, a connoisseur and dealer, whose collection later passed into the hands of Louis XIV almost intact, purchased several fine pieces. Mynheer van Reynst, a wealthy patron of art, bought several items which after his death were bought by the Netherlands and presented to Charles II. There were many British buyers, members of Parliament, noblemen and merchants.

Finally, much was accounted for by the Fire of London, after the Civil War and dispersal had done their worst. Many of the portraits rescued by Cromwell and many fine Holbeins perished in this way.

Many, during the eighteenth and nineteenth century, have lamented the loss to England of all these paintings. At the time, however, such laments were confined to the small circle of art lovers and connoisseurs. It was not until towards the end of the nineteenth century that art, like everything else, was drawn into the wake of nationalism, and art-deals which led to the export of works of art were stigmatized as 'betrayals of the nation' and 'contempt of the nation's proper claims'. Museums and galleries then became focus-points of national pride and moral superiority. It was in this new perspective that the fate of Charles I's collection aroused the feelings of wider circles.

The final paragraph of the book by Claude Phillips, *The Picture Gallery of Charles I*, well expresses this attitude and its relation to the art market:

'Regrets are, no doubt, vain things, and we shall be told that our country in the eighteenth century, and the earlier part of the nineteenth, gained, in the wonderful private collections of many illustrious families, an equivalent for what she lost when Charles's pictures were scattered; when many of Lord Arundel's most famous possessions remained abroad; when the Duke of Buckingham's collection was almost wholly absorbed by foreign buyers. Still, to recall that England held, though only for a short quarter of a century, collections of pictures and works of art in many respects above rivalry, and as a group certainly without any equal in their own time; to see how, deliberately loosening her grasp on them, she enriched eager rivals whose gain has been permanent, is—it must be repeated, though the cry should become monotonous—even now to suffer an intolerable pang.'

Among Charles's like-minded contemporaries and advisers was Thomas Howard, Earl of Arundel. He too was an important collector of pictures, and he was also the first Englishman to buy in the grand style and the first to introduce Greek and Roman statues to England; it has been said of him that he 'transplanted ancient Greece to England and filled the gardens and galleries of Arundel House with statues'.

Like other rich collectors he employed a number of agents and buyers, of whom the most competent was a Mr Petty. Thomas Roe, the English ambassador to the Sublime Porte, may have been the first who, at his request, sent him Greek marbles from Greece and Asia Minor, but Petty in 1625 was commissioned to make a first tour of the Levant, in the course of which he visited Pergamum, Ephesus, Smyrna and Athens. Then, when he was on his homeward voyage from Samos he not only lost his whole cargo of antiquities in a violent storm but was also held a prisoner for a time by the Turks on a charge of spying. After being set at liberty he went to work again and this time successfully brought back 'the first large, authentic and important collection of classical art to reach Europe outside Italy. For a long time it remained the only really important collection of antique art in Europe, at first in the galleries and gardens of Arundel House, and later at Oxford, where even today as the *Arundel Marbles* it arouses the liveliest admiration for such an achievement.' The inscriptions on Petty's acquisitions were deciphered by John Selden and published in 1628 as *Marmora Arundelliana*.

Arundel was known in England as 'the father of virtu'. His portrait was painted by Van Dyck. Although he was Earl Marshal he utterly despised politics and was exclusively concerned with questions of art. As a Catholic he was involved in the same difficulties as those that harassed Charles; but being less tied and less closely watched he was able to remove himself and his treasures to the continent before it was too late. When he saw the Revolution approaching he emigrated with his whole family and a large part of his artistic possessions to Italy, and thus saved his collections from sharing the fate which overtook those of Charles. It was impossible to remove all the immense accumulations of many years; a half, perhaps, perished during the

Civil War; part was clumsily and ignorantly restored, and part used as building material. Yet a magnificent collection remained, unrivalled until Lord Elgin's achievement a hundred and fifty years later.

Arundel possessed pictures by Raphael, Titian and Tintoretto. But his great glory was the finest collection of drawings by Leonardo which has ever been in private hands. Rubens did paintings for him and visited him in England; Charles owed to him his acquaintance with Van Dyck. He admired Holbein and Dürer, and when, in 1636, he was sent to Germany by the King on a mission connected with an attempt to end the Thirty Years War, he took the opportunity to buy the library of Willibald Pirkheimer in Nuremberg.

His withdrawal from the court began soon after this, and in 1642 he left England for Antwerp—one of the many Catholics of those times who found in the Catholic Netherlands the possibility of being true to their faith without endangering their lives. His admiration of classical art soon drew him to Italy, where he lived, mostly in Padua, until his death in 1646. His passion for Italy and Italian life as well as his dislike of his own country were deepened by the Civil War, although he was very little concerned for the fate of Charles. He ended by becoming completely Italianized, the first of the many Englishmen who have made their home in Italy.

He had left a large part of his collections behind in the Netherlands where his wife lived. Being in need of money, she sold some of his statues, and these are now in Oxford. An inventory of 1655 and records of an auction in 1684 give some idea of the paintings of the Dutch School possessed by this great collector, besides his invaluable Italian and German masterpieces; there were at least two Rembrandts. Yet he included the Dutch principally as 'a decorative element'.

10

Marlborough's Requests for Pictures

lunder takes many forms. The mercenaries of the sixteenth and seventeenth centuries could invoke written law when they rifled a conquered town for its valuables, and even while they plundered they were bound by a code of honour and strict rules of discipline, any disregard of which might mean that they were summarily hanged on the very scene of the crime. In the Second World War the 'Einsatzstab Rosenberg' justified robbery and plunder by the National Socialist philosophy, and if any questions of right or wrong arose, they were settled by Göring's announcement: 'I am the court of appeal.' Napoleon and his commissioners justified their robberies in Italy by the claim that Paris had supplanted Rome as the hub of the world and the Russians in 1945 plundered German museums and galleries as part of their war on capitalism and the middle classes, and in pursuance of the aim of educating the world in socialism.

But history also affords many examples of statesmen and commanders of armies who had scruples over making off with whatever they took a liking to, particularly when, as in the Thirty Years War, it might be a question of robbing their allies and dependants. In such cases it sometimes happened that gratitude took a tangible form and even that the gift was chosen by the beneficiary, who was thus spared the painful predicament of having either to take it by force or go without. This technique must not be confused with the behaviour of Charles in Spain. In his case it was his long and profound admiration that induced Philip IV to give him one painting outright and to offer a second in the hope that he would have the tact to refuse. But that was too much to ask of such a lover of art: Charles took both back with him to England with unfeigned gratitude.

The pictures given by the Emperor Joseph I to Marlborough in 1706, on the other hand, were offered quite unequivocally in response to a simple demand.

This gift had its origins in the difficulties from which the Emperor Leopold was delivered by the victory of Blenheim, when the French were defeated by the Duke of Marlborough, Prince Eugene and the Margrave of Baden, the *Türkenlouis*. Marlborough's military skill had rescued Austria, freed Germany and rudely shaken the power of Louis XIV. In gratitude for these achievements the Emperor made him a prince of the Holy Roman Empire and created for him the principality of Mindelheim in Bavaria. In his own country, too, Marlborough received his reward. He was given the manor of Woodstock, where the building, at public expense, of the magnificent Blenheim Palace was begun in 1704.

Marlborough's victories were resumed in 1705, when he barred Louis XIV from the Netherlands, and in 1706, when he won the battle of Ramillies, in recognition of which the Emperor Joseph, who had succeeded Leopold upon his death in 1705, made him vice-Regent of the Netherlands. Marlborough foresaw the difficulties such an elevation would bring in its train, and turned his thoughts, 'always a little bent on his own advantage', as a recent biography says, to 'more tangible rewards'. He let Joseph I know through a former ambassador of his in London that he would gladly accept some pictures from the collections at Munich as an outward mark of the Emperor's satisfaction and gratitude. From Munich, it must be noted, not Vienna, by which it was adroitly hinted that a share in the plunder of Bavaria might be considered his due. But he did not intend to leave anything to the unprompted generosity of the 'giver': he told him straight out that the equestrian portrait of Charles I by Van Dyck, which had reached Munich owing to the dispersal of Charles's pictures, would give him particular pleasure. The Emperor, who was not directly the loser by this gift, gave orders in his own hand that some pictures from the Munich gallery, including the portrait, should be handed over to Marlborough. The English ambassador at the Emperor's court, following Marlborough's explicit instructions, chose, in October 1706, two paintings by Rubens, *Mars and Venus* and *Lot and his daughters*, which, with a third, were to accompany the equestrian portrait. The Emperor's commissioner in Munich, however, found this demand excessive and the ambassador's interference unwelcome, and refused to part with these three additional pictures. The ambassador therefore had to be content with the portrait only, valued at 8,000 talers. The three others together were valued at 10,000.

A lively correspondence followed. The Emperor, generous and confused, spoke of three or four and then of 'some' pictures which Marlborough was to have besides the Van Dyck, but his officials were more precise and did all they could in the way of prevarication, obstruction and delay. Marlborough at first took no part in the discussion, leaving it to the English ambassador, who was all the more active because he desired Marlborough's recommendation for his sister in her ambition to be made an abbess in Germany.

Finally Marlborough stepped up his demand to include four additional pictures, the two Rubenses already mentioned, another one by Rubens, *Venus and Adonis*, and a *Last Judgment* by Tintoretto. To make his demands more palatable he offered the Imperial commissioner in Munich, Count Wratislaw, a portrait of Queen Anne and one of himself, both by Kneller. On November 5, 1706, Count Wratislaw gave instructions that these four pictures were to be handed over. Marlborough had attained his object and on November 8 he wrote to his wife:

'I am so much in love with some pictures which I am bringing back with me that I wish you had somewhere to put them until the gallery at Woodstock is ready for them, for it is beyond a doubt that no such fine pictures are to be found in all England as some of these are, particularly King Charles on horseback by Van Dyck. It belonged to the Elector of Bavaria and was given me by the Emperor. I hope it is by now in Holland.'

He was not, however, content with these five masterpieces. He had seen that the Emperor as well as his courtiers and officials were open to persuasion, and so, on the very next day, November 9, he sent through the British ambassador a new, revised and extended list, consisting of eight pictures: *The Massacre of the Innocents, Lot and his daughters* and two sketches of *Venus and Adonis* by Rubens, and also four hunting pieces, the painters of which are not known.

These demands were found intolerable by the Keeper of the Munich Gallery, Count von Loewenstein. He expressed his downright refusal to surrender any more pictures to Marlborough in an exasperated letter and wrote as follows to Count Wratislaw:

Munich, November 23, 1796

'In reply to your Excellency's favour of the 17th, His Majesty's approbation concerning the four pieces of painting given to the Duke of Marlborough over and above the *Charles Stuart*, namely (1) *Mars and Venus*, (2) *Lot and his daughters*, (3) *Venus and Adonis*, all by Rubens, and (4) *The Last Judgment* by Tintoretto, has not yet come to hand, for which reason I have again asked for it. It seems, however, from the enclosed from Mr Stepney—which may indeed have been written before he knew that the above four pieces desired by him had in fact been despatched—that still more pieces of painting are demanded, concerning which, however, there is this to be said, that the one noted as No. 1, the *Massacre of the Innocents*, is painted on wood, so thin and vulnerable that it could not suffer an hour's journey without risk of total destruction; the *Lot* under No. 2 he has already received; the four hunting pieces grouped under No. 3 were valued at 20,000 taler and are the best in the whole collection, so that if they are to be given away there will be scarcely anything of peculiar merit left; *Venus and Adonis*, No. 4, may also be

106

worth two to three thousand taler. It only remains to say that the *Venus and Adonis* under No. 5 has already been sent off. I will tell Mr Stepney in reply by tomorrow's post that as his Imperial Majesty's gracious command extends only to the *Charles Stuart* and three or four other pieces, I cannot send more without fresh orders. Should his Imperial Majesty not wish to make a present of the pieces mentioned above, the lack of further orders will be my sufficient excuse,

your humble servant . . .'

On the following day he informed the English ambassador, Stepney, that without the Emperor's orders he could not hand over any more pictures, and moreover the picture of the *Massacre of the Innocents* was too fragile to stand the journey. With this, the incident was closed; neither Marlborough nor Stepney ever returned to it.

All the same, Marlborough had successfully 'requested' those five pictures from the Emperor: one Van Dyck, three Rubenses and one Tintoretto. It is of interest that people writing in the first half of the nineteenth century who saw these pictures at Blenheim and mentioned them—they were noted in the catalogue—say that the equestrian portrait by Van Dyck was bought by the Duke in Munich, whereas the other four are stated, with an approach to accuracy, as 'presented by the Emperor'. The further history of these paintings—the Van Dyck went to the National Gallery in 1885—does not concern us here. They are mentioned only as one example of the most well-bred way of acquiring works of art as booty, the way of firmly asking for them as a present.

Of Prince Eugene, the great companion in arms of the Duke of Marlborough, there are no reports of similar behaviour. So far as his interest in art goes, such biographies and monographs on him as mention it at all, admittedly only those written by Austrians, dismiss him as a complete innocent in this alien sphere. But this leaves much to explain.

Thus, in a work devoted to him as patron of art, we read:

107

'At Eugene's death his property in Marchfeld came to 600,000, his two Vienna palaces to 200,000, the library 150,000, his bank deposit 200,000, cash 200,000, his silverware 170,000, his jewels 100,000, pictures 100,000, property in Italy 150,000, in all 1,870,000 gulden.'

This is confidently described as too low a valuation, because one of his picture rooms alone was worth 200,000 gulden, a lustre 40,000 and a chimney piece 20,000. But all the same the account proceeds:

'He was a poor man when he came to Austria and he never enriched himself in the old style by plunder and spoliation. Therefore if Eugene was one of those who acquired what for those days was a notable fortune, it was honestly and honourably earned and a mere trifle, after all, in comparison with the deserts of one whose name is made illustrious by such titles as Centa, Peterwardein, Luzzarn, Turin, Höchstadt, Malplaquet, Lille, Oudenarde, Belgrade, and the equal of that of the greatest heroes of history.'

But even granting that Prince Eugene never took his share of the plunder, the Duke of Marlborough was by no means the only commander who did so during those years between the end of the Thirty Years War and the death of Louis XIV in 1715. Dutch and French art historians have more than once pointed out that the wars of Louis himself did more than anything else to transfer Dutch pictures to French collections. No doubt this occurred now and again in the ordinary course of the art trade: the great Condé, during his campaign of 1673 and again in 1678, bought pictures and works of art at high prices in Utrecht and other places, and it is known, too, that officers—Colonel Salis for example, the commandant of Rees—commissioned paintings from Dutch masters. But, as in every war, many a picture changed hands by force and was then either added to a private gallery or offered for sale.

11

Art Plunder and the Art Market

It has often been pointed out that the sale of plundered works
of art, or the removal of works of art from one country to
another owing to the approach of the enemy, has had the
effect of overloading the market and even caused loud complaint
among native artists. It is worth while, then, giving a glance
at a section of the great European art market during the period
under review.

Towards the end of the seventeenth century the city of Hamburg did a considerable trade in the export of art, principally to the
countries of the north and east. Whole collections of coins, of
curios, medallions and pictures went abroad, particularly to
the court of Peter the Great in St Petersburg. French furniture,
too, reached Russia via Hamburg.

Of art treasures known to have been exported from Hamburg
before 1700, we find that 57·8 per cent could still be identified in
Russia in 1911 and 8·5 per cent in Scandinavia. Of the products
of about 1700 and soon after, Russia in 1911 accounted for
27·9 per cent, Germany 63·2 per cent and the rest of Europe
8·4 per cent. The art collection of the Moscow Patriarchate, which
contained no acquisitions of an earlier date than 1700, was
'stocked' to the extent of 67·2 per cent from Hamburg.

If, in the period after 1700, this eastward exportation of art
declined, that probably means not a quantitative but a material
change. Before 1700, princes and church in Russia were eager not
for 'art' but for 'treasures'; in the eighteenth century the Czars and
the nobility were more and more concerned, in encouraging the
westernizing of Russia, with pictures, drawings, furniture, lustres,

porcelain, etc. The Hamburg art market in the eighteenth century was not, therefore, less, but more important than before, only it wore a different appearance.

The entire export of art from Germany to north-eastern Europe at the turn of the seventeenth century has been estimated to be in the proportion of 40 per cent to Scandinavia and 30 per cent to Russia and Poland respectively. Half a century later only about 10 per cent was going to Scandinavia, 20 per cent to Poland and 70 per cent to Russia.

There is no room here to analyse these exports, but it is certain that after 1650 they contained a varied assortment of works of art thrown on the market by the Thirty Years War; and also that the same thing happened in a larger geographical setting during the wars of Louis XIV in the seventeenth and eighteenth centuries.

The art market was much livelier, however, in Italy round about 1700 and for the next half-century than anywhere else. The whole of Europe, socially as well as geographically, was buying art there, antique and modern, at this time. All who made the Grand Tour, the *giro d'Italia*, whether young nobles, army officers, rich merchants' sons and heirs, or churchmen eager to see the Pope and Rome, the centre of Catholic Christianity, brought home keepsakes at the very least. But many went further than this; the sight of antique statues and mosaics, of temples and palaces, of works by Titian and Leonardo infected them with a love of art and made them life-long collectors in one branch of art or another.

Immense quantities of works of art crossed the Alps during those decades and passed into Germany and Scandinavia, Hungary, Poland, Russia, France and England, and Italian writers often complained that Italy was being stripped bare by visitors from beyond the Alps. Foreign art lovers, too, in letters and diaries, published and unpublished, expressed their astonishment at the seemingly inexhaustible riches of Italy, which enabled collectors, dealers and agents to supply their clients and patrons with all they wanted and still leave as much behind.

Forgeries, of course, were even then not unknown: by no means all antiques reaching England, Germany or Scandinavia were more than six months old. In Rome, Naples and other towns the fabrication of forgeries kept pace with the provision of accommodation for strangers, and this trade reached a peak at that time and again in the nineteenth century. Enthusiastic amateurs from northern Europe as a rule understood next to nothing, or nothing at all, about art. Their enthusiasm went far beyond their capacity to distinguish the genuine from the false, and besides, it had in many cases a social origin: up-to-date, enlightened princes thought it the right thing to collect art and to play the Maecenas, and now merchant princes also felt that the antique gem or statue, the 'genuine' Titian or the Gobelin tapestry gave them the stamp of culture. Besides, it soon became evident that a judicious art collector was investing his money as wisely as by buying shares in an East India Company or mortgages on land. The price of works of art went up rapidly.

Princes were of course in the first rank as buyers. Their number was not large; but in each generation there were always some hundreds of German rulers of small independent states, all eager to follow the example of the great. They normally had considerable fortunes at their disposal and as long as a war was not actually raging or the threat of bankruptcy impending they could lay out something year after year on works of art which they acquired either in person or through their agents. These agents often served several princes at once, which must have strained even a divided loyalty; but there were also many cases of an agent who had only one master for whom he scoured all Europe, but principally France and Italy. He kept his ears open whenever the art trade was discussed and visited dealers sometimes as a poor scholar, sometimes, if it seemed more advisable, as a prince travelling incognito and well provided with money. The death of any well-known collector sent him off to find the heir, who was very likely to sell off some part of his inheritance, and it was naturally important to be first on the scene.

111

Works of art also reached the market from Asia in the seventeenth and eighteenth centuries, and from Egypt too. Towns like Alexandria and Cairo, Constantinople, Tabriz and Ispahan were combed by the agents of Trading Companies as well as by travellers and emissaries. India, China and Japan sent shipload after shipload of old and new porcelain, of lacquer, from the tiniest box to the largest cabinets, from the massive chest to the costly screen, pictures and tables and bronzes of every size.

Here, too, plunder played no small part. Apart from war, to which, however, we shall return with the Sack of the Summer Palace in Peking in 1860, there were the rivalries of the colonial Powers; they captured each others' ships on the high seas, and though the losses on each side may have cancelled out, many a cargo of hundreds of thousands of pieces of porcelain, precious lacquer, whose layer upon layer of paint had cost years of patience, fine silk garments of ancient workmanship arrived at Rouen instead of London, at Dublin instead of Amsterdam or Copenhagen, and vice versa.

Augustus the Strong and his son were among the greatest lovers and patrons of art that Germany has known. The creation of the Residenz at Dresden, an obscure garrison town, which the King adorned with a jewel of rococo architecture, is one of the greatest achievements of European art. Augustus took an even greater interest in pictures. Even allowing for the not inconsiderable collection he inherited at his accession, he still remains the creator of the finest gallery of Germany. No sooner had he come to the throne than he despatched his emissaries in all directions to buy pictures. In the forty years of his reign several hundreds of pictures by the greater and lesser Dutch masters, by Rubens and Jordaens, by Giorgione, Palma, Titian and Guido Reni arrived in Dresden. The pick of these paintings were assembled in a special gallery.

To him, too, Dresden owed the finest collection of classical sculpture of the time, especially as he acquired the so-called Brandenburg collection from King William Frederick I of Prussia in exchange for a few strapping recruits. There is some

7. St Elizabeth's Reliquary in the National Historical Museum, Stockholm.

8. Algarotti, by Jean-Etienne Liotard.

reason for what was later said: 'The origin of Frederick the Great's hatred of the Saxon electors and Polish kings may perhaps be found here; Frederick took the antique to be the essential element and principle of art, and he had later to replace at enormous cost what Berlin had lost owing to his father's passion for soldiers.' Augustus also secured the famous collections of Bellori and Chigi and lastly the greatly admired thirty-two antiques possessed by Cardinal Albani.

The Dresden Gallery admittedly did not attain its highest glories before the reign of the Elector Augustus III, who was also King of the Poles. This prince, owing not least to his Jesuit upbringing, was such a devoted connoisseur and collector that he handed over, or left, the conduct of affairs of state to his father's chief minister, Count Brühl, and covered 'the earth with the web of his agents and experts' in case any prize might escape him.

In the year 1742 alone, in the midst of the Austro-Prussian dispute, no fewer than 715 pictures were bought by Augustus III, and the inventory for that year listed 1,938 pictures of the first rank, and more than 4,700 in all. His correspondence on matters of art quickly out-distanced his correspondence on political questions. Sometimes forty, sixty or a hundred pictures arrived at once, brought either by his own agents, or by art dealers, or even by obscure go-betweens; in 1745, for example, the world-renowned collection of the Duke of Modena was gathered in, with four pictures each by Coreggio and Veronese, *The Tribute Money* by Titian and other paintings by Holbein, Rubens and Velasquez. Other works by Titian followed, not to mention the 268 items in the Waldstein collection, including masterpieces by Vermeer, Franz Hals and Van Dyck. Paris supplied Rembrandts, Rubenses, Watteaus and the loveliest examples of Wouverman. But the masterstroke was the acquisition of Raphael's *Sistine Madonna*.

One at least of the most important agents of those times may be mentioned here, Count Algarotti, who carried out his missions with such ardour and with successes of such extraordinary brilli-

H   113

ance that their results, at least according to the conceptions of our own day, must be regarded in a metaphorical sense as art plunder. To Count Algarotti, a somewhat impenetrable, remarkably adroit, not exaggeratedly honest, but extremely cultivated and, socially, highly esteemed Italian, Augustus owed his most important successes. Algarotti had an astonishing memory for works of art and their history, and an untiring persistence in the pursuit and capture of them in the interest of his patrons, first Frederick the Great, then Augustus, and finally Frederick again, and of his own pocket and reputation.

It is not surprising that Augustus, Brühl, Algarotti and all the others of that circle 'imported' artists as well as works of art into Saxony. Of these the best known are the sculptor, Permoser, and the painter, Bellotto, whose pictures of Dresden in the days of her glory are a legacy to her impoverished heirs. Dresden too was the nursery of Winckelmann, the founder of modern art criticism, and of the excellent painter, Raffael Mengs.

The Seven Years War put a sudden and tragic stop to this brilliant period of patronage and encouragement of art. Political reverses, lack of money, military weakness, sickness, ill will, vanity, envy cast their shadow on great achievements; more than all, the rococo style favoured by the princes and nobility was neither liked nor understood by the smug generation that followed.

Algarotti's letters to the Minister, Count Brühl, 'give an inside view of the eighteenth century's fine concern for art, which, pursued with unstinted energy and backed by powerful resources, created new and prolific nurseries of culture in the north. They shed light on one of the most fascinating examples of the passion for collecting in the Europe of this epoch, the creation of the Dresden gallery. They also bear witness to the remarkable personality of one who played a brilliant part as friend of the great of his time, as accomplished man of the world, as scholar and connoisseur, distinguished as much for the charm of his disposition as for his grasp of the intellectual interests of his day; he was in touch with all the great minds of Europe; from his youth up he

114

was on terms of lasting friendship with Voltaire and Frederick the Great, who gave him an unalterable love and admiration which bridged all gaps and accompanied him literally to the grave.'

'*Le dieu du génie et de la bonne compagnie*' was the art-loving Hohenzollern's description of Algarotti. If we turn to his letters we find in them a vivid and detailed account of his journeys in Italy, buying pictures for the court of Saxony. Frederick the Great gave Algarotti a friendly invitation to Prussia a few days after his accession, an honour he shared with Voltaire, the Marquis d'Argens, the learned Maupertuis and Count Kaiserling. At the end of June 1740, Algarotti left London for Berlin, where he quickly became a favourite of the young King and was consequently courted on all sides. 'Algarotti is pampered like a mistress, but'—it is added—'he profits little by these marks of favour since they are not accompanied by any more solid tokens.' When war broke out and the King was preoccupied by political and military concerns, Algarotti turned to Dresden and Augustus III whose love of Italian art and Italian music was well known.

He was not yet thirty when he arrived in Dresden, a desertion which annoyed Frederick and led to a sharp exchange of letters in a tone, on Algarotti's side, which caused Frederick to write in a 'final' letter of September 10, 1742:

'The rules of good taste would forbid me to reply to your letter. Its style and expressions are so immoderate that silence would certainly best become me. But a residue of goodwill towards you induces me to ask you (for the last time in my life, mark you) whether you will come back to me and on what terms. Put all official duties out of your head; they do not suit you; think only of a good pension and your liberty. If you reject this offer, please think of me no more——'

Five years later, when the Saxon episode had closed, the correspondence was resumed.

From September 1742, Algarotti was employed by the Saxon court; in October he presented Augustus III with an excellent

115

memorandum on 'the extension and completion of the Royal collections' and was thenceforward in the King's full employment, principally as buyer; he procured copper-plate etchings, of which Augustus was an excellent judge and assiduous collector, drawings, medallions, cut gems and cameos, statues, busts, and lastly pictures and more pictures. At the same time he designed a large museum for the display of the paintings and sculpture.

On February 15 he was instructed to inspect the Pallavicini collection, and then, after he had reported favourably, he was instructed further to buy it and other pictures as well. Commissions to make similar purchases followed one after the other. He became a practised hand at thwarting the intrigues of rival dealers and experts. One of them, a coarse but artful man called Rossi, wore a mask to confuse dealers or owners, or passed under a false name, and went all over Italy buying up old pictures by the dozen, which he disposed of preferably in Dresden. The period of Algarotti's great purchases, of which he was particularly proud, when he bought works by Palma Vecchio, Titian, Holbein and Marrata, began in August 1743. He wrote in one letter:

'These pictures, with those I have already bought or would have bought if Rossi had not got in front of me, are the pick of an enormous number seen up to date in Venice. I have ransacked every corner in case anything might escape me, and I have been on the search for famous paintings in all the great palazzi. In the course of all this I have been shown many copies, many fakes, many poor and patched up and badly preserved originals. But, with me, the brew soon clears. My collection, by the excellence and splendour of each several work, shall be to other collections what the green diamond in the royal treasure in Dresden is to all other diamonds, their assay-piece and measure.'

In all, from 1743 to 1746 he bought thirty-four pictures in Italy for the Saxon court, twenty-three of which were still in the Dresden Gallery in 1931. After making four tours of Italy in the service of Augustus III, he found that his services were neither appreciated nor adequately rewarded; his great plans for Dresden were wrecked and with them his hopes of a permanent livelihood. He therefore turned to Frederick the Great once more and, in April 1747, he was restored to the service of Prussia. At Frederick's court as a member of the celebrated Round Table of Sans Souci, as an intimate friend of the King and his adviser in all artistic matters, he soon forgot the disillusionments of Dresden. Yet at the age of forty-one, in 1753, he had to seek the milder climate of Italy and died in Pisa, presumably of tuberculosis, in 1764.

Frederick, with whom he exchanged letters to the end, erected a memorial to him in the Campo Santo with an inscription of his own composition:

> Algarotti Ovidii Aemulo
> Newtoni Discipulo
> Fredericus Magnus

Algarotti may be regarded as the real creator of the *plus belle collection de l'Europe*, as the Dresden collection was once called in 1790, whereas the gallery of St Petersburg was described at the same time as being *sans contredit la plus nombreuse en Europe, mais bien loin d'etre la premiere pour la choix des morceaux*. Frederick's collection, on the other hand, was given only the fourth place among German galleries in 1777, the year after the Silesian War.

Dresden, which had been growing in splendour year by year, was twice occupied by the victorious Frederick the Great, as Berlin too had been in the course of the Silesian War by the Austrians and the Russians, but neither the Prussian King nor his enemies had laid a hand on the galleries and collections in either of the conquered and occupied cities, and it looks as though a new code, or at least a new attitude to artistic treasures, had come in since the seventeenth century.

It is true that no reliance was placed on this change of heart in advance, and therefore in 1759 the Dresden pictures were stored for safety, under the threat of the advancing Prussians, in the castle of Pommersfelden, which belonged to the Arch-bishop-Elector Lothar-Franz von Schönborn. The hiding-place was betrayed and a number of pictures were ruined or damaged, but it is known that none was stolen.

Similar incidents must have occurred on other occasions as the inevitable penalty of war. But another phenomenon connected with the influence of war is especially noticeable in the career of the Margravine Caroline-Louise of Baden. This princess was famous as a collector in the second half of the eighteenth century. A catalogue drawn up in 1784 after her death lists over 200 pictures, but she had possessed many more and a fine collection of drawings as well. From her correspondence alone 180 paintings can be identified. Of these, seventy-eight were bought in Paris, fifty-seven in Holland, fifty from their German owners, ten from Italy and two from England. It is worth noting that she was collecting 'during the Seven Years War, a period very favourable to her as collector, because it precluded the rivalry of the big guns, England, Prussia and Russia, and kept prices down.'

Here then we have a new phenomenon, one at least which catches the eye for the first time in these days of the growing power of capital: the art market shows a new sensibility to peace and war. While the warring powers were endangering each other's picture galleries—but not robbing them—the neutrals and the petty princes had the opportunity of acquiring many a work of art that in normal times the buyers commissioned by the greater and richer princes would have put out of their reach. Algarotti's acquisitions for Dresden are, after all, an example of the same thing. While Frederick the Great and Maria Theresa were either actually fighting one another or anxiously repairing their finances for the next bout, it was comparatively easy for him to buy good pictures for Augustus III at fairly reasonable prices. There is abundant evidence to show that many private collections came on the market during the hard times of the Seven Years War; and as this long war was not merely an Austro-Prussian conflict but also and still more one between France and

118

England, the Paris art market was unusually busy. 'From one month to the next it grew in interest and importance.' The Margravine Caroline seized the unexpected opportunity and gave free rein to her passion for collecting. Her last purchase took place significantly in 1769 when she bought a picture from the collection of a Councillor Ehrenreich of Frankfurt-am-Main. But by that time her agent was already writing from Paris on the subject of buyers from Russia: '*Quelle douleur de voir sortir et passer dans les mains des Scythes des choses si précieuses, que dix personnes au plus admireront en Russie et dont toute l'Europe clairvoyante a été apportée de jouir ici. Tout le monde peut aspirer au bonheur de voir les bords de la Seine, et peu de monde est curieux de visiter ceux de la froide Neva . . .*'

The Margravine's biographer observes: 'In the later years of the Princess's activities as a collector, particularly after the Peace of 1763 when England, Prussia and Russia were once more active in the art market, we often hear Caroline bitterly lamenting the shocking rise in prices. Her agents had to return empty handed from the most famous auctions, because her resources were no longer able to keep pace.'

The effect of the war on the art market may be seen also from the vendor's side.

Clemens August, Elector of Cologne, was one of the best known patrons of art in the Rhineland of the eighteenth century; his fame as a builder of fine buildings in Bonn and Brühl and as a patron and protector of architects, sculptors, painters, plasterers and other artists and craftsmen will not be forgotten. Rembrandt's *Man in a gold helmet* was probably at one time in his possession. Shortly after his death in 1761—a severe blow for his company of artists—an inventory was made of all his works of art and other possessions, and the first sale took place in that same year. After this there was a pause which lasted until 1764, due no doubt to objections made by the legatees, but also beyond any doubt because the reserve prices were not reached either for the porcelain, which included superb pieces from China and others of celebrated European manufacture, or for the silver.

119

In some cases no bid was made, in others the bids were far below the valuation. The long war and the consequent depression, which, starting in Amsterdam, quickly affected the whole of Germany, naturally did not spare the Rhineland. Finally a celebrated hunting-service of solid silver, made in Paris, weighing more than ten hundredweight, was probably consigned to the mint, when not a single bid was made towards the reserve of 36,000 talers. The sale of the pictures, between 750 and 800, brought in all told 40,121 talers, 'a miserable result', upon which this observation was made: 'The art market [in 1764] was for the moment thoroughly unfavourable, and further weakened, perhaps, by these very sales, coming one on top of the other, occasioned by the Bonn inheritance.' Rembrandt's *Man in the gold helmet* was valued in 1761 at seventy talers and was sold in 1764 for seventeen. But other paintings, too, by unimportant painters, esteemed at that time far more highly than Rembrandt, valued at 1,000, 2,000 and 3,000 talers did not bring in a fifth or a sixth of those sums.

Let us end with one more quotation of wider reference from the account of this generous and cultivated prince and Maecenas and of the dispersal of his collections: 'These sales, spread over seven years, throw a last brilliant illumination over the most lively and the richest princely court of the Rhineland, showing it up like a fire-work castle, blazing in coloured light against the night sky before vanishing in darkness. Rococo was dead!'

Rococo was dead—and with it a whole attitude to art, its patrons and the passion for collecting. What followed in the age of the French Revolution was destined to produce something quite different, a complete transformation of the conditions of ownership of art and of the circumstances of creative artists, brought about in the first place by unequivocal robbery, depredation, dispersal and public auctions, and also a new or more emphatic nationalizing and politicizing of all judgments of art and artists, art collections and art sales, a transformation which recurred towards the end of the nineteenth century and is still in process to this day.

But before we come to the French Revolution and Napoleon, one episode remains which it is not easy to fit into the scheme of the account, for the reason that it has been regarded at different times in very different lights and judged, to a greater extent even than in the case of the events narrated up to now, in very different ways.

12

The Elgin Marbles

The story of the Elgin marbles, Lord Elgin's world-renowned collection of sculpture, falls chronologically within the Napoleonic era; and the political events of that time, the wars between England and France, Napoleon's occupation of Egypt, the outcome of the Battle of Aboukir, the British occupation of Malta, and the Peace of Amiens in 1802, undoubtedly had a considerable influence on the acquisition of these works and their transport to England. But essentially Lord Elgin's enterprise had nothing to do with the attitude to art of Napoleon and the French of those days: it had its roots in a quite different, entirely independent and individualistic soil, the tradition of Charles I and Lord Arundel. The national idea played no part at all in the make-up of this nobleman, who lived his life according to his own ideas in a 'splendid isolation'. It mattered nothing to him that his travels in Greece, Egypt and Asia Minor happened to coincide with Napoleon's stay in Egypt and the emergence of France in her new role as the mistress of all Europe. He made use, certainly, of the political set-up, but its inner significance escaped him. In his eyes, the fact that his hunting-grounds lay within the Ottoman Empire meant only that passports and export licences had to be seen to and also that the works of art he was set on collecting were exposed to the greatest risk in their present situation, owing to the barbarity and insensibility of the inhabitants. He was not thinking only, or indeed at all to begin with, of acquiring these treasures for himself, but of rescuing them from decay and dilapidation for the benefit of civilized and artistically minded persons.

Today, when there are laws to forbid or regulate the export of works of art in almost every country, the removal of a single piece of sculpture, let alone the many hundreds which Lord Elgin had carefully packed up and sent to England, would arouse the indignation of governments and editors and evoke ancestral glories; which shows how far political susceptibilities have invaded the domain of art since those dilettante days. But for the moment we are concerned to show how the Elgin Marbles became not only a British possession but also a spiritual possession of all admirers of classical art.

Thomas Bruce, seventh Earl of Elgin and eleventh Earl of Kincardine, was born in 1766, went to two of England's most famous public schools, completed his studies in Scotland and Paris, went into the army in 1785, and retired in 1835 with the rank of general, without ever having seen active service. He embarked on a diplomatic career in 1790 and was entrusted with a special mission to the court of the Emperor Leopold II. In 1792 he was minister in Brussels; envoy extraordinary to Berlin in 1795; and ambassador to the Sublime Porte in 1799. He died in 1841.

His appointment to Turkey at the time of Napoleon's occupation of Egypt involved him in many important political and diplomatic events. Yet he was chiefly interested in the acquisition of important specimens of the art of classical antiquity. He said himself that when he was appointed ambassador in Constantinople in 1799 his first thought was that he might devote his time there to the 'service of art'. An architect named Thomas Harrison, who had done work for him in Scotland and had spent many years in Rome, observed to him one day that although the public had a rough idea of the artistic glories of Athens, casts of the originals would be widely welcomed and would greatly deepen the knowledge of them.

'Whereupon,' Lord Elgin later said, 'I got into touch with friends in London and brought the matter to the attention of Lord Grenville, Mr Pitt and Mr Dundas, pointing out that here was a matter of such importance to the nation that the government ought to take it up, and also see that it was undertaken by the best artists available. The government answered with an unqualified refusal, as there was no money to spare for fanciful schemes of the kind . . .'

Elgin, having had the first prompting to this singularly fruitful enterprise from his architect, now took it on his own shoulders as his appointed task. He dedicated to it his attainments, his personality, his private fortune and the advantages of his official position in Constantinople. The whole course of the operation is amply documented by letters and reports from himself and his wife, and from the artists, agents, travellers, architects, sea-captains and others who were employed on it; and all go to show that it was carried out on an ever increasing scale by a regular expedition enlisted and instructed for the purpose. But this, it must be clearly understood, was at first, and for long after, confined to the locating of ancient buildings and sites, making drawings of surviving remnants of classical art, plotting them out, copying inscriptions, and lastly to making casts of the most interesting pieces for taking back to Scotland. There was no thought at first of taking possession of any originals.

The expedition was not, in fact, the first of its kind, in so far as its original aim goes: Stuart and Revett had been at work in Athens, in spite of political disorders and the plague, from 1751 to 1753; and in 1754 and 1755 the Society of Dilettanti had sent an expedition to Asia Minor, principally to collect inscriptions; it returned, however, with many ground-plans, drawings, etc., and also with a few pieces of sculpture. The present expedition, though a private venture, soon surpassed in its scope all previous ones with similar aims. In the prosecution of these aims, particularly when, as we shall see, they were greatly enlarged, Lord Elgin was able to make good use of his official position.

He set out in 1799, visiting Naples on the way, where Sir William Hamilton, well known and even famous because of the association of his wife with Lord Nelson, was the British chargé d'affaires. From here, Elgin's private secretary, William Richard Hamilton, to whom a large share of its success must be credited, organized the expedition, a task which bad postal communications made very laborious. He assembled his collaborators, painters who were practised in making topographical drawings, an expert in making casts and an artist who was good at figure drawing. There was also an architect to supervise works of reconstruction, and even an Italian guitar player.

Lord Elgin was in Constantinople early in 1800, leaving Hamilton still occcupied with his arrangements. When these were at last completed and Hamilton had drawn up detailed instructions in a document of twenty-two paragraphs, the possibility of actually acquiring the originals first dawned on his mind. Bad sea communications delayed the arrival of the expedition in Constantinople until the middle of May. The greater part of it proceeded to Athens at the first opportunity; the rest remained behind for some time in Constantinople.

Athens in 1800 was a small, dirty, sleepy town of very little importance, lying to the east and north of the Acropolis. The Turks had enclosed the town including the Acropolis and the Temple of Theseus with a wall about ten feet in height, in which there were six gates. This was chiefly as a protection against pirates and robbers. Between the town and the wall there was a strip, about 200 yards in width, which was cultivated, and some of the houses had gardens. Altogether there were about 1,200 or 1,300 houses, of which about 400 were inhabited by Turks; Greeks and Albanians occupied the rest. There were also half a dozen families from western Europe, who were described as 'Franks' and were under the protection of the French Consul. There was not a single house which could have been called substantial or of modern construction. There was no hotel. It was considered a bold venture when a tavern was opened in 1810. European travellers either rented a house or lodged with one of the European families, unless of course they found refuge in the Capuchin monastery.

This, then, was the scene in which Lord Elgin's artists and craftsmen set to work. They were industrious and devoted, but continually interfered with by the Turks, who either forbade access to the ancient sites or made martial demonstrations, although a daily fee of five pounds sterling was paid for the permit to reside in the town. This monstrous charge, as it has been justifiably called, was followed up by various other annoyances, and nothing could induce the Turkish authorities to recognize the peaceful intentions and entirely unpolitical character of the proceedings. They had plenty to do to keep them busy; besides the Parthenon, which had suffered severe damage from the explosion of a powder magazine during its seige by the Venetians in 1687, the Erectheon, in which the highest Turkish authority resided, the Propylaea, the temples of Nike and Theseus, there were many other buildings of smaller importance.

Reports were sent to Lord Elgin, now installed in Constantinople, on the progress of operations and the difficulties put in their way. Complaints were made of the distrust and superstitions of the Turks and the endless negotiations with the authorities. Nevertheless, the drawings, the topographical plans, and the casts were methodically continued.

In March 1801, Lord Elgin was presented by the Sultan and Caputan Pasha with two very fine marble statues from a church which many eighteenth-century travellers had described with admiration. These then formed the nucleus of his celebrated collection, which now took more and more of his attention. It was his daily experience to see how statues of great beauty and historical interest, sometimes with inscriptions, were not only exposed to the weather and by now almost effaced, but also made use of for all sorts of practical purposes, the chief of which was to pound them down for mortar. They might also be built into walls without alterations; and beautiful marble basins were used as mortars in which grain was ground until at last they broke up.

Up to now, Lord Elgin's plan, as he himself described it, had been 'to measure every surviving piece of classical sculpture come across, to draw it and to take mouldings of selected specimens of architecture. For example, I brought home a description of every column, as well as of the capitals and ornamentation.'

During the course of operations both he and his helpers could note the great number of works of art which had been lost or destroyed in the half-century since the tour made by Stuart and Revett. An ancient temple on the Ilissus, for example, had simply vanished.

'Every traveller,' Lord Elgin said, 'contributed to the mutilation of any statue or other piece of sculpture within reach. There are fragments in London today which were broken off in our day. The Turks have disfigured the heads of statues throughout the whole time of their rule. They have often told me that they have pulled statues down to make mortar of them. These circumstances and the feelings they called up induced me to remove as much of the sculpture as I conveniently could: it was no part of my original plan to bring away anything but my models.'

In these words we have the turning point, the originating cause of the Elgin Marbles. To pursue this new aim an extended permit was of course required, and this expressly covered 'the removal of any sculpture or inscription not incorporated with the buildings or the walls of the citadel'. We do not know precisely how the ambassador put through this wish of the art collector to the Sublime Porte, as the request was made by word of mouth. Anyway, Lord Elgin received the required firman, later described as a momentous document.

'It is our wish that on receipt of this letter you do all in your power to meet the wishes of the said ambassador during the time the five artists in Athens carry on their work, going in and out of the citadel of Athens, erecting scaffolding against the ancient temples, taking mouldings with chalk and plaster of the ornaments and figures visible there, measuring the ruins and foundations of other buildings, or, if they think it necessary, exposing the foundations in order to look for inscriptions among the debris. These people must not be hindered, either through the Disdar, the commander of the citadel, or by any other person, or by yourself, to whom this letter is addressed, no one shall interfere with them in their work or prevent them taking away fragments with inscriptions or figures. Do as you are ordered herein.

Seged Abdullah Kaimacan.'

This order, into the bargain, was sealed to mark its importance.

Lord Elgin later commented: 'With this the opportunities for me and all British travellers were increased, and by the middle of 1801 all difficulties had been overcome.' The important part played by the political situation in this result has never been disputed. Napoleon at this very time was plundering Italy of her art treasures at sword's point; and, further, Nelson's victory of Aboukir after Napoleon's landing in Egypt, and the defeat of the French by the English in Egypt, very greatly strengthened Lord Elgin's hand.

He wrote at once to his people in Athens: 'You now have permission to dig and this opens up a wide field for medallions and for fragments of sculpture and buildings.' He urged them on to renewed efforts and also had his plans for his castle in Scotland altered to accommodate the acquisitions of ancient art he could now look forward to.

The difficulties which had to be overcome are almost unimaginable today. All journeys had to be made on foot or on horseback and were handicapped not only by primitive conditions but the threat of bandits and cut-throats. Sometimes a find had to be abandoned owing to the risk of plague. Once in Gallipoli when they had come upon a portion of an inscribed column which was used as a mortar for grinding corn, plague-infected Turks collected round the 'Frank' who was busy copying the inscription. Who can blame him if he put his life before the inscription? Nearby the same man unexpectedly found a clothed torso and was able to carry it off.

In Athens the temple of Minerva was stripped of its finest and most important pieces, which had for long been the admiration of scholars and artists, and were now carried off as Lord Elgin's property. Even today, after more than 150 years, the letters

9. Lord Elgin, by G. P. Harding after Anton Graff (*c.* 1795).

10. A painting by A. Archer (1819) showing the Elgin Marbles as originally displayed in the British Museum.

and reports from Athens, the replies and instructions from Constantinople enable the reader to share the excitement and enthusiasm in which all who took part lived during those months. Pieces of sculpture were dug up, drawn and measured, reliefs sawn from their beds with any saw available until proper marble saws were procured, carefully let down to the ground and packed. Next there was the transport to the quay-side and the shipping, for which a regular service had to be organized; Lord Elgin bought and chartered ships, and even contrived that a warship should pay a visit to Athens and take off some of his cases, cases containing Jupiters, Minervas, mounted warriors, a much admired Victory, the torso of a remarkably fine Hermes, and many another priceless treasure. While the work of rescue went tirelessly on in the heat and dust and the risk of various diseases, the Turks were equally busy a few yards away pulling down portions of the Parthenon for the lead clamps holding the blocks of marble together; they wanted these for melting down as bullets. 'I am convinced,' wrote Lusieri, Lord Elgin's representative, 'that in fifty years time not one stone will be left standing on another. It would be as well, my Lord, to ask for all that is left . . .'; that is to say, for the whole of the Parthenon!

Operations had soon extended far beyond Athens. In Negroponte, Thebes, Arcadia, Elis, Olympia and Eleusis, where the great bust of Demeter was acquired, and in many other sites, works of art were unearthed, drawn, measured or carried off. But it was not always so easy. Occasionally the prices demanded were too exorbitant. Sometimes, too, the disposal of them was prevented by their reputation as talismans.

The greater the success and the larger the haul, the higher rose the enthusiasm of Lord Elgin and of his helpers.

An idea of the vast numbers of works of art which reached England in this way can be obtained from the mere bulk for which shipping had to be arranged. Periodical reports state that now thirteen, now eighteen cases have left by warship or merchantman, either direct to England, or sometimes by way of Smyrna or Egypt. Every case was marked in bold letters:

'Property of his Excellency, Lord Elgin. Ambassador extraordinary and Plenipotentiary at the Porte, London, Downing Street.' The cases were therefore diplomatic baggage, which no tax collector, customs officer, inspector or exciseman would dare interfere with, and no bandit either, it was hoped.

As in the case of any other cargo, way-bills and descriptions of the cases and boxes were made out. For example, on September 15, 1802, when the *Mentor* left Athens for Malta, her way-bill had the following entries:

Nr 33 Two reliefs

Nr 35 Portions of the Parthenon frieze

Nr 36 Two other reliefs

Nr 43 Part of a statue and fragment of a column

Nr 46 . . . and fragment of a column

Nr 47 . . . and fragment of a column and of a porphyry column

Nr 48 . . . and fragment of a column and three small inscriptions

Nr 49 . . . and fragment of a column and part of a male torso found in the Parthenon

Nr 50 . . . and fragment of a column and part of an arm found when digging below the pediment of the Parthenon

Nr 51 . . . and fragments of a column and two other pieces of the frieze

Nr 52 Corner piece of the frieze, two inscriptions, part of a shoulder from one of the pediment groups

Nr 54 Part of the large relief taken from the northern wall of the Acropolis

Nr 55 Another part of the same

Nr 56 Case containing the marble seat from the Archbishop's palace

However, the Elgin Marbles were not brought home without disappointments and losses. There were breakages, and the *Mentor*, which left Athens with the treasures listed above, was wrecked while attempting to make port in a storm. Crew and passengers were luckily saved, and next day all persons of importance in the neighbourhood were notified to stand by and help with the salvage, as the law required. But in spite of voluble assurances nothing was done. So for the time being the whole cargo, which included some Egyptian papyri, was given up for lost; and efforts to raise the ship failed owing to the great depth of the water.

On January 25, 1803, Lord Elgin left Constantinople, and his journey, to his great annoyance, took a very long time. He had only just reached Paris when all British nationals between the ages of eighteen and sixty were declared prisoners. He was arrested on the 23rd, but in July he was given permission to reside at Barèges in the Pyrenees and then, in October, to move to Pau. For a time he was confined to a fortress near Lourdes as an act of retaliation on the part of the French government. He was a prisoner in France until 1806.

These years were an interruption in his diplomatic career and also in his activities as a collector, but they did not interrupt the work of his expedition, even after all communications between him and Lusieri had been broken off, Lusieri carried on, his chief concern being to forward all the specimens which were still awaiting shipment in Greece, Egypt, Malta, Smyrna and other ports, to England. Often there were long intervals between one consignment of money from England and the next; French rivals naturally took advantage of the ups and downs of war; Turks stole and sold valuable vases, and once, on his return from a journey, Lusieri found his whole house gutted. On the other hand, he was able to report to Lord Elgin that in 1803 and 1804, after many difficulties, all his treasures in the *Mentor* had been salvaged, including the papyri. For the time, certainly, the cases had had to be stacked on the shore covered with seaweed and brushwood weighted by stones, and the moment the place was left unguarded the inhabitants came along and removed the stones for building huts or marking field boundaries.

As soon as Lord Elgin was set at liberty he sent suitable presents and material of all kinds out to Athens for the further garnering in of his acquisitions. But finally even his financial resources gave out, and in 1812 he had to tell Lusieri to abandon the proposed excavations at Olympia, and all other plans of the kind; he was now to restrict himself entirely to collecting together and despatching what had been already recovered. Lusieri's task was soon concluded. He died on March 1, 1821, almost exactly twenty-one years after he had taken on the direction of Lord Elgin's historic enterprise. He had been employed for more than twelve years on the assembly of a unique collection, in the course of which there were at times more than 300 men under his orders. His last drawings went down in H.M.S. *Cambrian* and with this disaster the story of the transport of the Elgin Marbles, often via Malta, was closed. It had included statues, inscriptions, pieces of marble, casts, sarcophagi, metopes from the Parthenon, parts of its frieze, horses' heads, corner pieces from the Erectheon, twenty-three cases of marbles, vases, parts of tombs, caryatids, porphyry columns, bricks, terracotta tiles, reliefs, bronzes and earthenware.

The subsequent history of the Elgin Marbles, their exhibition, the world-wide admiration they aroused, the commission appointed by Parliament to enquire into the circumstances of their acquisition and the taking over of the whole collection by the state, is not our concern here. We need only revert to the question already touched on: Was Lord Elgin's operation rescue work or robbery, or both? The Commission had to decide whether Lord Elgin had acquired his collection as a private person or as ambassador and whether it could be classed as private property or had been the property of the state all the time. The bargaining was all the more protracted because the price of works of art had risen steeply since 1812. Lord Elgin protested with energy that he was only one of many collectors who had obtained firmans, passports and export permits, that he had never in this connection made use of his official position, and that all expenses had been paid out of his own purse; however, the Commission decided that 'only an ambassador could have acquired such extensive privileges,' and paid him £35,000 for the collection, a considerable sum which, nevertheless, did not cover half his outlay.

Lord Elgin himself in a letter of 1831 to the Society of Dilettanti expressed the aim and purpose of his undertaking in these words: 'The motives which induced me to carry out this operation in Greece proceeded entirely from the wish to secure for Great Britain, and hence for Europe as a whole, the best possible knowledge, and the means of improving it, through the most outstanding works of Greek art in sculpture and architecture.'

In *Lord Elgin and his Collection* A. H. Smith sums up the achievement of a great collector as follows:

'The operations were carried on with a single-minded enthusiasm for the promotion of knowledge and art, and it is beyond question that in this direction their influence was profound. The effect of the marbles upon the minds of the artists has been sufficiently indicated in the foregoing narrative. In archaeology it is unquestionable that by the opportunities of study opened out to western Europe new standards were set up, and that the whole view of ancient art was permanently modified and corrected.'

13

Land Grabbing and Art Plunder

Stanislaus Augustus Poniatowski, the last King of Poland, tells in his memoirs how from his earliest childhood everything to do with art had quite an extraordinary attraction for him. During his youth the customary visits to Paris for education and pleasure added further inducements to make the acquaintance of artists and works of art, and also of patrons and protectors of the fine arts. His education by the Italian Theatines in the College of Vilna and a journey to England were influences in the same direction. But his rapid conversion to the Anglomania of the day must be attributed rather to his admiration for the political and social institutions and circumstances of Great Britain than to her artistic achievements.

In 1764 Stanislaus Poniatowski became King of Poland and at once despatched persons of trust to buy pictures for his castles and to decoy capable artists to his court. His correspondence about the buying of pictures and the visits of foreigners who informed him about art in their own countries or offered pictures for sale took up so much of his time that people soon talked of a *régime artistique*, one which inclined more and more to the *grand goût* of the court of Louis XV.

At the end of the reign of his predecessor, Augustus III, the pictures which had belonged to the Saxon royal house had been transferred to Dresden. For the time, therefore, Poland was left with nothing but a few second-rate historical paintings. But Stanislaus had from the first intended to have one of the finest galleries in Europe, and he got the Italian, Bacciarelli, who later became his closest friend, to draw up a plan for the purchase of

134

paintings up to the limits of the Royal purse. As the King was in more of a hurry than Bacciarelli allowed for, his purchases quickly outran his means, although he did not succeed in acquiring any really first rate works. He relied at the outset on dealers in Poland and other countries, but in 1787, like so many other princes, he sent his own agent and buyer, Bacciarelli, to Italy. It throws light on the importance of art purchases in those days that a trade agreement with the Pontifical State should have been negotiated by Poland, providing for a lower rate of export tax on Italian works of art.

Stanislaus Augustus rose to his greatest heights as a collector during the years between 1780 and 1790; and Bacciarelli had frequently to restrain him to prevent his debts reaching even more dizzy heights. We have nothing now but the catalogue of 1795 to go by in judging the value of his collection, made with such love of art and at such cost, only to be scattered far and wide a few decades later. It numbered 2,289 pictures of which today a fifth at most can be traced. It consisted principally of paintings of the seventeenth and eighteenth centuries, the 'moderns' of the day, and was representative therefore of the average taste of contemporary collectors between 1750 and 1790 rather than of a superior discrimination. Fragonard's *The Stolen Kiss* was one of its highlights.

These 2,289 pictures were not assembled in one gallery, but distributed among the various castles and palaces of Warsaw; the historical works chiefly in the castle of Warsaw, the Dutch in the Lazienki Palace, those of less worth in the Belvedere and one other castle.

The first and second partitions of Poland in 1772 and 1793 when Russia, Austria and Prussia robbed the kingdom only of territory on their borders, severe though these losses were, did not destroy Poland's integrity or deprive it of Warsaw. But the year 1795 brought the dispersal and removal of Stanislaus Augustus's collection. If ever there was a literal case of art plunder occasioned by land grabbing, it was the third partition of Poland, the deliberate dissolution of a thousand-year-old kingdom by the very powers who in the west, in France, were upholding 'ancient right' and the 'old order' for the benefit of Louis XVI and his dynasty, while in the east they carried their own desire for territorial expansion to such lengths that they simply annihilated a state which was in no way concerned in the struggle between the Revolution and the *Ancien Régime*.

In 1794, after the defeat of Kosciuszko, who tried to save Poland, the plundering of the royal collections began. It is true that an official distinction was made between the personal property of Stanislaus and the property of the state, but is it any less unjust and immoral to rob a state than to rob a private person, especially when it is an open question whether or not the king's 'private possessions' were bought out of his private means? Moreover the powers implicated in the dismemberment of Poland did not only rob the Polish state or the Polish people: they also robbed each other. Prussia, having agreed that Cracow was to fall to the share of Austria, made haste to steal the crown jewels from the castle while Prussian troops were still in occupation. The Russians too stripped Warsaw of all that might recall its past or had artistic value before handing it over to the Prussians. In December 1794, Suvorov and Buxhoevden, the Russian generals, removed all the furniture of value from the Palace, excluding the 'private possessions' of Stanislaus Augustus. But the Prussians would not even recognize the right of 'the king without land' to this property, and long negotiations followed with a so-called tripartite commission set up by the Convention of St Petersburg on January 15, 1797, and composed of representatives of the three powers.

Stanislaus Augustus tried to anticipate the findings of the commission by the sale of all his works of art and other possessions in Warsaw to the King of Prussia, who, however, after long haggling rejected the offer, no doubt from the conviction that it was foolish to pay for what he would sooner or later get for nothing, or at any rate much more cheaply. The Prussians therefore dragged out the proceedings of the commission by insisting that the furniture of the castle was the property of the state, on the dissolution of which it automatically became the property of Prussia. This led finally to the appointment of another commission, charged with the task of distinguishing between state property and private property, and at last, after protracted negotiations, the Prussian demands were rejected.

Stanislaus Augustus died on February 1, 1798, in St Petersburg and his heir, Prince John Poniatowski, carried on the negotiations with the Prussian court, partly with the aim of having his uncle's Warsaw possessions put at his free disposal, if the sale of them to the King of Prussia did not come off, and also to obtain compensation for the buildings which Stanislaus had erected partly out of his 'own' means. Discussions went on year after year until the defeat of the Prussians at Jena and Auerstedt, and the creation of the Arch-Duchy of Warsaw, brought about a new situation and postponed the settlement of these questions to a distant date.

Meanwhile much had been destroyed. Russian troops destroyed part of the Palace in Warsaw in 1794. In 1796 Austria had removed everything in her 'zone of occupation', particularly pictures. Protests to the tripartite commission were useless. The pictures must be counted as lost today.

Stanislaus Augustus was heart-broken by the fate of his country, his collection, and by his own situation. Sometimes he despaired of any future for the Polish people, the Polish national character and the Polish language; he often declared that he was a man who had outlived himself. He gave up his collections for lost, or at most regarded them as a means of procuring for himself a modest subsistence abroad, now that he was reduced to poverty, and of paying some part of his huge debts. He had reckoned them at forty million gulden when they were taken over by the partition powers, but it was soon apparent that they amounted to fifty-eight or sixty million, and he wished to meet the difference by the sale of his castles, furniture and works of art—a vain proposal from a king without land or power, who had to accept any price he was offered. His collections were valued at 54,961 ducats in 1794; a year later the valuation had sunk to 41,203. Also the King wanted to keep 'some' pictures for himself.

A list drawn up by Bacciarelli gives 172 favourites, presents and keepsakes which Stanislaus wished to take with him to Rome, his future place of exile. He gave a larger number to former servants, and also recommended his court painters, but not his dearest friend Bacciarelli, to the Czar. His furniture and other valuables, including presumably the favourites among his pictures, were sold at his death. We cannot follow in detail the vicissitudes of the negotiations, their interruption during the Napoleonic wars and their subsequent resumption. The dispersal and scattering of the collections was continued in 1815, after many Polish nobles had already acquired single pictures in 1805, 1807 and 1810.

We hear of further sales, large and small, to nobles and merchants at different times in 1817, 1819 and even later. The final liquidation in 1821 brought in 175,000 gulden, but meanwhile many pictures had vanished owing to the dishonesty or negligence of the administrators. One of Prince Poniatowski's grooms of the chamber made a fortune in this way.

Thus ended a peculiarly flagrant example of art plunder a generation after the land itself had been divided as spoil. Many pictures found their way into the galleries of the Polish nobility, a certain number remained in the castle of Lazienski, some of the best arrived in Vienna. The Lazienski collection was 'evacuated' to Moscow during the First World War and was 'restored' in 1922 by the terms of the Treaty of Riga, minus *The Stolen Kiss* by Fragonard and a self-portrait by van Gelder.

The dispersal of King Stanislaus Poniatowski's collections could not be undone when Poland rose again. The territory of Poland remained, even though curtailed here and there; but once its art collections had been dispersed by the partition of 1795 they were scattered all over the world.

14

Art Plunder and the

French Revolution

1. *A new theory of looting*

The French Revolution and its immediate consequences open up an entirely new field of enquiry. The standards that had been applicable since the Middle Ages held good no longer. With the advance of the 'People', including their great protagonists, like Napoleon, into the position occupied before by the 'Princes', everything acquired greater weight and a more emotional quality. Looting became more radical, principled, all-embracing—and dangerous.

Princes who carried off treasures during the seventeenth and eighteenth centuries did so as individuals in their royal, electoral or ducal capacity; they wanted the stuff for themselves and sent or took it home with them. When king, emperor and czar came to the third and last partition of Poland during the French Revolution and robbed first Stanislaus Augustus and then each other, they were acting according to form; they were not actuated either by feelings of revenge or triumph, nor filled with either pride or shame.

It was quite another matter with revolutionary France. There, passionate feelings were uppermost and the right of property, regarded as sacred for centuries, was now supplanted by the right of revolution and national feeling. Emotions of revenge, of overweening power, of arrogance, of the desire for reparation, of the fervour of reform took the place of judicial considerations; there was, in fact, an entirely new 'justice', based on newly discovered

139

principles; Europe was to experience it during all the years of revolutionary rule in France, during the rule of Napoleon too, and even after his downfall.

With the outbreak of the French Revolution, which at first had a social-economic character but later took as definite a political turn, the domain of art shared in the general upheaval, and as time went on was given a new orientation. When in 1789 the French people created its new state on new principles, these principles found wide application in a new attitude to art. As all power proceeded from the people and had to serve it, works of art also belonged to the people and had to be at its service. The rationalistic centralization of the French Republic and the Empire extended very quickly to pictures, sculpture and all artistic property. Without the slightest concern for historical associations or respect for the rights of ownership, castles, churches and monasteries were stripped of their treasures, all of which were then accumulated in Paris, the home of the Revolution and the seat of the rule of the people. The haul was so immense that it would have been quite impossible to house more than a small part of it in any one large museum. It was not until five years later that provincial museums were instituted and a considerable advance made, it must be admitted, towards the acquaintance of the people with art.

This accumulation of more or less valuable works of art of all kinds—in 1794 there were 1,122 pictures stored at Versailles—was not only derived from the royal collections: it came as well from rifled churches, monasteries, houses of lay brotherhoods, archiepiscopal and episcopal palaces, from the houses of émigré families, particularly of noble families, which were over-run and despoiled in 1789. The 1926 catalogue of the Louvre still contained a special list of objects confiscated from émigré families, with notes of origin and dates of appropriation by the state. Only a few, among them the Duke of Orleans and Calonne, once the King's minister, succeeded in getting their art treasures out of the country.

The lengths to which this expropriation or nationalization or, in the eyes of the sufferers, not unnaturally, this robbery, was carried is shown by the attitude taken up by *La Décade Philosophique* in its issue of January 29, 1795, where the complaint is made that the names of the aristocratic families to which many of the pictures in the National Museum formerly belonged were still to be seen beneath their frames. This National Museum, decided upon on May 26, 1791, was already in existence only three and a half years later.

It is also of interest to observe that as long as works of art belonged to the king, to a bishop, or to a marquis, no questions of ownership arose. But as soon as the Revolution had taken the first step in over-riding ancient rights of property, no standard remained except the highly unreliable emotions of the mob. Many interested parties, for example, at once laid claim to the pictures from the Palace of Versailles. The nation with its government in Paris claimed them for the central or national museum of the Louvre. On the other hand, the commune of the town of Versailles considered itself the direct heir, and also pointed out that revolution had its negative sides in that the inhabitants of Versailles already complained of the damage done them by the abolition of the court, and were now apprehensive of suffering further financial loss by the removal of the pictures. Finally, at the end of 1793, the town of Versailles was conceded 'a gallery of the French School'. We know today, from first-hand experience, that these revolutionary expropriations cause irretrievable losses owing to the thirst for revenge, the reckless desire to obliterate the past, the lust of destruction and the dead weight of indifference, and without conferring any great benefits on the individual, or the nation, or art, or even on the revolution itself. But in France these losses, whatever they may have been, were quickly made good many times over, both in quality and quantity, by the plunder of Europe's masterpieces, brought to Paris by the armies of the Revolution almost as soon as the opening of the Louvre Museum showed the people what it owed to the looting of its own country.

Had the king, the nobles, the church, that is to say, the elect, used their privileges to enrich themselves without scruple at the cost of the people, who now resumed possession of what was originally theirs, or was it the people, who having abrogated law and order by insurrection and revolt, now stole whatever excited its greed? It makes no difference that a great deal of the plunder—much was sold to satisfy the state's creditors— found its way into the Louvre. The Louvre was from the first much frequented; but for seven days in every ten it was reserved for artists and only open to the public on the other three. In the course of the next few years, works of art belonging to condemned and executed persons, of unequal value but considerable in number, were added to those which had been confiscated at the outset. Even to possess works of art might in those days be extremely dangerous, particularly when their aristocratic possessors tried to go underground and take a bourgeois name. Although many members of the Third Estate had been prosperous before 1789 and owned libraries, sculpture and pictures, there were certain possessions which were confined to persons of noble birth, such as those services of porcelain imported since the seventeenth century from China, on every piece of which the coat of arms of the family was painted. This practice had been copied by French manufacturers of china. These precious collections, running often to hundreds and sometimes to thousands of pieces, were buried, hidden or even smashed to prevent their being silent witnessess of former grandeur.

2. *The Netherlands and the Imperial territories west of the Rhine*

The Austrian Netherlands, later Belgium, had already in the days of Emperor Joseph II, son of Maria Theresa, been forced to yield up many valuable works of art. Count Rosa, Director of the Vienna Art Gallery, points out that pictures, once in the possession of the Jesuits there, were sent to Vienna in 1774 on the dissolution of that order. Two years later twenty-five pictures worth more than 57,000 gulden arrived in Vienna. In 1783 the Hapsburg government in the Austrian Netherlands secularized a further 162 monasteries and abbeys. The works of art found in them were nearly all sold abroad. Joshua Reynolds went to Belgium in 1795 to buy pictures formerly in the possession of religious houses at reasonable prices, and wrote home that he had acquired 'every picture from Brussels and Antwerp which was for sale and worth buying, with one exception' (the exception was a *Rape of the Sabines*). It is not surprising that the author of the catalogue of the Ghent gallery saw only a final blow in the depredations of the French.

We mention these 'legal' events here to show that, even before the arrival of the French, works of art in this region, at least, had shown a tendency to migrate. The reforms which enlightened despotism, represented in this case first and foremost by Joseph II, introduced might have as their aim the liberation of the peasants or the suppression of the Jesuits, but the blow they aimed at ancient usage did not rest there: it raised a doubt of the eternal validity of right, and suggested that it depended on power politics and the philosophy of the moment, and was therefore neither unalterable nor immune to influence. This experience, and the observations it led to, were the best preparation for the views which the French revolutionary army brought with it when it invaded the country.

When the French first came in 1792, the looting was merely looting; Danton, for example, was later charged with having carried off works of art. Two years later when the revolutionary troops made their second appearance, the Revolution itself accompanied them: all religious corporations were abolished and their possessions confiscated. This time plunder too was organized.

In June 1794, the French 'Committee for the education of the People' proposed sending 'knowledgeable civilians with our armies, with confidential instructions to seek out and obtain the works of art in the countries invaded by us'. Passing over the question whether this order came from the government in Paris or from the army command, it is on record that on July 18, 1794, the following army order was issued:

'The People's commissioners with the Armies of the North and Sambre-et-Meuse have learned that in the territories invaded by the victorious armies of the French Republic in order to expel the hirelings of the tyrants there are works of painting and sculpture and other products of genius. They are of the opinion that the proper place for them, in the interests and for the honour of art, is in the home of free men. They therefore make the following order . . .'

Whereupon Citizen Barbier, lieutenant in the Hussars, and Citizen Léger, an assistant of the adjutant for General Affairs, were instructed to keep a look-out for masterpieces of art, and all officers and officials were ordered to give them every assistance. These were the first instructions for organized plunder by French revolutionary armies abroad. They were signed by the distinguished chemist, Guyton de Moreau.

The commissioners named above were no connoisseurs and set about their job in a clumsy and haphazard fashion. Thus the geologist, Barthélemy Faujas, and the botanist, André Thouin, reported to the Provisional Art Commission in Paris: 'Citizens, since our last consignment of 28 Vendémiaire (October 19, 1794) in charge of Citizen Bonnet, we have searched one by one the towns and villages of Verviers, Spa and Aix as well as the mines, manufactories and all the neighbourhood. These tours have brought in a convoy of more than twenty wagon-loads.'

Albrecht Dürer was in Aix on October 23, 1520, and noted: 'In Aix I saw the proportioned columns of green and red porphyry which Charles brought from Rome and set up there; they are really fashioned as Vitruvius describes.' All the finest pictures were taken out of the churches and every work of art that could be removed was removed from the Cathedral, including the wolf and the artichoke, its national symbols, the Proserpine sarcophagus, and the bronze Virgin and Child above the west door. They also packed the Carolingian screen of the octagon, and then forgot to despatch it. Then in October the columns of Charlemagne were dislodged. Forty-six columns, mostly with their capitals, reached Paris after being months, years rather, on the way. At the beginning of January 1800, they were still in the courtyard of the Palace in Liège.

The commissioners found the booty of Cologne 'much more abundant than the above-mentioned . . . The guns, the antique remains, the coins, the sketches and drawings, the manuscripts in various languages, the printed books of the fifteenth century, the valuable works on the natural sciences, the arts, and history found in this city were collected and will now be added to the libraries and galleries of the Revolution.'

Next, in November 1794, the commissioners despatched the valuable city library, the famous altar-piece by Rubens, and also many works of art belonging to émigrés, from Cologne to Paris. Likewise the Cologne arsenal yielded its store of antiques, the former Jesuit school lost its 1,400 Greek and Roman silver coins, its cut gems, its bowls and vases, its natural history collection of nuggets of solid gold from Peru, silver ore, coral and many curiosities, brought back by members of the order and its friends from their travels abroad. What the commissioners could not take possession of on the spot—there was much which had been sent eastwards for safety—was either laid up in store or else sold for what it would fetch. Art in those days was merchandise, to be judged by money standards, not taste, whether it was acquired lawfully in the old-fashioned sense or was the reward of robbery.

In October 1794, *La Décade Philosophique* was able to announce the arrival in Paris of the first convoy of works of art. More than a hundred pictures, it was stated in the next issue, were still on the way to the capital of the Revolution, destined now to be the home of art and the focus of all artistic effort.

In October the Committee for the Education of the People congratulated the representatives of the people in the National Convention on the haul of works of art from conquered and occupied countries, and from the correspondence laid before it on that occasion it is clear that the initiative at least, if not the first promptings to the plunder of art, came from the army and

K

not from the government. It was in the Austrian Netherlands, then, that the precedent was set by which every army in a foreign country confiscated all works of art found there and despatched them as booty to Paris.

Second-rate works, which were naturally in the majority, were sold on the spot for the benefit of the state. The description of any work as second-rate was purely arbitrary and opened the door to unlimited peculation. But in any case, the result was the same: the art market was flooded once more. When in Brussels alone about fifty religious houses and churches were despoiled, it is obvious that there can have been no lack of bargains to be picked up for years afterwards. Picture dealers, such as von Nieuwenhuys in Brussels, from whom the Boisserée brothers of Cologne bought Dutch and Flemish paintings, prospered. Not until peace was concluded in Paris after 1815, when numbers of rich English and Russians visited Belgium, did the supply gradually dwindle.

The history of the Ghent altar-piece by the van Eyck brothers is in several respects typical of the fate of Flemish works of art. In 1781, the year of his mother's death, Joseph II, thinking the two side-panels of Adam and Eve shocking, had them removed. Then, in 1794, the French commissioners carried off the four middle panels to Paris. In 1815 they were returned to Brussels, but, as though recent experiences had infected them with unrest, they were unable to settle down. In 1817, in the absence of the Bishop, the Brussels art dealer, Nieuwenhuys, bought six side-panels. Soon afterwards he sold them to an English merchant, and in 1821 they were acquired by the Prussian Government, together with other pictures from the English merchant's collection. After the First World War, Germany was compelled to hand them over to Belgium, although they had neither been carried off from Belgium nor bought from a Belgian. During the Second World War the whole altar-piece was stored in an Austrian salt-mine.

French troops penetrated further into Holland under General Pichegru in 1795. William of Orange, the Stadholder, took refuge in England, leaving his officers and officials free to conform to the principles of the Revolution. The Provisional Government of the Netherlands, by the decrees of March 5 and 25, confiscated the property of the Stadholder, but the French had anticipated them; their civil commissioners had already made a start with the inventory of his possessions. In May the pictures in his cabinet were packed up and by June 7 they were on their way to Paris. The French did not take possession of any other pictures in Holland, but the Dutch Republican Government, on the other hand, sold off all works of art from the religious houses as well as many hundreds of other pictures and works of art. This went on until 1798, when Alexander Gogel, Minister for Finance, succeeded in founding a 'National Art Gallery' on the French model, in which were assembled the pictures from the various castles and a considerable number of others acquired for the purpose; and in 1800 the Gallery was declared open to the public. The catalogue of 1801 contains 201 entries, mostly historical pieces and portraits. At the end of the same year the number had risen to 252, and in 1804 to 315. The first Rembrandt was bought for the gallery at this time. Four years later, on April 21, 1808, Louis Bonaparte, Napoleon's brother and then King of the Netherlands, provided for the establishment of a royal museum in Amsterdam and allotted a large sum for this purpose. On his abdication, the kingdom of the Netherlands was incorporated with France and no money was forthcoming for the upkeep of the Museum.

3. *Italy*

In March 1796 Napoleon Bonaparte became commander-in-chief of the French army in Italy with the task of driving the Austrians and their allies out of the country. To understand the situation of the army at that moment it must be remembered that it relied for its upkeep entirely on contributions levied on occupied territory; when Napoleon arrived at his headquarters in Nice, the soldiers had had no pay for months; everything was lacking and some regiments were reduced literally to rags. This state of affairs was naturally bad for discipline, and plunder was the first aim of the army of the Revolution.

Napoleon's correspondence shows that he did his utmost to curb the excesses of his soldiers. An order of April 22, 1796, may be taken as an example of many more:

'Headquarters, Lesegno, 3 Floreal, Year 4. The Commander-in-chief commends the army for its bravery and for the victories it has wrested from the enemy day after day. He sees with horror, however, the frightful looting committed by worthless wretches who only join their units when the fighting is over, because they have been employed in committing these excesses.'

He gave warning of severe penalties. An order of the day of June 11, 1796 runs:

'The Commander-in-chief is informed that in spite of repeated orders looting in the army continues and houses in the countryside are gutted and laid waste.'

He ordered that any soldier found looting should be shot in front of the ranks; and, further, no commissioner might raise levies on the country without his personal orders or those of certain specified authorities.

Yet the Commander-in-chief did not feel bound to obey his own orders. What he forbade to others he perpetrated himself without scruple. He plundered the country far and wide with a thoroughness of which history affords no parallel; but it was done not for his own personal gain—which distinguishes him from many earlier and later conquerors—but for France.

Works of art formed a large part of his plunder, his confiscations, or to call them by their true name, his robberies, since it was not dukes, kings and tyrants who were penalized in conformity with the principles of the Revolution, but ordinary people, those very people whom this army and its commander-in-chief were pledged to free from their oppressors.

While the commissioners, the officers and men went for works of art, pictures, bronzes, coins and so forth, in a small way, Napoleon's operations in the same field were on a larger scale and in a different style. After his unprecedented successes in the field, he concluded an armistice with the Duke of Modena on May 17, 1796, on the following condition among others: 'The Duke of Modena undertakes to hand over twenty pictures. They will be selected by commissioners sent for that purpose from among the pictures in his gallery and realm.' But what was to prevent the commissioners packing and carrying off other pictures as well? Or who would object if they despatched eighteen to Paris and kept two for themselves? Or again they might make a profitable bargain with the Keeper of the Duke's gallery and leave his most valuable pictures in return for a present of gold, bronzes or ancient coins. There was nothing, in fact, to stop the plunderers and their agents deceiving one another.

In Modena the commissioners confiscated, in addition to the twenty pictures for the Republic, the Duke's collection of cameos and other pieces for themselves. Wicar, one of the commissioners, appropriated no fewer than fifty pictures and many of the Duke's drawings. It needed Napoleon's arrival on the scene to put a stop to this private looting, but what was done could not be undone; on the contrary, Napoleon joined in on his own account and chose two pictures for himself, a portrait of Prince Eugene and one of Caesar as a military commander.

Parma had to surrender twenty paintings, Milan twenty-five. Venice, towards the end of 1797, lost its famous bronze horses, mentioned above in connection with the Fourth Crusade, the lion from St Mark's, a bust, a bas-relief, an exceptionally precious cameo, sixteen pictures, 230 incunabula and 253 manuscripts. When the fortress of Mantua fell on February 2, 1797, Mantua had to hand over four pictures, five drawings, three marble busts, fourteen manuscripts and forty-six prints. An altar-piece by Rubens, already cut up on account of its size, was retrieved on its way to France by the unruffled Director of the Academy; but several pieces of it were irrecoverably lost.

149

The few but on the whole precise details we have show that the choice of works of art to be handed over was made by men who knew what they were about. They did not make wholesale confiscations, but selected the best. The French insisted later that the French Republic in its dealings with Italy proceeded always by treaty and with the agreement of the Italians. But that is an argument which Hitler, Göring and Rosenberg might equally well have served up. For the conquered it is all the same whether their possessions are looted or handed over by enforced agreement.

In 1796 Napoleon invaded central Italy. The King of Naples was perhaps the most apprehensive and certainly the most far-seeing of his possible opponents. As soon as Napoleon appeared on the horizon he made peace with him on terms which, owing to the distance which parted them and the as yet untried and untarnished valour of his army, cost him remarkably little.

The Pope, on the contrary, had to make heavy sacrifices for peace. Terms were reached in Bologna on June 23, 1796, by which the Holy See had to pay twenty-one million livres in money and goods. Article 8 is unquestionably the most eloquent:

'A hundred pictures, busts, vases or statues to be selected by the commissioners and sent to Rome, including in particular the bronze bust of Junius Brutus and the marble bust of Marcus Brutus, both on the Capitol, also five hundred manuscripts at the choice of the said commissioners.'

These conditions were inscribed in the Treaty of Tolentino, and the Holy See agreed to carry them out promptly. If Napoleon's insistence on the two busts was linked with his Caesar complex, we can recognize in it, as in so many other instances, the desire of the French Republic to challenge a comparison between its own political way of thinking and that of republican Rome.

In addition, there were of course levies and deliveries of works of art from the other and, in many cases, very rich Papal dominions. Forty pictures were commandeered in Bologna and ten in Ferrara. Napoleon wrote proudly, 'The Commission of experts has made a fine haul in Ravenna, Rimini, Pesaro, Ancona, Loretto and Perugia. The whole lot will be forwarded to Paris without delay. There is also the consignment from Rome itself. We have stripped Italy of everything of artistic worth, with the exception of a few objects in Turin and Naples!'

The King of Piedmont and Sardinia possessed a gallery which ranked as one of the most important in Europe: every traveller of note visited and praised it. The agents of Frederick the Great had likewise paid it visits, as had other rich collectors, and made an occasional acquisition. Now Napoleon compelled Charles Emmanuel to abdicate. When General Clausel came back with the news, he brought a painting by Gerard Dou as well, the picture of the dropsical woman, regarded as the most valuable of the whole collection. Later he explained to the Directory that Charles Emmanuel had given it him in recognition of the delicacy and tact he had shown in the matter of the abdication. Nevertheless, we read in the catalogue of the Turin Pinacoteca of 1909 that the King's reply to the arrogant demands of the general was that, if he had to surrender all he possessed into the hands of his enemies, he at least refused to agree to being looted. However that may be, the result of Clausel's mission and the King's abdication was the establishment of a provisional government and the despatch, up to April 19, 1799, of forty pictures from the gallery to Paris. This takes no account of the satisfaction of the private desires of the generals and commissioners who had taken up residence in the town. General Fiorilla appropriated in three days twenty-five pictures and thirty-four miniatures. After a temporary evacuation, an Executive Commission under General Dupont was set up. When the French had to surrender Turin once more on August 15, 1800, the 'Chief of the Government' purloined ten pictures from the royal gallery.

These years saw many other appropriations, or thefts; an unknown French commissioner was the recipient of three paintings, and the Italian members of the official commission were not so busy as to neglect their love of fine things. The historian, Carlo Botta, for example, possessed himself of ten pictures. The in-

habitants fully believed by this time that the Royal Palace had
been stripped bare; but this was not yet the case, although when,
in 1804, Napoleon gave orders that the castle was to be made
ready for his occupation, the bailiff of the castle had to procure
pictures from the academy and other public buildings, and at his
desire General Menon on June 4, 1804, made an ineffectual
order that anyone who had 'acquired' pictures, furniture or
other objects from the castle was to hand them over to the mobile
guard.

Napoleon organized the plunder of art on the state's behalf
with the thoroughness he devoted to his military operations.
Two days after that first enforced picture-deal with the Duke of
Modena, he put an agent at the disposal of the army in Italy
with instructions to commandeer works of art and scientific instruments, and to arrange for their transport to France, after
giving a precise inventory to the army commander and the
government commissioner attached to the army. A record of
each confiscation had to be made in the presence of an official
person recognized by the French army. The booty, when possible,
had to be conveyed to France by army transport and only in case
of necessity by transport requisitioned for the purpose. The cost
of the removal, packing and transport had to be met by the army,
and was often so heavy that twenty years later the original
owners were in many cases unable to pay for the return of their
property, and either abandoned it to the French or sold it to the
Allies far below its value.

At the head of these organizers, who remind us not a little of
the *Einsatzstab Rosenberg*, was citizen Tinet, an 'artist attached
to the Tuscan Embassy'. The Directory had also appointed the
geometrician, Monge, the botanist, Thouin, and the painter,
Wicar, to help in the selection of paintings and other works of
art, two at least of whom must have relied on their proficiency
in other spheres than those of art—or else on their good relations with influential revolutionaries. We have no knowledge of
the impeccability in artistic matters of the two first named, but
it is known of the painter Wicar that he appropriated to himself

'a fortune, particularly in jewels and drawings' from the palazzi of Rome.

Tinet's task was not an enviable one: he was always in need of more transport than he could get hold of. Eighty-six wagons left Bologna alone. When the Austrians advanced in 1796, Napoleon reported to Paris that his convoy of pictures, Italian master-pieces, had had to turn back after Coni, because it would other-wise have fallen into the hands of the *Barbetsa*—the nickname given to the enemy on account of their fur caps. Pictures were in any case sometimes 'lost' during convoy, as happened to two Raphaels, *The Madonna of Loretto* and *The Crowning of St Nicholas*. Much damage, too, must have been done on journeys of hundreds of miles, with mountains and rivers to cross, in wagons without springs and little protection from wind and weather.

Transport by sea also, as Lord Elgin discovered at about this time, had its dangers. A merchant vessel carrying Venetian works of art ran into heavy weather, and Titian's magnificent altar-piece of the death of Peter the Martyr, although it was securely packed in a case, was waterlogged for several days; the wood panel swelled, the painting became detached, and the famous restorer, Hacquin of Paris, had the utmost difficulty in transferring it to canvas, a task which was almost beyond the technique of those days. Another danger was British sea-power, which Napoleon was never able to break or even restrict.

The statues in Rome were mostly so heavy that transport over the Alps was impracticable. Napoleon therefore proposed to the Directory that they should remain ready packed in Rome for the time being. Then, early in the months of April, May, June and July, four convoys set out from Rome for Leghorn, consisting of about a dozen special vehicles, painted red, drawn by ten oxen each, and followed by smaller wagons containing tools and spare-parts. Artisans and soldiers in plenty accompanied the convoys. The Vatican, from whom these works had been stolen, had to pay for the transport, to the tune of about 800,000 livres. The whole consignment was loaded on to a particularly heavily armed frigate in Leghorn and reached Marseilles in safety. Citizen

Vistal was responsible for the further journey in six ships to Paris, for which he was paid 174,000 francs.

There is no exact record of the whole amount of works of art looted from Italy. Even the figures for the official confiscations vary. Napoleon gave forty pictures for Bologna, whereas thirty-three is the figure given by a historian a century later. Apart from Rome, the rest of Italy must have sacrificed at least 241 pictures to the French Republic, the choicest in each case from the galleries, monasteries, churches and palaces concerned. It is impossible to say how many works of art were taken by soldiers and commissioners on their own account. The *savant* Wicar is frequently described as dishonest in the contemporary sources, but when hundreds of persons were dealing with works of art with little or no supervision, it stands to reason that many must have been misappropriated. We learn from Passavant, for example, that 'in the days of the Revolution a copy of a Leonardo was misappropriated by a Frenchman who took it to Milan and sold it. Nothing more was heard of him;' and the opportunities for similar deals must have been endless. Many a work of art after being stolen was sold on the spot, or elsewhere, to an Italian and so remained in Italy. Such local sales must have been frequent in towns like Verona which were given over to plunder.

The plundering of Rome in 1798 is a good example of what was occurring in Italy at that time. Here Napoleon's restraining influence was absent, and also the loot was the richest and choicest Europe had to offer. Moreover, Rome, the capital of the ancient world and of the greatest empire in history, was now to be superseded by Paris, and the French Republic, in whose eyes it was the hotbed of the Catholicism they detested, while at the same time the new régime in France, seemingly at the height of its power, was in fact corrupt and beggared and tottering to its fall. All this combined to make the conquest of Rome the greatest exercise in looting of the Napoleonic age and the most complete Rome had experienced since the spoliation by the Vandals and the Sack of Rome, though not the most bloody.

We are well informed about the events of 1798 because of Rome's unique position, and also because so many foreigners were there to put on record what they saw.

On February 10, 1798, the French General, whose troops were encamped on Monte Mario, made a proclamation to the inhabitants of Rome to the following effect: 'All subjects of the Papal State may rest assured that their persons, their property, their Church are under the protection of the French Army.' Revolutionary fervour and the necessities of France caused a noticeable alteration of tone when the Government of Rome was addressed. Article 6 of General Berthier's declaration went on: 'The Government of Rome will pay an extraordinary contribution in three decades of four million piastres in cash and two million in goods according to his (the General's) choice . . .' Article 14: 'Such pictures, books, manuscripts and works of art will be confiscated in the city of Rome as are thought worthy [sic] of despatch to France in the judgment of a commission appointed for this purpose by order of the Commander-in-chief.'

Five days later, on February 15, 1798, a tree of liberty was planted on the Capitol, and Berthier, in all the pomp of victory, paid homage to the 'Manes of Cato, Pompey, Brutus, Cicero, Hortensius on the Capitol where they so often defended the rights of the people and adorned the Republic of Rome.' Addressing the inhabitants of Rome, he said:

'The Roman people has now resumed the rights of sovereignty. It has declared its independence and, in conformity with the government of ancient Rome, constituted itself a republic. The Commander-in-chief of the French Army in Italy declares that he recognizes the Republic of Rome as an independent state under the special protection of the French Army . . . The French General Cervoni is made responsible for law and order in the city of Rome and for the setting up of the new government.'

On the same day Pope Pius VI celebrated the anniversary of his accession. While High Mass was being held in the Sistine

Chapel in honour of this event, General Commissioner Haller and General Cervoni entered and informed the Head of the Church that his temporal rule was at an end and that his place had been taken by a directorate of five consuls, who took their orders from General Cervoni.

The French then put their seal on all the Pope's possessions to show that they were confiscated, and also on anything of value belonging to his officers and household. Finally, on February 20, they removed the Pope to Siena and were able now to draw up a complete inventory of everything in the Vatican and Quirinal. When this was done, a number of men of business, chiefly from Marseilles and Lyons, who had put up the capital, no small sum, for Napoleon's first crossing of the Alps, were invited to take their pick of the contents of both palaces, naming the prices they saw fit to pay.

The English painter, Duppa, was present at one of these so-called public auctions. In spite of the publicity he found it difficult, if not impossible, to discover who were the buyers. The celebrated Brussels tapestries from designs by Raphael, for example, were priced, at the request of one of the Frenchmen, by one of the officials employed in the Vatican. The figure he named was 1,200 piastres. 'Bravo, my man,' the Frenchman replied and added fifty, which brought each piece out at 1,250, or £218 sterling.

When the 'consuls' heard of this deal—they had not been informed of the 'public auction'—they endeavoured to recover the tapestries. But the exchequer was so broke that the consul for Internal Affairs, a reputable archaeologist named Visconti, was unable to pay the price now asked. It was not until early in 1808 that the tapestries came to light again in the possession of a dealer of Leghorn, from whom the Pope himself bought them back, as we learn from the correspondence of Wilhelm von Humboldt with Caroline.

Besides the Vatican and Quirinal, the Pope's castles at Monte Cavallo, Terracina, and Castel Gandolfo were also gutted; so too were the palaces of his nephews and of several cardinals, and the possessions of all the noble families who had taken to flight. At first only English, Scottish and Irish churches and religious houses were abolished, but on May 11, 1798, the rest followed, and the property of all was swallowed up by 'the State'. The celebrated *Propaganda Fide*, the most important mission institute and language school in Europe, shared the same fate. Its presses and type, and even its teachers, students and printers, were all carried off to Paris. Duppa reports of the Villa Albani: 'Every statue, every bust, every column, every chimney-piece, every bit of marble of decorative value or practical use was torn from its place and either sent to Paris or taken there by the commissioners as presents for the members of the Directory.' The loot from this villa alone filled 290 cases.

Lastly, all the churches of Rome were stripped of their gold and silver. St Peter's alone produced 4,000 pounds of silver and seventy of gold. Whatever might have been overlooked on the first occasion in the way of lamps, reliquaries, cups and monstrances, was taken a few months later. Even the dead were not left in peace: the grave of Philippo Neri, the Roman saint, was opened, because he had been put in a silver coffin. According to the French themselves, the yield of the first plundering of precious metals and jewels came to thirty million francs. What was not kept back for themselves by the commissioners and officers was either sent to Paris or was minted in Rome. What was not suitable for either destination was stored in a disused monastery and, if no French dealer would offer, it finally found its way to the Roman ghetto.

Living artists too were held to ransom. Tribute was paid to them in public, whether they were of French, Italian, English, German or any other nationality, but their work was mulcted all the same, particularly if it had been commissioned by patrons belonging to enemy countries, and whether it had been paid for or not. This brought many of them to destitution, notwithstanding the fine professions made to them. Duppa relates the story of how the commissioner, Haller, paid a visit to a celebrated woman painter who was a friend of his, admired her work, enquired with the utmost politeness about the owners of the pictures he saw and took his leave 'with a shower of compliments'. He returned a week later and explained that to his keen regret it was his duty to confiscate all works of enemy ownership. He then recommended her to give him a present of £40 sterling if she wished to be spared similar annoyances in the future.

Other commissioners insisted on the sacrifice of works of art after having first extorted contributions and loans. Officers frequently took pictures from the houses where they were billeted, or demanded them as presents. The great palazzi suffered very severely in this way. 'For this reason,' Duppa reported, 'many princes parted with their most valuable things for quite small sums. Actually, it is owing to these circumstances that our own country (England) possesses the *Altieri* of Claude Lorrain, which was sold, while I was in Rome, to an Englishman for the trifling sum of £500 and sold again for £7,000 on its arrival in London.'

There is, of course, no excuse for the looting, extortions and thieving of all these officers and commissioners—the common soldiers were credited with greater honesty—but pay was bad and irregular. When the news came at the end of February 1798 that General Berthier was giving up the command of the army in Rome, the officers' pay was six months in arrears. What they now feared was that they might have even longer to wait, or to sacrifice that half-year's pay altogether. They did not actually mutiny, but they held a meeting in the Pantheon and drew up a statement for the General's benefit. In it they contrasted the gallantry, selfless devotion to duty and poverty of the majority of his troops with the looting and excesses of a small minority, and demanded the punishment of 'crimes which disgraced the name of France'. They further demanded their arrears of pay within twenty-four hours and 'the restoration of all property confiscated under various pretexts in the houses and churches of foreign neutral powers and that all buildings shall be restored to the state they were in before our troops marched in. Apart from our pay, we insist on the chastisement of the robberies committed by high-ranking monsters, corrupt and degenerate officials who wallow day and night in luxury and dissipation.' On the next day these same officers issued a proclamation to 'the people of Rome' in which they declared that it was not they but certain 'shameless wretches' who were guilty of all the extortion. 'Let each man come to the Pantheon and state what contributions and forced loans he has been the victim of and what property of his has been seized. We came to give you freedom, not to plunder you of all you possess.'

Since there was no further talk of these promises once the officers had had their pay, they may well have felt, once their own demands had been met, that there was no further reason to plead their cause.

As regards 'acquisitions' by the state, it is known that nineteen marble and two bronze statues from the Capitol arrived in Paris. The Vatican lost sixty-two antique sculptures, including the Apollo Belvedere and the Laocoön group. The Papal galleries and various churches had to surrender seventeen pictures to the Louvre. About 150 works of art from various places in the Papal states went the same way. In November 1799, Sir William Hamilton, British Minister at Naples, told Lord Elgin that the French had taken 'nearly all statues of any worth' and that 'most of the best pictures are in Paris too.' But three years later the historian and painter, Gottlieb Schick, wrote to the sculptor Dannecker: 'Rome has not lost much of value for the artist; the museums and galleries are still crowded with works of art of every sort, and it is hard to say whether animate or inanimate Nature is the lovelier.'

In Naples, the French troops plundered the museum on the Capo del Monte and sold the proceeds in Rome. Generals Ney and Championet appropriated some of the king's pictures. But many of the most valuable pieces had been removed to Sicily in good time, among them 'over a hundred packing-cases of the best things from Portici, a few marbles from the Museum, a large number of pictures and other things'. So later visitors, among them Wilhelm von Humboldt in 1807, found a large collection of the finest paintings as well as a good number of excellent and many less good statues, and a magnificent collection of vases.

Once they had been warned, many Italian owners of works of art naturally tried to save them from the French by removing them to some place of security, generally to the south or north-east. But if transport was lacking, or the roads were already unsafe, smaller objects, such as pictures, vases and small figures were concealed in some more or less safe hiding-place nearer at hand. Then, when the danger had passed, they were taken out and secretly sent abroad, where they often had to be disposed of at very low prices.

In this way six cases containing 174 pictures belonging to Cardinal Albani arrived in Vienna early in 1800. He himself had taken flight at the approach of the army of the Revolution and now offered his pictures to the Emperor, the director of whose gallery, Rosa, selected thirty-one works, which he valued at 2,000 ducats, certainly no great consolation to the Cardinal-connoisseur in the hour of his need. Later on Rosa acquired other paintings from this collection; the rest must have gone to private galleries. In this same year 141 pictures from Bologna were acquired by the Emperor, but they mostly remained in store; only one group in marble was thought worthy of exhibition.

But not all owners accompanied their possessions abroad or were in a position to obtain transport once they were there. They distributed them in their own country, or sold them because money was more easily concealed or more urgently needed.

The news quickly spread through Europe that conditions in Italy were favourable for picking up bargains, treasures which had lain hidden for centuries in private hands, almost forgotten, or at any rate unknown to the general public. Letters from travelling Englishmen, making the Grand Tour and taking advantage of the market, as well as the reports of dealers and agents, show that Italy was swarming with buyers of every description. Until the arrival of the French, Italian collectors and owners considered

12. A marble bust of Marcus Brutus in the Capitoline Museum, Rome.

11. A bronze bust of Junius Brutus in the Palazzo dei Conservatori, Rome.

13. The triumphal entry of the art treasures from Italy into Paris in 1796. From a contemporary engraving.

14. The French Commissioners listing the contents of the Academy at Parma, May 1796. From a drawing by Meynier at Versailles.

the sale of works of art abroad, to an Englishman or even a Russian, as a barbarity. But after 1796 this notion was quickly abandoned and did not return. The poverty of Italy was now apparent for the first time, although it had existed in fact for centuries. With the discovery of America and the ocean route to India and the Far East, Italy had lost its place as the centre of the world and had grown no richer under its petty princes and the representatives of foreign powers. The campaigns since 1796 and the following years of French rule inflicted such damage that the eagerness to sell works of art grew, and it mattered no longer who the buyer might be. The confiscation of the possessions of the churches in Northern Italy in 1805 and 1811 gave a further fillip to the market. Pictures were the principal items and many were bought for public galleries; the great majority by the authorities of France and the Kingdom of Italy. The English dealer, Solly, who later settled in Berlin, bought over 3,000 pictures in those years, mostly by Italian masters of the fifteenth century. Wicar, the commissioner and 'collector' already mentioned, made probably the largest haul of drawings at this time. His most formidable rival was the painter Antoine Fedi of Florence, who dispersed his collection in 1823–4 and sold a considerable part of it to Wicar. Wicar sold many of his drawings to the English painter, Lawrence, and left the rest, a collection of 1,436, all Italian with the exception of fifty, to Lille, where he was born.

German agents and collectors also bought many Italian works of art at this time. The dealer, I. B. Schiavonetti, who had settled in Berlin, announced in a Berlin journal of July 4, 1815: 'I have just received from Italy a consignment of old original paintings, among which are several by the most famous masters, Raphael, Albano, Domenichino, Parmigiano, Titian, and others.' The Roman dealer, Grossi, visited Leipzig Fair with a number of valuable pictures in 1811. Numerous German nobles are known to have bought many works during their Italian travels. The diplomatic service was naturally in a particularly favourable situation. Wilhelm von Humboldt and his wife bought reliefs and sarcophagi at auctions, and his predecessor in Rome, Uhden, paid court to his king's mistress by means of several consignments of pictures; the Bavarian minister, Haffelin, bought on behalf of the Crown Prince. This Bavarian prince was the richest and most zealous collector in Germany at that time—in 1813 he acquired the famous Barberini Faun—and employed a large number of artists as his agents. But he was far surpassed by some English collectors.

By degrees the Italian authorities came to the conclusion that the continual traffic in works of art was hardly distinguishable from the wholesale looting of the French. The Vatican tried to preserve what was still left in the Papal states, and already in 1802 had forbidden the export of old or of good modern paintings, but it was not until 1814 that the enforcement of the decree was possible.

4. *Central Europe*

The plunder of Italy both in quantity and quality gave the French their most important winnings; but they did not spare the rest of Europe. To realize the scope of their operations in this region, that is principally in Germany and Austria, one must bear in mind that since the sack of Prague in 1648 no plundering of art on a big scale had occurred there.

But since 1796 French armies repeatedly crossed the Rhine; accustomed to live on the land they took whatever pleased them or excited their animosity. Works of art of a secular character had the first effect and those of a religious character the second. The rich religious houses of south Germany suffered the most from the godless soldiers of the Revolution. Their records are full of complaints of the losses in money and church silver suffered at the hands of the common soldiers and the robbery or works of art by officers and commissioners. In 1800 General Joba had the whole gallery of the Prince-Bishop of Bamberg, with the exception of a few worthless pieces, packed up—and lost. This same 'friend of art' took part of the precious library and the painting from the high altar of the monastery of Augustinian Canons at Rebsdorf.

A wild 'flight of art' to the south and south-east was the immediate result, first to the provincial capitals, since it was thought that the castle of an electoral prince, a duke or king, would be a sufficient protection. Thus the various collections of the Wittelsbachs of Mannheim and Düsseldorf, treasures which had already been taken to Glücksburg on the approach of Bernadotte, had since 1805 joined those of the Castle of Karlsberg near Zweibrücken in Munich. These removals, when they were not carried out by the conquerors' orders, often took a long time; the Düsseldorf gallery, despatched to Munich in May 1805, did not arrive there, in twelve four-horse wagons, till 1806. Karlsberg Castle had an important gallery of pictures. The castle fell into the hands of the French in 1793, but Mannlich, the keeper of the gallery, had hidden the most valuable of its pictures, and as soon as it was freed by the Prussians and Hessians he had the whole collection packed up. 'Thirty men were kept at work night and day,' he writes in his memoirs. It was then removed to Mannheim by degrees as transport could be made available in the ravaged countryside; and there the pictures were unpacked and hung. The French eventually arrived there too, but the Palatinate Minister Salabert got General Pichegru to answer for the safety of the collection, and he kept his word.

Early in 1798 Duke Maximilian succeeded the Electoral Prince Charles Theodore on the throne of Bavaria. He wished the gallery at Mannheim to follow him to Munich, but the French re-occupied Mannheim by a surprise attack and found in the castle 200 cases containing the finest of the pictures awaiting removal, and the remainder still on the walls. They immediately sealed the door of the gallery and posted a sentry outside. But two of Mannlich's assistants succeeded, in the course of eleven nights, in abstracting all the pictures from the walls and hiding them; when the General commanding the French army came to inspect his booty he found the walls bare and the cabinet of engravings empty. He tried to console himself with the library. Soon afterwards the French re-opened the

Mannheim theatre and gave the scene-painter, Quaglio, permission to procure the necessary properties from the castle. This was the opportunity for removing the cases of pictures too, under the very eyes of the sentry; they were taken to the theatre and hidden there. Next, the Court Chamberlain, von Gohr, disposed of 'about twenty cases' of the pictures in his baggage, for which the French ambassador, a distant relation of his, gave him a pass. Thus some of them finally arrived unmolested in Munich.

Nevertheless, in 1800 a part of the Bavarian collection was once more on the move. Mannlich, meanwhile promoted to director of the Electoral Prince's galleries, put a painter named von Dillis in charge of the removal to neutral Ansbach. Early in 1801 General Moreau occupied Munich, and on the very first day his junior, General Lecourbe, had the state rooms of the castle opened and took possession of some of the pictures, the value of which he promised to deduct from the forced levy, as in fact he did.

Soon afterwards a professor of drawing from the Ecole Polytechnique, named François-Marie Neveu, called on Mannlich and informed him that he was 'Commissioner for the arts and sciences in Germany' and was empowered to confiscate the most valuable pictures in Munich for the French Republic. Mannlich's account goes on: 'He showed me his authority at the same time, and his orders to perpetuate the memory of the victories of the *Grande Armée* by the acquisition of works of lasting value, as had been done in the case of the masterpieces of Italy, thanks to the victories of the army there.' He at once with his own hand chalked '*Republique Française*' on the back of three pictures. On their way through the castle garden to the gallery, the two men were joined by several generals and their wives, who wished 'to be of assistance' to Neveu in his selection. 'They fell like harpies,' Mannlich wrote later, 'on the portfolios of engravings, which had been taken from me along with our pictures.' On the next day Mannlich had to accompany Neveu and his friends to Schleissheim. There he had to look on while 'the generals and their ladies insisted on the Commissioner taking more and more,' and it was clear, he added, that 'this was not the first time he had yielded to their pressure.'

As the requisitioned works were left for several months in Munich, Mannlich had the opportunity of coming to terms with Neveu, who consented to the restitution of several valuable Wittelsbach portraits, which were not of particular interest to the Louvre. Finally, seventy-two pictures were despatched, at the expense of Bavaria for the packing and for transport as far as Mainz. In return Neveu promised that the Munich Gallery should be indemnified by works of equal value from the Louvre. For the next seven years Mannlich kept on requesting works by masters of the French school. 'The director of the French Gallery, however, never gave a sign of life, let alone sending us the promised equivalent.'

When war broke out again in 1809 and Munich was occupied in October by Napoleon, the 'famous Denon', as Mannlich writes, was in his train.

This is our introduction to one who was perhaps the most expert and certainly the most artistic, industrious and genteel personality in the whole history of art plunder—Dominique Vivant Denon, born in 1747 at Chalons-sur-Saone. Thanks to his excellent education and his good connections, he made an early appearance at the court of Louis XV. He was put in charge of the King's cameos and was Madame de Pompadour's 'professor'. Later he was in diplomatic employment in St Petersburg and Naples. He drew and etched after the old masters for seven years in Italy before his return to France in 1788. The painter David rescued him from the guillotine a year later and soon afterwards he was commissioned to design uniforms for the Republican army. In 1798 Denon was one of the official artists who accompanied Napoleon to Egypt, for the purpose of examining its antiquities—but not, it may be added, with the purpose of 'saving them from destruction'. After this he accompanied him, as general and emperor, on nearly all his campaigns to select works for the Louvre in all the conquered, annexed and occupied countries. From 1804, when Napoleon became Emperor, Denon was Inspector General of French Museums. It will never be known who first nicknamed him *l'emballeur* (the packer), but he certainly gave apt expression to the mixture of ridicule, distaste, resentment, apprehension and hate which Denon aroused. He was the man who packed up all the art of Europe for despatch to Paris, the political, military and artistic hub of the continent. He was a fanatical upholder of the idea of French supremacy, a born official, a man of personal ambition, determined to concentrate the art of Europe in the hands of one man; a crude instrument, but one that was perfectly adapted to carry out the policy of the Emperor. Napoleon, not alone among the generals who have made history, judged pictures and sculptures by their size and the exactness with which they reproduced the object they represented and he found Denon's comprehensive knowledge, organizing ability, industry and resourcefulness exactly what was needed for the creation of a French empire of the Fine Arts within the military empire he had created for himself.

Continual invasions, forced levies, plundering and spoliation also led many in Germany to think of selling to foreigners, principally rich Englishmen. The Elector of Bavaria, Charles Theodore, had never trusted Napoleon since 1795, when peace was concluded at Basel; he offered his Düsseldorf collection, removed for safety to Glücksburg, to an English Duke, but the deal fell through. When Duke Maximilian of Pfalz-Zweibrücken lost all his land and was in need of money he sold his collection of engravings for a song to an art dealer of Mannheim, his coins for the worth of the metal, his jewels for even less—but his collection of sticks and pipes, at very high prices, to the officers of the Austrian army. Mannlich, the gallery director already mentioned, prevented the dispersal of valuable works of art by continually postponing the preparation of a catalogue designed for English buyers.

The Hapsburg treasures in Vienna were saved for a long time by the comparative remoteness of Austria. But in November 1805, when a French army was approaching, the most valuable of the pictures were packed in forty-eight cases and sent down the

Danube to Pressburg. When the French occupied Vienna they left the gallery of the Belvedere intact. As soon as they had withdrawn, the pictures were brought back from Pressburg. Füger, the director of the Emperor's collections, had just announced their return on July 17, 1806, and started on the preparation of a catalogue, when the French appeared once more; this time fifty-four cases of pictures left for Hungary. On May 11, 1809, French troops were in the suburbs of Vienna and at one o'clock the same day an officer and twenty-one men were at the gate of the Upper Belvedere with orders to occupy the castle. Füger, on June 6, had to account for the missing pictures to the Governor-General, Andreossi. On being told where they were, he replied: 'You did your duty. But they can't all have gone.' In the evening of the next day the Chief Commissioner, Daru, presented himself at the Belvedere, accompanied by Denon. They went through every room until far into the night, and prompted by previous experiences Denon did not leave the Austrians a moment for rescue-work; at dawn he was back again to make a complete list of the pictures, backed up by an order of Napoleon, which Andreossi had drafted in the following words: 'His Majesty the Emperor and King has instructed M. Denon, the Director-in-chief of the Museums of France, to make him a list of the objects in the Belvedere worthy of selection and sequestration. Herr Füger, Director of the Academy of the Belvedere, will therefore give M. Denon all necessary information without reserve and put all the objects selected by him at his disposal. This is His Majesty's express command. Vienna, June 9, 1809. Andreossi, Governor-General.'

Twenty years had passed since the outbreak of the French Revolution and the confiscation of the treasures of Louis XVI, of the nobility and of the Church, thirteen since Napoleon's first sweep of Italy; instead of the revolutionary justification for the looting of Rome and Naples, plunder was now by 'the express command of His Majesty'—but nothing had altered: whatever was worthy of selection was still sent off to Paris, the great repository of European art.

And Denon, who had to travel all over Europe gathering in the harvest, could no more spare the time for taking the wishes and feelings of his victims into consideration than could the victorious generals. There was no trace of that accommodating spirit we noted at Munich. Next day, June 10, the delivery of what was left in the Belvedere was exacted without prevarication or apology as the commercial consequence of military victory. Füger pleaded in vain as art lover and champion of the traditions of European civilization; Denon did not listen. Rubens's large *Assumption of the Virgin* was taken down, sawn into three pieces and packed up with the rest, forty in all according to his list. (He 'forgot' to enter the Turkish tents and some other items which he took all the same.)

The castle was soon emptied. When later the French departed, the pictures which had been taken to safety were brought back; but the building had suffered so severely from military occupation that the cases were not opened nor the pictures hung until 1811.

Now that it was possible to take a survey of what had been saved and what had been lost, it was seen that the losses were fewer than had been feared. The large number of pictures carried off had, as Füger wrote in 1816, given rise 'to the widespread impression' that many of the Belvedere's most important treasures had been removed to Paris. The belief in this 'wholesale loss' had aggravated the resentment felt in Austria against Paris and, for political reasons, the misapprehension was never corrected, although this might long since have been done. Denon, in fact, had arrived too late; a large part of his booty never got beyond the depots, and the cream of the collection had been removed to safety at Pressburg, including all the works of Salvator Rosa, Guido Reni and Caracci. The reason why only fifteen of the thirty-six Titians fell into Denon's hands was not due to negligence, but to the low esteem in which his paintings and those of other Renaissance masters were held at that time.

Of all German and Austrian galleries, the luckiest was that of Dresden. Saxony was saved from the revolutionary armies by its remoteness, and from Denon by the treaty between the Elector and King, Frederick Augustus, and Napoleon. Denon would have been ready enough to plunder Saxony as a member of the Rhineland Confederacy, since he quite logically made no distinction between voluntary and involuntary satellites. He therefore hurried to Dresden, drew up a list of its most valuable items and placed it before the Emperor. But when the Emperor showed it to Talleyrand, that sagacious statesman, who understood the importance of imponderables and the value of art as propaganda, was strongly opposed to the removal of a single work from Dresden—and Denon had to submit.

In the summer of 1803 the Hanoverian government took the precaution of sending its state treasure, its most important state documents and sixty-nine cases of 'silverware, some linen and pictures' to St Petersburg. When the French arrived, their first haul was part of the valuable stud and, next, fourteen bronze busts from the park of the castle of Herrenhausen, representing Roman generals and emperors; these naturally delighted the victorious generals of France, but were of little artistic worth. They were set up in the imperial castle of Laeken in Belgium.

When the French occupied Cassel in 1806, Prince William I of Hesse-Cassel had his forty-eight most valuable pictures packed up for despatch to a place of safety. But a dispute over the cost of carriage caused such delay that the pictures finally fell into the hands of the French, and General Lagrange, who had been appointed Governor of Hesse, appropriated them. Later they came into the possession of the Empress Josephine, whose heirs sold them to the Czar. Robbed, sold, bequeathed, sold, lost—such was the fate of this first and most valuable batch of pictures from Cassel.

Then, in January 1807, Denon came on the scene. True, he could make little use of the catalogue he found, as he did not know German. But that did not prevent his making a selection to the number of 299 pictures for the Musée Napoléon which 'did honour to his artistic judgment', according to the 1913 catalogue of the Royal Gallery of Cassel.

Cassel was plundered for a third time after its inclusion in the kingdom of Westphalia, created for Napoleon's brother Jerome.

A letter from one of the maids of honour at the court of King Jerome, or King *Lustig*, as he was called, contains an allusion to the royal collections and to the mother of Napoleon and Jerome, a lady whose thoughts were generally occupied with the increase of her fortune. 'When Madame Mère came into the room where the jewellery and precious stones were kept, the Keeper of the Gallery who was standing near her heard her say to herself, *"Ici il faut voler"*. The King went up to the Keeper and congratulated him on the excellent arrangement of the museum, and Madame Mère then took some of the pieces out of the cases and examined them. When the royal party had gone and the Keeper checked the exhibits, he found that a valuable diamond ring was missing. He at once and very courageously made investigations, but they were cut short by the son of the too appreciative lady.' Of all German territories Brunswick suffered most at the hands of the French plunderers, since the Duke had made himself hated as early as 1792 by his famous manifesto. The days of the Revolution were certainly long past but, as commander-in-chief at Jena, he had been the opponent of Napoleon as well—and that more than doubled his offence. Brunswick was rich in art treasures; according to a catalogue of 1776 the castle of Salzdahlum contained 1,129 pictures. In Brunswick itself the Duke had 18,000 antique coins, 1,500 cut gems, a very valuable collection of Limoges work of the sixteenth century, bronzes, majolica, etc. On the approach of the French, Professor Emperius, whose account of these events is of great interest, had a celebrated onyx dish, some other precious things, 'valuable minerals' and the collection of coins packed up and sent away. After an adventurous journey across the Danish border, the boxes and cases reached England. But 'objects of greater bulk and weight could not, owing to lack of time and transport, be got away, and soon afterwards the roads were considered too unsafe.' Ninety pictures were removed from Salzdahlum to Brunswick, but there was no means of sending them on from there, and so they also fell into the hands of the French.

Denon of course was on the spot on this occasion too. In

September 1806, he commandeered 278 pictures and many other works of art besides. The taste he showed in his selection is a matter for astonishment. Emperius writes that he wanted to be shown everything; 'however, he was often persuaded by the representations made to him to leave us this or that.' It served Emperius well that he had, like many other Germans, visited the collections in Paris, and so could point out that they already had far finer specimens of one sort or another to show. Denon was accompanied during his inspection by representatives of the commander-in-chief, who persuaded him to take various showy items of little value—obviously not for the benefit of the public collections in Paris. On one occasion, Denon, according to Emperius, described four antique marble busts as modern copies in order to save them for Brunswick. He even went so far as to advise Emperius to hide some pieces of value to avoid trouble in the future. We have to take the word of Professor Emperius for such astonishing statements; and he had made friends with Denon.

In any case he was filled with admiration for the skill and adroitness Denon showed in ransacking every cupboard. He took six busts and sixty small figures from the collection of antiques; and from the collection of majolica he chose over 900 pieces. 'He maintained,' Emperius wrote ten years later, 'that they incorporated a great number of ideas and drawings of Raphael and the Roman School, of which there was no other surviving record.' Emperius could not convince him of the untenability of this assumption. He also confiscated a great number of works in enamel; he admired their wealth of motifs, all the more because, in his opinion, they would give so many ideas for engravings. 'He thought that the use these works of art would be put to in Paris would console us for losing them.' As a great connoisseur of drawings, he did not overlook the opportunity of taking 250 examples, but left the engravings and the collection of natural history intact.

This rich booty was received in Paris in March 1807, together with a hand-written catalogue of the Wolfenbüttel Library, from which the Bibliothèque Nationale might take its pick at leisure—as indeed it did. Jerome had the castle of Salzdahlum gutted and then pulled down. Two hundred and fifty-two of the pictures were sent to Cassel and over 400 were sold by auction in the town of Brunswick in 1810. Jerome had promised the town 200 of the best of them, but instead it received 200 of poor quality. However, they did at least remain in the town, and were used in furnishing a residence for the King.

Meanwhile Denon, *l'emballeur*, continued his tours of Germany, inspecting, listing, packing and despatching whatever he thought suitable; from Schwerin, for example, out of a total of 695 works of art, he took no fewer than 209. Naturally he did not overlook Berlin. Unfortunately, the keeper of the collection of antiquities, the Protestant Minister, Henry, had sent the most interesting of the gems and ancient coins to Memel. The King's silver, various pictures and a case containing objects from the treasure cabinet followed by sea to Kustrin on October 16, 1806, and from there to Memel. Four cases containing seventy pictures, mostly from Sans Souci, took the same course on October 23, as far as Kustrin, where, however, they fell into the hands of the French when that fortress surrendered. But most of Berlin's art treasures remained. Denon selected 116 pictures, 204 statues, busts and reliefs, over 500 gems and cameos, over 7,000 Roman bronze coins, 5,000 ancient and medieval silver coins as well as terracottas, inscriptions and small bronze figures. From the treasure cabinet he took twenty-five carved ivories, twenty-three pieces of worked amber, twenty-two West Indian curios (originating perhaps from Maurice of Nassau), statues and busts of Frederick the Great, numerous engravings and maps, wood carvings, and finally modern works of art and copies of the antique. He had inset cameos and precious stones torn from cabinets which did not attract him in themselves. But he never neglected to give a formal receipt for each object 'removed'. Two convoys took the booty to Paris.

Denon confiscated officially for the state; the French officers robbed on their own account. 'Wherever they were billeted, either singly or as part of the Emperor's immediate entourage, objects of value were later found to be missing.' The behaviour of General Vandamme at Potsdam and Sans Souci was the worst, but an unruffled Prussian official with the help of the French Commander-in-chief succeeded in retrieving most of the loot from his billet. It was not so easy in the case of the connoisseurs who accompanied Denon on his tours of inspection and slipped into their pockets coins and trifles which he had noted as interesting but not suited to his own requirements. Among them was a certain Prince Isenburg-Birstein, who was recruiting soldiers for Napoleon in Berlin at that time. He repeatedly filled his pockets under Denon's eyes, but when the Keeper, Henry, protested and pointed out that this thief had not even the right of a conqueror, Denon would not support him.

Nothing was passed over that was worth mounting, hanging, or exhibiting, or even keeping in store for distribution among provincial museums. Each sacrifice had to be looked upon as final since no one imagined that within a few years Napoleon would be overthrown and imprisoned, that Denon would be stripped of his powers, and that commissioners would be appointed in Paris for the contrary task of tracking down and restoring the treasures he and his like had stolen.

5. *Spain*

Ten years after the Napoleonic era, the British art dealer, W. Buchanan, observed in his *Memoirs of Painting*: 'French generals had little scruple in picking out many of the best works from the (Spanish) monasteries.' He describes how General Belliard in 1809 carried off copies of the Ghent altar by Michael Coxie, which were at that time very highly valued, and—very wisely—sold them one by one in Brussels. Marshal Soult 'acquired' Murillos from the city of Seville while he was governor of Andalusia.

There can be no doubt that Spanish works of art were in much greater danger from the year-long vicissitudes of war than were those of Italy, and consequently their owners were even more inclined to dispose of them at low prices. The supply, therefore, was inordinately large. It was added to by the booty which soldiers put straight on the market.

Buchanan himself was in an unfortunate situation, as several Madrid banks had failed; they were unable to cash their British client's cheques and he found himself without hard currency just at the moment he might have invested it to the greatest advantage. This meant that his French rivals had the field almost to themselves. The Parisian dealer, Le Brun, toured the whole of Spain in 1807 and 1808 and bought up all he could find, either personally or through his agents. By 1810 he had collected no fewer than 160 pictures, among them some which had been brought from Northern Italy for safety from the French.

And lastly there was of course the usual plundering by the French authorities. The castles and religious foundations round Madrid alone sacrificed fifty pictures. Other parts of Spain are known to have had similar losses, although it was not possible to give the exact figures. A remarkable windfall fell to the lot of the English army in Spain. King Joseph Bonaparte when he fled the country took a number of pictures from the Escorial with him. His carriage was captured at the battle of Vittoria in 1813, with a large quantity of gold vessels and a torn book of drawings by old masters which had been used to protect the paintings underneath. The canvases had been cut from the frames and laid one on another. The Duke of Wellington gave orders that the coach and all it contained should be sent to the Duchess in London. When it arrived and was inspected by experts summoned for the purpose, the surprising discovery was made that the paintings were selected and in some cases world-renowned pictures from the royal palace in Madrid, a discovery which had eluded Wellington on the battle-field. In the following year, 1814, using the British Minister in Madrid as an intermediary, the Duke informed the restored King of Spain, Ferdinand, of his intention to return the paintings; but the King replied that he wished the Duke to keep them. 'His Majesty,' wrote Count Fernan Nuñez, 'touched by your delicacy, does not wish to deprive you of that which has come into your possession by means as just as they are honourable.'

The looting and capture of works of art in Spain and the appearance of them on the market had at least one good result: the Spanish masters became known to the rest of Europe for the first time. Before this they had scarcely crossed the frontier and few connoisseurs had visited Spain. The astonishment and admiration were all the greater. An English art dealer went so far as to say that the works of Murillo acquired by Marshal Soult would revolutionize painting in England.

6. *French 'Confiscations' seen through contemporary eyes*

> What the art of Greece created,
> Let the Frank by dint of battle
> Carry to his vaunted Seine.
> Let him in superb museums
> Show the trophies of his valour
> To the marvelling citizen.
> Never will they break their silence,
> Nor, their pedestals forsaking,
> Mingle with life's throng.
> He alone enjoys the Muses
> Who has ardour in his bosom,
> To the barbarian they are stone.

These lines were written by Schiller and first published in 1803 with the title, *Antiques to Paris*. The following come from Schlegel's Elegy addressed to Goethe:

> Warring the world reels on, and now fresh perils beset you,
>> Art-cherishing land, most favoured descendant of Hellas;
> Once more the Proconsul heaps his plunder in ships,
>> Proudly exacting tribute.
> Barbaric pomp leads genius weeping and chained
>> Once more in triumphal array.

But such severe comments were by no means the rule in

Germany at that time. In general it was enough to describe the plunder of art as 'uncommon and even unexampled' and wrong. Naturally the losses suffered by one's own country were felt most keenly and the stripping of its museums particularly resented, but the spoliation of Italy aroused the greatest indignation among lovers of art throughout the world. While the French were in occupation, journals and periodicals were of course silent or at least restrained; it was only later that accounts could be published of all that had been stolen, carried off, extorted, or destroyed, and indignation freely expressed. On the other hand lovers of art, connoisseurs and artists could now recognize the worth of the art collections of Paris and had to admit Denon's great achievements. The concentration of works of art in one place enabled the student of art to appreciate and compare pictures and sculptures, many of which had hitherto been in private collections and inaccessible to the ordinary traveller. The much-travelled doctor of medicine, Edouard Meissner, observes in his *Notes from a doctor's diary* of 1819:

'Anyone who lived in the metropolis of the world of that time had the exhilarating feeling of living in the midst of the art of all ages and of collections embracing every branch of art; he could find some excuse for the systematic looting by the French, just as an artist in London might overlook Lord Elgin's high-handedness more easily than could the privileged few who were able to visit Athens. The French seem to have robbed not so much for themselves as for the convenience of the world at large. Collections which were open to Parisians on certain days were open to foreigners every day. Precious possessions such as gems and manuscripts, which in Italy had been guarded as jealously as the Golden Fleece, were more accessible to those who wished to inspect them than engravings were in many public libraries.'

This opinion is borne out by the testimony of many other contemporary visitors to Paris. In 1814, the Louvre was visited

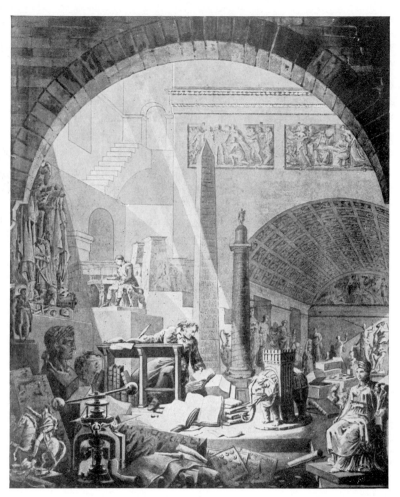

15. Denon in his studio, by Zix.

16. A French déjeuner set (*c.* 1810), formerly belonging to Joseph Bonaparte and captured at the Battle of Vittoria (1813), in the Wellington Museum.

by the monarchs of the victorious nations, who congratulated Denon on the way the works were shown. It is remarkable that at the very moment when the restoration of the plunder was being discussed, Denon could still pride himself on his personal integrity and on international approval of his misdeeds.

The French, at the time and ever since, have vigorously defended their behaviour. Even in 1926, in the second volume of the catalogue of the paintings in the Musée du Louvre, it is emphasized that the charge of depredations or robberies made by foreigners must be contradicted. The soldiers had the right to seek some compensation for their sacrifices in blood and toil, and if they carried off pictures, one could only say: '*Leur avidité était singulièrement idéaliste.*'

This point of view, held in perfect good faith, need not be taken as the retrospective condonation of past misdeeds; it is rather the logical consequence of national pride and the conviction that the French nation was called upon to preside over the civilized world. Barbier, a lieutenant in the Hussars, who was in command of the first convoy of works of art from Holland to Paris, and assuredly no profound and original political philosopher, addressed the National Convention in September 1794, as follows:

'Too long have these masterpieces been sullied by the gaze of serfs . . . these immortal works are no longer in a foreign land . . . they rest today in the home of the arts and of genius, in the motherland of liberty and sacred equality, in the French Republic.'

An order of the political commissioner, dated Brussels, July 18, 1784, made it known that the true home of works of art must, for the honour and advancement of art, be in the home of free men. Naturally it made no difference that the Netherlands, having just been liberated, was now a participator in the blessings of the Revolution and might just as well have been allowed to keep its works of art. Nevertheless, it would be a mistake to think that in the early days of the Revolution it was simply and generally a matter of sheer robbery. Covetousness, revenge and megalomania played their part, but the men who gave orders for the removal of works of art to Paris should not be identified with those who took the chance to secrete a miniature or slip a diamond ring in their pocket.

The conquest and occupation of Italy, and above all of Rome, gave an excellent opportunity of airing the merits of transporting works of art to Paris. Antoine Chrysostome Quatremère de Quincy, student of art and member of the Academy, published a pamphlet of seventy-four pages in which he opposed the removal of works of art from Rome; he said that they could only be properly appreciated in their own surroundings, that they made their effect as a whole and should not be split up and separated, since the meaning of Rome lay in its being a storehouse of art. To understand her statues properly, there was need of the Pantheon, of the Colosseum, of Trajan's column, of the frescos of the Sistine Chapel and of the galleries of the Vatican. This same courageous scholar wrote, in a petition addressed to the Directory, that the arts and sciences of Europe formed a republic whose servants all had the same aim—the advancement of learning and of civilization. All means thereto were the common possession of the nations, none of which had the right to make a prescriptive claim on the common heritage of art or to divide it up arbitrarily. But if one country made this exclusive claim, then it must bear the reproach 'of barbarity and ignorance for thus damaging the common property'. Eight members of the Academy and forty-three artists signed this petition. On October 3, 1796, a counter-petition appeared in the *Moniteur*, the official organ of the government: 'If we demand the assembly of masterpieces in Paris, it is for the honour and glory of France and for the love we feel for those very works themselves.' Such arguments might be dismissed as altogether too ingenuous, but in practice they made it impossible to say a word against the looting of art without being guilty of treason to France and of discrediting the Revolution, especially when other perfectly logical considerations were added.

178

'We form our taste precisely by long acquaintance with the true and the beautiful. The Romans, once uneducated, began to educate themselves by transplanting the works of conquered Greece to their own country. We follow their example when we exploit our conquests and carry off from Italy whatever serves to stimulate our imagination.'

In six years, according to the opinion of a Frenchman in 1806, French painters would surpass the masters of the Italian Renaissance.

It was pointed out too that Italian works of art might otherwise be sold elsewhere, to English connoisseurs for example. The King of Naples had taken the treasures of the Farnese Palace to Sicily, the Emperor had robbed Lombardy of its masterpieces and an Englishman had already acquired the Negroni collection. 'We must therefore hasten to bring all we can to Paris: in six months time there may be nothing left in Rome.' The war, and particularly the war with England, were arguments which could not be altogether denied. And finally they went so far as to contrast the effeteness of Rome with Parisian competence; Rome was a 'lazy and superstitious city' under a 'wretched and corrupt government' . . . 'The French Republic, because of its power, the superiority of its men of learning and artists, is the only country on earth which can offer these works of art an unassailable refuge.' It was the hub of the world, and if works of art were assembled there 'all nations will come to us to be instructed in the fine arts, and with the same eagerness as they came before to imitate our frivolity. And as soon as we have conferred on them the blessing of peace, they will hasten here to benefit by the wisdom and good taste which these masterpieces diffuse.'

As governments changed, further considerations came to the fore. 'Citizens of all classes observe that the government desires that everyone shall have his share in so rich a booty . . .' Instead of the princely gallery, there was to be the democratic museum open to all. The recently conquered 'provincial' cities too, such

179

as Brussels, Cologne, Mainz and Geneva, were allotted their
share for public exhibition, and so would learn to value their
dependence on France. 'Now that they are subjects of France,
they must share in the prosperity of the Empire,' wrote the
politician, Armand Gaston Camus, after a journey through the
new departments in 1802. And finally the sight of all these riches
assembled in museums was designed to impress on the public
that, whether as soldiers or workers, whether in peace or war,
their hardships and privations had not been in vain. The treasures
brought from Rome were like a decoration which Napoleon had
pinned to the breast of the whole nation. His personal attitude to
art might be elementary, but he was well aware of its power over
the minds of his contemporaries, and, supported by Denon, he
made magnificent use of his plunder.

The sufferers and even the neutrals were naturally less
enthusiastic. The Englishman, Henry Milton, went to Paris
immediately after the fall of Napoleon to see all that he and the
Revolution had gathered in, before much of it was returned to its
original owners. In his *Letters on the Fine Arts* he wrote with
admiration and enthusiasm of all he had seen in the Musée
Napoléon, but added:

> 'Bands of practised robbers who could not find an outlet for
> their talents in their own country were sent abroad to commit
> their crimes under another, less discreditable name. . . .
> Hordes of thieves in the form of experts and connoisseurs
> accompanied their armies to take possession, either by dicta-
> tion or naked force, of all that seemed to them worth taking.
> Their adroitness was as remarkable as it was merciless.'

7. *English profit from French plunder*

Was Henry Milton's indignation completely justified? Quite
apart from all those cases of marbles which were being despatched at this very time by Lord Elgin's orders from Athens
to London, and whether it was a question of robbery or rescue,

there were alert and knowledgeable British dealers and agents in Italy and all over the continent, ready to fall on the harvest of fine works of art put at their disposal by the revolutionary armies. It did not occur to them to offer these pictures and sculptures, which they had as a rule picked up for next to nothing, to their former owners; on the contrary, they were delighted with their windfalls and added them with joy to the art treasure of their country. They were not art robbers in the literal sense, but they took what they were offered.

Let us consider first the works of art acquired from emigrés; it was not for them to recognize the principles of the Revolution; they emigrated precisely because they refused to submit to it, and, if they could, took their possessions with them.

The English had not been very fortunate in their acquisitions of works of art up to 1789. They had themselves dispersed the collection of Charles I, and that of the Earl of Arundel had been sacrificed to religious conflicts, or else to its owner's lack of principle. And when, in the eighteenth century, the nobility and gentry set about procuring paintings on the continent, they were often planted with copies, for which, in their inexperience, they paid high prices. Even Hamilton, as Buchanan points out, although far above the average as a connoisseur, could only acquire very few important pictures, because before 1789 'only copies or works of secondary importance were procurable' in Italy. It need not surprise us that the correspondent of the Meusel 'Museum' found nine Raphaels for sale in London in 1789. Contemporary taste did not favour Raphael and in any case the authenticity of each of these works was disputed. Buchanan wrote in 1824 that, before the French Revolution, England possessed 'only a few genuine paintings of the Italian school', whereas after 1824, according to him, there were as many in England as in Rome. In 1831 the German art critic, Passavant, even came to England to study Raphael, and in 1843 the painter and connoisseur, Wilhelm Füssli, declared that the 'love of art among the great' was 'a national characteristic' in England.

What a change within thirty years! One, too, which only a

fortunate conjunction of circumstances could have brought about. Just at the moment when English trade and colonial expansion had reached record heights, when its agriculture led the world and enriched the landowners, and the industrial revolution was promising even greater prosperity in the future, the French Revolution stirred up the ancient accumulations of art all over Europe and set them moving in the same direction as was taken by emigrants, refugees and capitalists who sought safety in England, where even the most violent commotions were unlikely to endanger them.

The British people were also better prepared to appreciate these works of art than ever before. The first volume of Gibbon's *Decline and Fall of the Roman Empire* had appeared in 1776 and had had an enthusiastic reception. The traditional continental tour of the young Englishman was given a new and powerful stimulant. Museums had sprung up in the 'sixties and 'seventies, and an interest in the antique, in the Renaissance and in contemporary art was spreading.

And then came the French Revolution. Philip, Duke of Orleans, who had joined the leading revolutionaries, hoped in 1790 to secure the throne, and needed a great deal of money for the prosecution of this aim. He therefore set about selling his important gallery of pictures. The Prince of Wales and some of his friends quickly showed that they were interested and a price of £100,000 was agreed to; but the deal was suddenly broken off because the partners of the prince and of two dukes were afraid that the splitting up of the gallery necessitated by the purchase would be prejudicial to their interests. Two years later, when the political situation in France had entirely altered, the Duke of Orleans came to his final decision to sell. The revolutionary government could only regard this as a misappropriation of French national property, whatever doubts might have been possible in 1790. A Belgian banker offered 750,000 livres for the Italian and French pictures, and an Englishman, Thomas Moore Slade, 350,000 for the Flemish, Dutch and German; but the Duke's many creditors, backed up by the artists and art lovers

182

of France, refused to allow them to leave the country. Slade as well as the Duke was therefore left in no doubt of the unlawfulness of their proceedings from the revolutionary point of view when Slade openly declared his intention of shipping the pictures to England from Calais. This, however, was a ruse, and in fact they were sent down the Seine to Le Havre, and thence to Chatham. Early in 1793 they were offered for sale in London and excited great interest, not least because of their adventurous journey.

The pictures bought by the Belgian banker finally reached London too. They were first bought by a Frenchman, Laborde de Mereville, who intended to restore them to France. But soon he himself was in flight from the guillotine. He was able to take the pictures with him and later sold them to three English noblemen. Thus the whole of the Duke of Orleans' gallery ended up in England. 'The interest aroused by this famous collection exceeded anything of the kind ever known in the country before.'

But this was not all. In 1787 the French minister, Calonne, went into retirement. When in 1795 he saw the storm approaching, he emigrated to England and from there gave such generous support to the French émigrés in Germany that he had to sell his collection of 350 pictures to satisfy his creditors. So these pictures too found English owners. Two years later, in February 1797, Christie's sold the pictures belonging to the American, John Trumbull, an attaché at the American Embassy in Paris, and also Madame du Barry's jewels.

And by this time a new current had set in, carrying pictures and other works of art directly from the continent to England. Numbers of Englishmen are known to have exploited the robberies of the French and to have been accused by the French themselves of marauding the art of Europe. A painter named Day got a choice collection together in a few weeks from the galleries of the celebrated Roman families of Colonna, Aldobrandini and Borghese, pictures which till then had been thought 'utterly unobtainable'. In 1800 Buchanan was equally successful in acquiring a hundred first-rate paintings. The most important of all the buyers in Rome mentioned in the memoirs of this exceptionally able man was a painter named James Irvine. In 1800 he brought the masterpieces he had collected in Rome during 1798–99 to London and caused a sensation; he returned immediately and made further purchases on his own account and also as agent for other people in England.

Sometimes Irvine worked with the English Consul-General for Sicily and the Ionian Islands, Fagan, a painter who studied the Italian masters for many years and made drawings and copies from them. In 1795 he moved to Rome and bought there a number of valuable pictures, two of Claude Lorrain's famous landscapes from the Altieri palace among them. This was before the French marched in; and when they came he walled his paintings up. He was obviously a cool-headed man, because he kept the hiding-place secret when he was thrown into prison, and as soon as he was released he and a friend of his took them along roads crowded with refugees to Naples, and finally by ship to Palermo in a cabin which he and his pictures shared with forty other persons. Nelson was there at the time with part of the Mediterranean fleet. Fagan's friend, Grignion, got an introduction to Nelson, whom he painted. Once when he was dining with him and Hamilton, he mentioned his anxiety for the fate of the Claudes, pointing out that they were as valuable financially as artistically. His account of the matter must have impressed Nelson, who cried out, 'This concerns the nation,' and wrote at once to the Governor of Gibraltar and arranged naval escort for the pictures.

If the French found the transport of their Italian booty to Paris difficult, the English dealers had risks to run as well in sending theirs through the Mediterranean to their home ports. Pirates and privateers from Algiers, Spain and France captured many valuable art treasures. A Titian reached Algiers and the offer of a large ransom was refused. Prizes of the kind taken by French warships were auctioned in Paris. The risks of transport by sea raised insurance rates to 30 per cent of the value, and even higher.

Companies were formed for the purchase of Italian works of art. From 1802 to 1806 inclusive they bought many first-rate paintings of the sixteenth and seventeenth centuries in conformity with British taste of the day; there are six instances, at least, to show that works by Raphael were not favoured.

After 1806, however, it was not easy to get works of art out of Italy, and it was regarded as a stroke of good luck when the French invaded Spain and opened up one more country to English dealers. As far as can be ascertained, it was in October 1807 that Buchanan despatched the first experienced and competent agent to the Iberian peninsula, provided with cheques on banks in Lisbon and Madrid. This was the painter, Wallis. Finding Portugal in a state of confusion, in dread of the arrival of French troops and war-ships, and with its currency in collapse, he went on to Spain. The purchases he was able to make there led him to say later that the proverb about fishing in troubled waters had a lot of truth in it, but that the fishing might be dangerous. He was once taken for a Frenchman and thrown into prison after being rescued from the fury of the mob. French officers, on the other hand, once they knew that he was a painter, came forward with offers at moderate prices, as they might not have done had they known he was also the agent of a dealer. His chief difficulty was not in finding good pictures, but in paying for them in good money when many banks were closing their doors.

His Murillos and Velasquez's, Rubenses and Salvator Rosas frequently arrived in England via Holland. The expense was far higher than in the case of Italian purchases, partly because of the long transport over land and partly because of the bribes and insurances, the value of which was in any case doubtful. One consignment of works bought in September 1808 only reached London in November 1809. Wallis had consigned them to Germany with French permits via Paris and they got past Macdonald's army shortly before the battle of Katzbach. Finally they were put on board a ship at Straalsund. Other pictures reached British ports as contraband. A French émigré named

La Fontaine, living in London, brought at least sixty-three pictures across the Channel in this way in June 1811.

All this led finally to a saturation of the English market. Even in 1803 Buchanan sent two pictures by Raphael and one by Parmigiano back to Rome, where Lucien Bonaparte paid a higher price than was offered by British collectors. This may in part be accounted for by the low esteem in which Raphael was held by English connoisseurs of the day, but it shows also that the supply was slowly overtaking the demand, a process which was aggravated even in England by the rising prices and scarcity of money which accompanied the last years of the war.

8. *Restoration of plunder*

In earlier times there had been no thought of redress for plundered cities and countries. At the Sack of Rome or when the Swedes and others plundered in the Thirty Years War, no one could hope that negotiations would ever be opened up for the return of stolen property, or that its restoration would be exacted.

In 1814 the situation was different in two respects. For one thing, standing armies with their strict discipline and regular pay were very different from the mercenary bands of the seventeenth and early eighteenth centuries. This development, however, was reversed by the French revolutionary armies in Italy in 1796, whose discipline was as far from exemplary as their clothing, commissariat and pay were below military requirements. But this was no excuse for the systematic robbery carried out by commissioners as servants of the state, or for the behaviour of officers of high rank, or of men like Neveu and Denon. The second and decisive factor was that the victims of these robberies now became the victors. They were able, therefore, to present Denon's receipts in Paris and insist on the restitution of at least some of their property even if much had simply 'vanished' or been destroyed, or found its way from Italy, Spain, Holland and Belgium to England.

186

By the beginning of February 1814, a list was drawn up in Vienna of the works of art taken by the French from Austrian territory; and a few weeks later a very precise list of Prussian losses was forthcoming.

The first claims were put in by the Pope and certain Spanish grandees in April. The Peace Congress was not of one mind about the general restitution of all works of art without exception. Talleyrand, in spite of Wilhelm von Humboldt for one, succeeded in imposing delays, until Frederick William III of Prussia was assured in a personal communication of May 30, 1814, from Louis XVIII that everything would be given back. This undoubtedly created a precedent. If the Prussians had all their works of art back, then all the other powers could make the same claim, and this was emphatically supported by the Prussians in the subsequent negotiations. Against this, the French representatives urged that their present government could not be held accountable for the actions of the revolutionary and Napoleonic regimes. 'The effect which the confiscation of the greater part of the Musée Napoléon (accumulated by plundering the whole of Europe) was likely to have on the people of Paris was a strong argument against the strict pursuit of justice.'

This was, in fact, a matter of some importance. The new King of France insisted, not without good reason, that the ordinary Frenchman would not easily tolerate the evacuation of the museums of Paris. Robberies or not, the things had been in Paris, in some cases for twenty years. The manner of their acquisition had long been forgotten; and was not even known to the younger generation. A king who was in any case overshadowed by the great Corsican would inevitably weaken his position with the public and even invite a successful reaction in favour of Napoleon if he gave up all these treasures without protest. Louis XVIII and Talleyrand had good reason to insist energetically on this point, whatever they may have felt about its abstract justice.

It put the victorious powers in an awkward situation. On the one hand, they wished to confirm Louis XVIII's hold on the throne and to restore the old order in general, and this consideration, as Talleyrand knew it would, forced them to yield to the wishes of the French. On the other hand, the Austrians, the Prussians, the Hessians and the rest expected their victorious rulers to restore the pictures, sculptures, drawings, coins and other treasures of which Denon had so unscrupulously robbed them. Their subjects, at least in intellectual and artistic circles, regarded this as one of the most important fruits of victory.

Only in one quarter did Louis XVIII find a sympathetic response from the start. Lord Aberdeen, British representative at the Congress, declared: 'I am convinced that a restitution would do more than anything else in the world to discredit the French Government. The withdrawal from the Netherlands and Antwerp will not be felt so keenly as a national humiliation as would the restitution of these spoils of victory.' The return of the works of art would also cause them serious damage. Lord Aberdeen was strongly opposed to their surrender. In a note of May 29, 1814, Castlereagh let the disapproval of His Majesty's government be known and left it to the judgment of His Most Christian Majesty to make reasonable compensation to the previous owners.

The motives behind the British attitude, though not openly expressed, were no secret. England wished to earn the gratitude of Louis XVIII and the French people at a cheap rate. She herself had suffered no such losses and so had no demands to make; and her support cost her nothing. On the contrary, the recognition of the principle of restitution might raise awkward questions about the acquisition of works of art by Englishmen in Italy, Spain, Holland and Belgium, or even about the auctions of the possessions of émigrés in London.

There was no mention of it in the terms of peace drawn up in Paris on May 30, 1814. Nor was there any recognition of the national justification for twenty years of looting; but the great museums of France were left intact. Louis XVIII, in the course of a short address to the Chamber on May 4, announcing the terms of peace, adroitly supplied the missing plea.

'The fame of the armies of France has suffered no diminution; the monuments to their bravery remain, and the masterpieces of art belong to us in the future by virtue of claims more enduring than those of conquest.'

When the Prussians persisted in their demands for the return of their works of art, their claims were not resisted, 'but,' as the French Minister, E. D. Pasquier wrote in his memoirs, 'ways were found of handing over only a part of them.' Again and again the surrender of pictures and other things was put off and the receipt of official communications denied. This gave Denon time to secrete many treasures and to put others in public exhibitions. It had been agreed with the express consent of the Prussians themselves, who were the worst sufferers, and the most insistent on a restitution, that only those works of art which were still in store need be given up, lest French *amour propre* and national pride should be wounded by an empty place on the walls. As, in addition, the Prussian representatives were instructed by their government, very illogically, to go about it 'as considerately and carefully as possible', it is not surprising that the French came out of it very well. The final result was that a compromise was arranged to which the Prussian plenipotentiary agreed on instructions from his government, although official confirmation was never given. Such were the concessions extorted by defeated France from her victors, thanks to Talleyrand, and in the domain of art to the equally brilliant generalship of Denon. He was insistent that no promises should be made to Prussia or to Bavaria, on which precedents might be based; and thus the French succeeded in dragging out the negotiations. By early 1815 the Prussians had retrieved only a very small part of their losses: fifteen statues out of twenty-eight, six antique busts and reliefs out of fifty-six, three out of seven modern works of art, forty-one out of 123 pictures; the showing in coins, medallions and jewels was even poorer. Above all, France retained the cream of her plunder because it was already displayed in her public galleries.

The French firmly declined to give the representatives of Hesse-Cassel access to the depots where works of art were kept in store, so they were unable to ascertain what possessions were to be found there in order to claim them. They did finally get into Malmaison, only to find that the plunder once stacked there had been removed long since. On the other hand, they recovered most of the objects stolen by the retinue of the ex-King of Westphalia from the castles and from what was left of the gallery, and also the books from the Wilhelmshöher Library and the pieces Jerome had taken with him from the museum on his flight in October 1813; these amounted to sixteen cases of works of art and also sixty-nine pictures. Brunswick got back about eighty out of 278 pictures, besides enamels and faïence. Negotiations with Bavaria were so protracted that they were cut short by the return of Napoleon. Austria scarcely bothered at all about her losses.

Thus Denon was able to boast in a report dated January 14, 1814, that the Louvre had only 'sacrificed' six paintings, forty-six marbles and fifty-two bronzes, 461 cameos, seven manuscripts and one Indian knife. Castles and provincial museums had suffered even less and had parted with almost nothing. Not a single private owner had been induced to part with his loot.

The public knew little of these obstinate and difficult negotiations, and when any news did come through, it was concerned more with such episodes as the return of the quadriga to the Brandenburg Gate in Berlin. Other works of art too were enthusiastically welcomed back and adorned with flowers. In Düsseldorf the military and civic authorities and many of the inhabitants turned out to meet the convoy, and the principal streets and squares were brilliantly illuminated. Salutes were fired and bells pealed when it crossed to the right bank of the Rhine. The people even took the horses out of the shafts and pulled the wagons through the streets.

Napoleon's return and the resumption of war naturally put a stop to all these proceedings. After the battle of Waterloo, when the English and Prussian armies advanced on Paris, there was great indignation at Blücher's Headquarters over the breach of the peace. This time there was to be a peace which gave full satisfaction to Germany's military and national requirements.

The terms of the truce now proposed by the French included the following article: 'Public establishments and monuments, museums and libraries and all institutions of the kind shall be respected.' On Blücher's intervention this article was crossed out and nothing put in its place. But the Prussian High Command made all the use it could of the brief interval before the occupation of Paris and the arrival of the sovereigns and the diplomats to commandeer the works of art which had been taken from Prussia, in other words to anticipate their restitution. The French did everything possible to gain time. Blücher and Gneisenau appointed their chief of commissariat, von Ribbentrop, as Prussian commissioner in matters of art; he was given three secretaries, one of whom, Eberhard von Grote, a volunteer officer of Cologne, he found particularly useful. When Ribbentrop informed Denon on July 4 that Prussia intended to recover all her art treasures, Denon, as general director of French museums, replied that some had only recently been returned and that the rest 'had by error been wrongly ascribed to Prussia'. Ribbentrop was not to be put off and his men made their entry into the Louvre. Denon, however, refused to hand anything over without an order to that effect from his government. The Prussian authorities rejected all further pleas for delay, and Ribbentrop wrote to Denon on July 9 to warn him that he would be arrested unless the objects claimed had been surrendered by the evening of that day. Denon hurried off to Talleyrand, who advised him to let the Prussians start packing up their statues and busts: this would take several days and meanwhile the 'military bluster' would subside and time would be gained. That evening Ribbentrop announced that if Denon persisted in his refusal an officer and twenty-five men would arrest him and remove him to Graudenz. Talleyrand made a protest and he as well as Denon continued their delaying tactics. It was not until mid-day of the 10th that Denon gave way; and that evening the removal began. Von Grote's authority clearly expresses Blücher's exasperation.

'I, the under-signed, hereby give Herr Eberhard von Grote, Prussian volunteer officer, orders and full powers to take immediate possession of all masterpieces now in Paris and formerly confiscated and looted by the French in the Kingdom of Prussia, and to restore them to the places where they belong —I hereby undertake to confirm whatever my above-mentioned plenipotentiary may do in the execution of this task.'

At six o'clock in the morning of the next day, July 11, two hundred Prussian soldiers presented themselves at the entrance of the Louvre. The French officials protested vigorously and appealed to the Russians for protection. While Grote was having the first pictures packed, eighty men of the National Guard arrived. The officer in command reported that he had orders to prevent by force the removal of a single article, and to summon reinforcements in case of need. When Denon reported that the Prussian soldiers' firearms were loaded, the ministry instructed him to allow the Prussian property to pass. By the end of the month most of it was once more in the hands of its owners.

Nevertheless, Denon had not procrastinated and protested, disputed, misunderstood and prevaricated, made deceitful, lying and exaggerated pleas of shortages of labour and packing material all to no purpose. Every day gained saw a more peaceable and humane disposition in the victorious sovereigns, and a diminishing regard for the Prussian officials. For example, only thirty of the Aix columns finally returned; the twelve finest are still in the Louvre today, and a few others have vanished.

The treasures of Brunswick as well as the 209 pictures taken from Schwerin in 1807 were rescued from the Louvre under the aegis of Prussian arms. When, under the same august protection, the representatives of Hesse-Cassel made their claim, Denon behaved like a madman. 'These gems are the property of the Museum. They are not to be given up!' By September 9, 1815, 272 of the 299 pictures Denon had taken had been restored.

The Paris museums suffered most, because Denon refused to hand over the lists of the booty distributed among provincial galleries, and they successfully hid most of it.

If it was difficult to recover pictures from the provinces, the recovery of valuables and literary treasures was even more difficult. Much had already vanished and, further, the Prussians made a point of taking only what was demonstrably theirs. The proof was not always forthcoming because, as in the case of the Rhineland in 1794, there was no written evidence whatever. True, the thefts were there before their eyes, but they hesitated to appropriate the stolen objects without justification and left them as a rule where they were. The heads of the departments of manuscripts and printed books in the Bibliothèque Nationale naturally asserted that not one of the works demanded was in their possession.

Nevertheless, the Prussians were not themselves innocent of looting in their turn. Blücher's Headquarters followed French example and made no scruple of appropriating works of art which belonged without question to the enemy. The Field-Marshal gave proof in this respect too of the 'Jacobinism' with which he is commonly credited. He took a very fine bronze clock and two pictures from the castle of Compiègne, ten pictures and a marble statue from St Cloud, giving in this case a receipt. And, just as Napoleon showed a preference for pictures of great Commanders, so did Blücher for portraits of the Emperor: David's *Bonaparte on the St Bernard* and seven other portraits. Eight more pictures disappeared on the morning the Prussians withdrew, four of them, it is true, burgled from outside after the windows had been broken. The French Government naturally complained, whereupon Blücher replied that they were taken as pledge for the return of Prussian property from the provincial museums. But they never returned to France. David's portraits of *Josephine* and *Bonaparte* later arrived in the royal castle in Berlin, and seven portraits and *Bonaparte on the St Bernard* were added to public galleries.

Prussia's allies, and the Pope too, took steps to recover their possessions; it might seem that the vigorous and successful exertions of Ribbentrop inspired in some of them the wish to do likewise. Certainly, such demands took up a great deal of the time during the sessions of the council of allied ministers in Paris, which were attended by Wellington and Castlereagh on the part of England, Metternich and Schwarzenburg of Austria, Hardenburg and W. v. Humboldt of Prussia, and Rasumoffski and Nesselrode of Russia. It would take too long to plot the vacillations of these gentlemen, almost every one of whom was in favour at one time of total restitution, at another of the opposite, and at others of a compromise, without ever losing sight of the fact that the discussions were essentially part of the game of international politics.

Pius VII and the city of Rome employed the celebrated sculptor Canova to state their case, a task he undertook with the conviction that he entered into it 'poor and denuded of hope'. But his great reputation enabled him to achieve more than he had expected.

He got into touch with W. v. Humboldt as soon as he arrived in Paris; he, however, dismissed all attempts as hopeless, 'since the Treaty of Tolentino had never been abrogated, and Russia and England were determined not to wound French susceptibilities.' But Canova was resolute, adroit and diplomatic. He exploited the prestige of the Pope and his own artistic reputation by turns, alternated artistic with political arguments, never forgot the key position held by Rome in art and history, or the unique authority of the Holy Father, and rounded off his long array of arguments with the reminder that it was not possible to revive the dubious right of conquest of ancient days, all the less because neither Charles VIII nor Francis I nor Charles V had plundered Rome. He astutely passed over the Sack of Rome. Even the ruthless Frederick the Great, who had twice taken Dresden, had been content with an inspection of its pictures.

Talleyrand, of course, was opposed to any sort of restitution and said that the Pope ought to have pressed his claim on the occasion when he came to Paris to crown the Emperor; he had missed his chance. Louis XVIII was equally unmoved by a written request in the Pope's own hand which, encouraged by Talleyrand, he stoutly rejected. But Canova made friends, meanwhile, with W. R. Hamilton and through him gained access to English legal opinion. He later made it clear that it was thanks to Hamilton that the works of art were finally handed over, after long, protracted and acrimonious negotiations, involving the exchange of memoranda of the greatest interest in which both sides brought forward arguments of the most remarkable kind.

The Austrians may well have been influenced by Canova's success when they followed German and Dutch example by claiming works of art taken from them, including those taken from Modena and Parma while under Austrian occupation.

At last, on October 2, 1815, Canova was able, without the formal consent of the French, to start packing the works of art belonging to Rome and to the Pope. The Pope always recognized the importance of the help he had received from England and showed his gratitude by 'magnificent' gifts to the Academy, to the Prince Regent, to the members of the Cabinet and to Hamilton. On a closer inspection these magnificent marks of gratitude are found to have been plaster casts, not originals, or else works by Canova. But Hamilton was given a Titian, and three years later Humboldt was allowed to take away three ancient baths dug up in the grounds of the Villa Negroni.

Denon, of course, fought every claim with tireless energy, whether Belgian, Dutch, Austrian, Spanish, Sardinian or Venetian. But he had to let the horses go from the Arc du Carrousel and return to Venice, nor could he prevent his life's work, to which he had devoted such determination, such knowledge of art and locality, such national fervour and collector's mania, crumbling bit by bit. Finally, after Canova had stripped the Louvre of all its Roman acquisitions, leaving it nothing but its purely French possessions, it was only the logical consequence when next day, October 3, he asked Louis XVIII to accept his resignation. 'My advanced age and failing health make repose necessary.' These were his pretexts. He was released, but spent ten more years in a house of ancient renown on the Quai Voltaire, surrounded by the treasures he had collected on his own account and his own engravings and drawings. He died in 1825, and with him there passed away the most important of all plunderers of art.

His successor was his secretary, Lavallée. On November 15, 1815, he drew up for the information of his superiors a list of the sacrifices suffered through restitutions to the victorious powers. According to this the Louvre and its annexes, not counting other public buildings and the provincial museums, lost 5,233 works of art, including at least 2,000 valuable pieces of sculpture. In addition, several hundred objects had had to be returned to French claimants.

This list has been disputed. Undoubtedly it was misleading in so far as it described as important many works which earlier were less highly esteemed, and entered many objects singly which before had been grouped together. But even allowing for errors in detail, it gives us a good idea of the extent of the plunder as well as of the restitutions. And, in spite of all, a considerable quantity remained behind in Paris—about a hundred paintings, twenty-one antique sculptures, the Pope's large cameo collection, six Etruscan vases, all the bas-reliefs from the Villa Albani, Prince Braschi's sculptures and a collection of about 800 drawings belonging to the Duke of Modena, to the value all told, according to the French estimate, of four or five million francs.

Even so, the proceedings were not finally concluded. As soon as the French Government saw that the original owners would not surrender their rights, it set about things in two ways; in the first place it claimed the return of pictures which it had itself given, to Brussels for example, when the gallery there had been a French provincial museum, and including some which it had not in fact even lent; in the second place, it bought in a number of works from their original owners who either had no room for them, or else were alarmed by the cost of transport. Napoleon had found the solution of this problem by employing military transport. Now in 1815 it was found that some countries and some private owners could not face the bill. The return of the Papal possessions, for example, was only made possible by the generosity of the British Government, which put 200,000 francs at Canova's disposal. The transport of works of art belonging to northern Italy was paid for by the Austrian Government, and in all, forty-one vehicles, with more than 200 draught-horses, left Paris on October 23 and 24, 1815. Sixteen of them were bound for Austrian territory, twelve for Rome, and eight for Turin.

Most troublesome of all were the four horses of St Mark's. They were of the so-called Corinthian bronze and had been despatched to Venice from Constantinople by Marco Zeno, the Venetian ambassador and plenipotentiary, in Domenico Morosini's galley as part of the Crusaders' booty. On arrival they had been left standing about for a long time in the arsenal and were several times in danger of being melted down. They owed their survival to Petrarch, who declared them to be *'antiqui operis et praeclari'*, and thus gave them their patent of nobility, though their place in history, their origin and subsequent career up to 1204 could not be ascertained. Presumably they are the work of Lysippus, who made them for Chios; it may have been Theodosius who had them removed from there to Constantinople. The Venetians placed them on the four largest arches of the façade of St Mark's. Since 1798 they had adorned the triumphal arch in the Tuileries, later named the Arc du Carrousel, where they soon became as dear to the Parisians as they had been to the Venetians. As soon as it was known that they were to be taken away again, there was an outcry such as no other restitution had caused. This was only natural. Pictures and statues were kept in closed galleries, books and manuscripts on shelves or in cabinets, and their disappearance was scarcely observed. But these superb, gilded steeds had been visible to all for nearly twenty years against the sky of Paris and were one of its chief glories. Now they were being cautiously and laboriously lowered from their magnificent pedestal almost as a symbol of humiliation. As a precaution, the work was begun after dark, but even so a crowd assembled and the National Guard and Gendarmerie had to be called out to protect the workmen from its rage. With daylight the temper of the mob grew more dangerous, and the government, who had no desire to underestimate it, said they were afraid that an insurrection was imminent. A protest was made to the Prussian commandant of Paris, and Metternich reported to the Emperor: 'Unfortunately these horses bring all parties into play. The Royalists resent an insult to the King because they are taken from the very Palace itself, and the Opposition cannot forgive an insult to the memory of the victorious army.' Work was suspended next night, September 30, but continued under the protection of bayonets during the following days.

The lion of St Mark's also returned to Venice. The five animals required five special wagons of the heaviest build, each drawn by six horses. The four horses were back in their places by December 13, 'on the very same Monday eighteen years earlier on which they had been removed from the *duomo*'. The lion was delayed because it had been damaged in Paris and needed careful repair. In the name of the Emperor, Francis I, who with his staff and the civic dignitaries attended the ceremony, the governor handed over 'these emblems of victory and of Venetian national honour to the City of Venice and its loyal inhabitants as a memorial to the love, solicitude and beneficence of their sovereign'.

The Pope, in spite of British help, had to pay 145,000 francs for transport up to March 1816. In the end, Canova had to leave part of the papal possessions behind in Paris and they were given to the King as a mark of His Holiness's friendship.

It was much the same with Austria, Parma and Florence. The Austrians exchanged a large painting for a smaller one, which though inferior was easier to despatch; the Florentines abandoned twenty-nine paintings by Botticelli, Cimabue, Fra Angelico and Giotto to the Louvre, because they did not think them worth the probable cost of transport.

The Roman nobility was even less able than the smaller states to raise the money for transport. Besides, it was very tempting just then, when so many foreigners were in Paris, to sell their works of art for high prices. Prince Albani offered Denon's successor twenty-eight statues, fifteen busts, four Herms, four columns, a basalt lion and two alabaster cups for about 307,000 francs. When Lavallée demurred, hoping to get them for less, the Crown Prince Ludwig of Bavaria stepped in. At the same period the Prussians bought the Giustiniani collection of pictures in Paris for 500,000 francs. Wilhelm von Humboldt wrote to his wife, Caroline, about this on September 27, 1815: 'There is so much to be had here at present that fine bargains can be had for 600,000 francs. The Crown Prince of Bavaria has done one very good deal with 2,000!'

In short, never before had Europe's stock of works of art been set in motion as it was between 1789 and 1815. Nearly every town and locality was drawn in whether to its loss or its profit— with the exception of Russia and the Scandinavian countries, which took no part; nor is it known that Americans benefited by this great mobilization of art.

The democratization of art is the second mark of this period. Say what one may of the creation of the public collections of Paris, they gave countless persons their first opportunity of becoming acquainted with great art. The same, even if in a different context, is true of the works of art that found their way to England. It is true that the greater part quickly vanished into private collections, the inaccessibility of which Passavant and many others have deplored. But all the same, most of these paintings and works of sculpture were on view before being publicly auctioned.

15

The Looting of the Summer
Palace in Peking

To say that up to the days of modern imperialism, after the middle of the nineteenth century, art plunder was confined to Europe and then crossed the oceans as the accompaniment of political and economic expansion would, of course, be an error.

There is no difficulty, for example, in reckoning what the Aztecs lost in great works of art through the Spanish wars of conquest. Today we see no moral distinction between the conduct of Spanish soldiers in Mexico and the conduct of their fellow-countrymen in the same years at the Sack of Rome in league with German mercenaries. To contemporaries there was all the difference: in the one case the capital of the Christian world was looted and the head of Christendom endangered; in the other it was a question of savages who were scarcely regarded as human beings.

In the following centuries too every hitherto undiscovered part of the world was plundered by Europeans. But here a new factor enters in: the products of the Tahiti islanders, of the Indians of North and South America or of the Malays were prized at best as curiosities or perhaps as rarities, and appropriated for the use they could be put to, or for their oddity, or for the money they would fetch, but certainly not because they were considered to be works of art.

This was not the case with Persia, India, China and Japan. Their inhabitants might be looked down upon, but Persian pottery and carpets, Indian paintings and sculpture and jewellery,

Far Eastern lacquer and porcelain were very often of the highest artistic perfection.

Yet even in these cases it was still a matter of 'colonial wars', of conflicts on quite another plane than that on which European wars were conducted. In the nineteenth century, moreover, the relation between the European Powers and peoples oversea was intensified by the pressure of world-trade, and this gave these contacts an entirely new character.

The disputes between Europe, represented principally by the British, and China, since the early nineteenth century, or at latest, after the Opium War of 1840, are a clear example. England and France found it necessary, for the protection of the lives and property of their nationals, to send an expeditionary force to China, where insurrections had broken out. The Earl of Elgin and Kincardine was given the command. But the operation could not be carried out until after the suppression of the Indian Mutiny, which had broken out in 1857.

Lord Elgin, in command of 5,000 British soldiers, and supported by 1,000 Frenchmen and a corps of coolies, arrived at Hong Kong in December 1857. Campaigns, battles, negotiations and treaties dragged on until 1860, when a fresh detachment of 3,000 British and 7,000 Frenchmen joined in. With these strong reinforcements the Taku forts were attacked from the land side and taken, but as the consequent negotiations were fruitless the allied forces marched on Peking. Stronger resistance had to be overcome. But the Emperor then fled to Jehol and soon afterwards the Europeans made their triumphal entry into the city. A few days later the Summer Palace in the neighbourhood of Peking was plundered and burnt.

Of this event, which may well be compared with the Sack of Rome, the looting of Prague in 1648, and the conduct of Napoleon's army in Rome, there are naturally a number of contemporary accounts. The most revealing of these is by a French interpreter, Comte Maurice d'Hérisson. He was an eye-witness of the plundering, but took no part in it.

His account starts with a description of the beauty of the

o   201

Palace before its occupation by the French, its accumulated treasures of art which owed their perfection to the tradition of centuries and had never been seen or touched by any but the Emperor and his immediate entourage.

A first court-yard led up three granite steps into 'an enormous hall . . . this was the waiting room for those who were privileged to approach the Emperor'. Another court opened out of this 'adorned with ancient porcelain jars over a yard high, which served as tubs for an amazing growth of carved foliage'. After this came the audience chamber.

'This formed one side of a square in the middle of which there was a garden where fountains played. To left and right were two other audience and ceremonial chambers, and the fourth side, facing, was the throne room. These three rooms revealed precious things of unbelievable beauty. It has to be realized that the Emperor's palace was at the same time a museum, or rather a treasure-house, in which the choicest productions of countless generations of a population numbering four hundred millions were collected, the tribute in kind owed to a demi-god, all the presents prompted either by the fear or the admiration of great and small alike. And to all this must be added the possessions confiscated from rebels or from subjects charged with rebellion. And lastly, it must be remembered that not a masterpiece was created in this vast realm which did not come to the Emperor as a matter of course and that every object of value fell into his hands by a sort of law of gravity. Everything that dutiful princes could offer as tribute in the form of precious stones or costly stuffs was heaped up there, and all the objects of luxury, or show, or curiosity that the kings and emperors of Europe had ever presented. Whatever simple merchants had laid aside for the Emperor in order to be allowed access to a port was kept with the same tender care . . .'

D'Hérisson gives a detailed description of the chambers, comparing their ebony pillars with the column of the Place Vendome;

of the superb lacquered furniture, of the roof of glazed yellow tiles, of the monstrous dragons at the corners, of the large tigers of bronze, of the countless jewel-cases, bowls, tables, seats, footstools of gold, lacquer and precious stones, and religious images of solid gold. And again he was reminded of the splendours of Louis XIV's court in the seventeenth century.

Wandering from room to room, he came from the throne room to the bedroom with its luxurious furnishings; he admired the private apartments 'spread over an immense area in the midst of gardens', where, in boxes, caskets, drawers, bowls and jars every precious stone in the world was found in every possible variety, gold and silver too and jewellery of the finest workmanship and settings. He penetrated to the apartments of the Empress and the concubines, and after he had traversed the whole vast array of rooms, halls and courts, he went into the park, in which were numerous temples, pavilions, pagodas, pyramids, smaller palaces, gates and colonnades, and all those artificial mountains and grottos, the lakes, islands and streams, with which Chinese prints have made us familiar; there were even observatories in this domain so well adapted to contemplation.

The intention was to have the most valuable objects selected by three English and three French commissioners for presentation to Queen Victoria and Napoleon III as their share of the plunder, according to ancient custom, and as befitted the courtesy of victorious warriors. Thereafter the rest of the booty was to be equitably divided among all ranks.

But by an irretrievable disaster which gathered with the momentum of an avalanche, all these precious things, the irreplaceable harvest of an almost immemorial past, were doomed to destruction. D'Hérisson tells us stage by stage how it happened.

'It was towards the end of the afternoon. The sentries stood with ordered arms at every gateway, while the commissioners were at work within. Every few moments soldiers who had been detailed for the task came out with their loads of precious things, which aroused wonder and admiration in the groups of men round the sentries. As soon as the men on duty had put down their loads they showed the sentries their passes and went back into the palace.

'The crowd which collected to watch these proceedings was composed of French and English foot-soldiers, riflemen, gunners and dragoons, of spahis, sheiks and Chinese coolies too, all watching with staring eyes and lips parched with greed; suddenly a rumour spread in all the various languages: "When they've had the best, it'll be our turn! To hell with that! We want our share of the cake. We've come far enough for it. Eh, Martin? Eh, Durand?" They laughed and barged forward—discipline began to give way . . .

'Suddenly a trumpet call was heard. A company fell in. What was that for? Nothing much. The Chinese from Hai-tien had got over the walls and into the park. It was a question of keeping them off the spoils.

' "Nobody'll take that amiss," said the soldiers. "But these Chinese'll have the lot if we're not careful. We'll see about that, though."

'Covetousness suddenly aroused in the Chinese a sense of patriotism; they told themselves that the hour of revenge had struck, and that—if I may be forgiven the expression—it would be the bread of life to rob the Mongolian dynasty and not to leave the whole windfall to the barbarian invader . . .

'The peasants of the district, and the common people of Hai-tien had come up to the walls too, or had slunk up, I should say, and there they joined up with our coolies and began talking to them. Our coolies had ladders. They put them against the wall and a crowd of thieves with black pig-tails hurried along the alleys to the palace.

'The job now was to chase them out. Hence the alarm . . .

'But the Chinese from Hai-tien and our coolies had tinder, bunches of straw, and all that was needed for setting fire to any palace, and they lost no time in getting to work.

'As soon as the soldiers heard the news, of course in a greatly exaggerated version, anxiety gave way to fury. First they said,

"The Chinese want to bag the lot"; and then, "The Chinese are going to burn the whole place down."

'A wild mob surged round the gates. The sentries were pushed aside, and the whole crowd, soldiers and civilians, poured in on the heels of the company which had been summoned to expel the intruders. At once everyone took what he liked.

'From the very first moment I had the opportunity of comparing the behaviour of the French and the English. The French pressed on with eagerness, each man obeying his own impulse. The more disciplined English, on the other hand, sized up the situation without loss of time and organized a system of looting.

'They came along in squads as though on fatigue, provided with sacks and marshalled by their NCOs, who were actually armed with touchstones. How the devil had they got hold of them? I have never discovered. But I repeat that they were in possession of these simple implements of which our jewellers and pawnbrokers make use, and for all I know they may have borrowed them from Chinese pawnbrokers.

'The English, of course, are well used to having their heel on the neck of Asiatic peoples; and it must not be forgotten that their army is composed of mercenaries who regard plunder as one of the elementary principles of war, and would, I am convinced, already have put it into practice in China if they had got there before us. Certainly, they would not have lost a moment in dispossessing His Imperial Majesty of his goods.

'They carried on with the looting up to the moment when peace was signed, and even after . . .

'So now English and French, officers and other ranks, joined the populace of Hai-tien and our coolies, who had already shown at the storming of the forts of Taku how they hated the Chinese of the North, and swarmed through the palace. There was also the band of marauders who followed the army like ravens, dogs or jackals and had clung to our heels ever since

Pe-tang, plundering, stealing and destroying whatever we ourselves had spared . . .

'To have expected our men to stand by while this human torrent, in which all races were represented, fell on the spoil would have been to expect a superhuman degree of self-denial.

'The General's concentrated powers of will could not have barred the way into the Summer Palace to his troops any more than Napoleon himself, demi-god though he was in their eyes, could have arrested the rout of his men at Waterloo.

'I was only an onlooker, a disinterested but curious onlooker, positively revelling in this strange and unforgettable spectacle, in this swarm of men of every colour, every sort, this scrum of all the races of the world, as they flung themselves on the spoil, shouting hurrahs in every language on earth, hurrying, pushing, tumbling over one another, picking themselves up, cursing and swearing, and returning laden with their loot. It was like an ant-hill disturbed by the toe of a boot when the black swarms have been roused up and hurry off in all directions, one with a grub, one with a tiny egg, another with a seed in its jaws. There were soldiers with their heads in the red lacquer boxes from the Empress's chamber; others were wreathed in masses of brocade and silk; others stuffed rubies, sapphires, pearls and bits of rock-crystal into their pocketss shirts and caps, and hung their necks with pearl necklaces, Others hugged clocks and clock-cases. Engineers had brough. their axes to smash up the furniture and get at the preciout stones inlaid in it. One man was savagely hacking at a Louis XV clock in the form of a Cupid: he took the crystal figures on the face for diamonds. Every now and again the cry of 'Fire' rang out. Dropping whatever they had hold of, they all ran to put out the flames, which were by that time licking the sumptuous walls padded with silks and damasks and furs. It was like a scene from an opium dream.

'When I returned to camp, night was falling; the men were coming back laden with booty, including the most unexpected encumbrances, from silver serving-dishes to telescopes and sextants, a mass of stuff they could never hope to take home with them.

'The English camp was busy too, but there the most perfect order prevailed. With us it was like a masquerade, gunners wearing the Empress's dresses with mandarins' collars on top. There, on the other hand, the stuff was piled in a heap in every tent and auctions were already in progress . . .

'One thing that struck me was that nothing is more tempting to soldiers than clocks and watches or indeed any sort of mechanical contrivance. Now the Chinese, like all oriental peoples and, in fact, all who are not very expert mechanics, have a passion for mechanical objects and particularly for clockwork toys. Our rulers and merchants have therefore indulged this taste of theirs for centuries past and sent or taken to China every new invention in the way of optical apparatus, and mechanical contrivances and clockwork toys. No one could ever imagine the accumulation in the Summer Palace of musical boxes, bird-organs, barrel-organs, clocks with intricate striking arrangements, hares as drummer-boys, pictures that came to life, clocks that turned the arms of a windmill, made hens pick corn, worked the arms of a man sawing. What an astonishing display of song-birds confined to cages of brass wire on mounts and provided with a key, of flautists, and monkey-violinists, of trumpeters and clarinettists, of whole orchestras of monkeys, diminutive rope-dancers, waltzing couples and so forth. The apartments of the Empress and the ladies were literally chock-full of these productions.

'Our fellows were either very knowing or completely childish. The knowing were in the minority, and it was they who collected the jewellery, the coins, the bonbon dishes, tobacco boxes, gold services, and pearl necklaces. The others, confronted by these mountains of undreamed-of riches, went for the mechanical toys of European manufacture, which the English generously left them.

'On the second night we were encamped outside the Summer

Palace the infernal racket was enough to drive anyone out of his senses. Every man was amusing himself, and the din was continuous, clocks striking all the hours in every variety of tone, and now and then there was the crack of over-wound clockwork. Hares were drumming in all directions, monkeys clashed cymbals, and the 4,000 songs and arias issuing from as many musical boxes were mingled with the chirping of birds, runs on the flute, blares from the clarinets and the shrill piping of decoy-birds. Trumpets, bagpipes and volleys of laughter added to the fun of our easily amused and gallant soldiers.

'With daylight looting was resumed.

'One of the two Buddhas of solid gold found in the Emperor's bedroom had been planted in front of the General's tent. It was for Napoleon III. The other fell to the share of the English. A large diamond on the top of it flashed all colours of the rainbow, and two sentries were on guard in front of this precious trophy. Yet scarcely two hours had gone by before the diamond had vanished. No one ever discovered how it happened.

'We were the victors and therefore all objects of value belonged to our nation, that is, to the Emperor for whom we were fighting, just as the Germans had the right to take from us our millions, and as Napoleon had the right to strip Italy of its masterpieces.

'The plundering of the Summer Palace was, therefore, a lawful act in so far as war can be lawful at all.

'The principle is incontrovertible. We can be reproached with the destruction, but not the plundering.'

16

A Berlin!

At the very time when French and English troops were engaged in the Far East upon one of the most extreme orgies of looting ever known, and setting in motion an apparently inexhaustible flow of oriental art to Europe, a new art journal made its appearance in France with the title, *Gazette des Beaux Arts, Courrier Européen de l'art et de la curiosité*. In the first number there was an article on *'Nos relations avec l'art de l'Allemand'*, which maintained that the two peoples were far too little acquainted with their respective works of art and artistic points of view. But, it continued, for some extraordinary reason the Germans were not so eager for a mutual acquaintance on those lines. They had not been at all forthcoming on the occasion of the Paris Exhibition. The *Gazette*, however, was not to be discouraged on that account, and went on to print an article on German artists, on the theory of art in Germany and on German art societies, which concluded: 'So if Germany will not come to us we will go to Germany until those who pursue the same studies and are one in a common enthusiasm for art, get to know one another and to value one another as they deserve.'

This no doubt showed a very praiseworthy disposition, but by the 'sixties these fine and noble aims had already vanished.

After the Franco-Prussian War, the defeat of France and the emergence of the German Empire, Europe enjoyed an astonishingly rapid and vigorous increase of prosperity, which did much to strengthen the spirit of nationalism and to foster narrow jealousies behind every frontier. This was by no means confined to economic, military and political affairs; it extended also to the whole domain of art. Diplomatic exchanges, legislation, and learned and scientific publications give only a veiled and indirect expression to this phenomenon; but from artists, writers on art, art critics, above all from the day-to-day dealings of the art market, especially in the writings and later in the memoirs of the great director of the Berlin gallery, Wilhelm von Bode, we see it in all its stark and undisguised reality. We see too that within a few decades the general interest in art greatly increased, while at the same time nationalism turned art traffic between one country and another, hitherto a matter for dealers, connoisseurs and collectors, into a battlefield of national rivalries.

There was plenty of money in Germany, partly owing to the five milliards of the French indemnity; the state, therefore, could take a hand in matters of art on a grand scale. From 1874 onwards it financed diggings, for example, at Olympia, and it assisted in the purchase of whole collections of art as well as of single items. The yield of taxation from a rapidly expanding economy and the immense growth of population, as well as Prussia's income from the state railways after 1879, meant that, with the eager concurrence of the Prussian Landtag and the German Reichstag, the museums and galleries of the whole country could play their part in foreign auction rooms. They could also extend old buildings and build new museums. All this did much to stimulate the art market. Thanks to his phenomenal memory, which enabled him to track down any important picture, and also to his extensive links with important dealers, Bode succeeded in acquiring many valuable works for Germany. Soon the Berlin museums enjoyed a reputation in Italy as eager buyers with money to spend such as only American private collectors enjoy today.

These activities brought Bode into touch with a class of men which before 1870 had been little known in Germany and not at all in Berlin: bankers, industrialists, and big business men; later he got to know shippers and exporters, who at that time were making big fortunes and beginning to take an interest in art, either for show, or as investment, perhaps from a genuine love of art, often out of a sense of the patronage owed to it by the rich.

Nearly all were ignorant and uncertain of their own judgment, and therefore they welcomed Bode's advice and help. In return they contributed to his funds, or promised to leave desirable items from their collections to some public gallery. In this way Bode became very influential in a widening circle of wealthy people all over Germany, but particularly in Berlin, which not only gave its support to his art-offensive and his purchases abroad, but was his indispensable ally. From this circle of donors, friends and dealers there emerged finally in the 'eighties the Kaiser Friedrich Museum Association.

Thus Bode achieved a position unknown in other lands. As head of the Berlin museums and also of the galleries of other cities, such as Frankfurt and Hamburg, as the artistic adviser of the Kaiser, of many German princes as well as of all the rich throughout Germany, he had acquired by 1900 an unprecedented influence and the reputation, among his enemies at home and abroad, of being the dictator of the art world.

Naturally, his travels abroad brought him into ever closer relations with his colleagues in France, Italy, Spain and England. 'My connections there,' he wrote in his memoirs, 'were always of a thoroughly friendly kind until England's hateful jealousy of Germany's advance made a difference.' Wherever he went he made a point of visiting private collections in the well-founded belief that before long many of the pictures and other works of art in private hands would come on to the market. This was already happening at that time, because their owners found in them an easily realizable asset.

Bode and the German Empire dominated the art market of the world thirty years after the Franco-Prussian War. But already on the horizon there was the distant threat of their being over-taken by the Americans. From year to year, indeed from month to month, Bode was compelled to recognize in the United States, after the victorious conclusion of the war with Spain in 1898, the same symptoms as in Germany after 1871. There was the same rapid up-surge of prosperity, the same great fortunes, the same determination to buy works of art. Pierpont Morgan, the chief representative of this new brand of acquisitor, was also the most energetic.

Was it not a possibility that these millionaires and multi-millionaires, these steel-kings, oil-magnates and Trust barons might set themselves the aim of buying up literally the whole art of Europe from the dawn of history to the present day, and therewith lay the foundations for a civilization of their own? There was cause for apprehension, but the danger passed. European periodicals, anxiously concerned with this problem after four or five years of hectic buying on the part of Americans and their agents, decided that it would take the Americans 'a long time' to catch up with the appreciation of artistic quality which it had taken Europe centuries to acquire. 'They bought pictures,' so Bode wrote in an article of 1903, 'in vast quantities,' but they missed the works of real artistic value, which alone were of interest to European galleries and collectors. They were neither experts nor amateurs in the European sense; they were buyers simply, and not, in the opinion of Bode and many of his colleagues, even buyers who knew their job. A few years later, however, Bode had altered his opinion; in 1907 he was concerned about the American peril in the art market; he was lamenting 'the emigration of fine works of art' and fearing that this tendency would increase. For the first time he considered the expediency of 'Draconian laws' to limit the excessive export of art. He had thrown out the suggestion, and now it was up to the government 'to take a strong line at least with the treasures in public ownership, in churches and collegiate foundations and so forth'. As for private owners, he appealed to their 'national feeling', which should prevent them from selling their works of art to America. The language he used was more suitable to trade rivalry not merely on a national but continental scale; even the vocabulary of military operations was drawn upon. The pictures fought for were not for museums or collections, but for America or Germany or Europe.

Bode did not at first observe that these despised buyers-in-a-hurry and mass collectors were employing much the same methods as had been employed by many sovereigns of the eighteenth century. He did not realize that they had the backing of extremely able keepers of museums and art critics, who were in touch with far greater industrial and commercial resources and far more important donors and patrons than Bode had ever heard of in Germany.

Meanwhile this vigorous concern with art on the part of Germany, and Bode's commanding personality led to an unexpected consequence. By 1910 no doubt was left of the Americans being the most formidable buyers in the European art market. American art dealers founded branches in Paris, London, Berlin and Rome; Europe did the same in New York, Boston and Chicago. But while the activities of these collectors and dealers met with understanding in England and toleration in France, every appearance of Germany and of Bode in the auction room came to be regarded as a crime and a menace. First Germany had conquered France in war, taken Alsace and Lorraine and exacted an indemnity, and now came this aggression on the art front, which was seen as another victory for German nationalism. It was hardly surprising, therefore, when, in 1909, one of the foremost art periodicals in England published a leading article with the heading 'A Berlin!', even though England had less cause than France for complaint. In this article Bode was stigmatized as the wielder of an 'extraordinary authority' over the experts of the day. He was certainly buying the best pictures for Germany; only the other day an important Rembrandt had gone to Berlin instead of to America. And even more formidable than Bode himself was the organization he had built up; the Kaiser Friedrich Museum Association, one of his most important achievements, enabled him to buy what he liked for Berlin, while England had to look on helplessly as one masterpiece after another was sold abroad.

Not long before, such facts would scarcely have been noticed; but since 1871, and even more since 1898, the trade in art had become a matter of national interests and national prestige. An international race was on, not one between lovers of art. The tariffs which excluded the products of agriculture and industry in the interests of trade warfare offered a precedent for similar measures in the case of art exports.

This reaction cannot be considered surprising. Year by year the number of international buyers and agents increased. At the end of 1912 a Paris newspaper complained of the concourse of 400 German dealers, museum directors and collectors at an important auction. A German art periodical might consider this complaint a provocation and a sign of 'the campaign against Germany and the Germans conducted for the last year by the whole French press', but, looked at impartially, such an occurrence might well seem an invasion and fill the French, who were conscious of the greatness of their past, with alarm. Every country in Europe was striving to defend itself against the aggression of every other country, but chiefly, of course, against those with more money and more determination; and these were Germany and America. A few months before this there had been a sale in London of valuable tapestries from Hampton Court; nearly all the important dealers of Europe were present, and it was only owing to the resolute intervention of an Englishman that they were thwarted.

Art periodicals at this time frequently published articles on the national origin of works of art now in the possession of some other country; it might be French pictures in private hands in America; or the statistics of the Customs would be examined simply to track out sales of pictures, followed up by comments on American interests and the reactions of European owners. Looking through these periodicals of the years before the First World War, you find, under 'Passing Events' or some such title, indignant or anxious reports of important works 'leaving the country', and always in terms of emotion more suitable to military operations. It was only by degrees that any difference was perceived between these depredations and the looting carried out by the French in Napoleon's day. Then it had been the preponderance of armed force, now it was that of money. The result in the long run was the same.

The article with the sensational title 'A Berlin!' was justified seven years later, by the celebrated writer on art, Karl Scheffler, in his magazine, *Kunst und Künstler*. On the occasion of Bode's seventieth birthday in 1916, he described him in an article as a representative of a generation of unsentimental adventurers, a political realist of art—a Bismarck of the world of museums, in whom Prussian thoroughness was wedded to American pushfulness.

Some years later, after the First World War had ended, the situation was reversed: it was for Germany to feel alarm over the sale of her works of art. A motion was proposed in the Prussian House of Representatives to give them legal protection, but the government did not take it up. Bode expressed the opinion that such measures would in the long run be more to the detriment than to the advantage of Germany. No prohibition, therefore, was put into force. Sweden, on the other hand, passed a law to this effect on June 20, 1918, and other countries followed suit.

17

War and Art Conservation

It was not only in military matters that the First World War ushered in a new era. It did the same for art plunder.

As reported in the *Kunstchronik* of October 1914, the French Government confiscated the German section of the Exhibition of Art at Lyons and auctioned it for the benefit of the city, but what was more significant was the appointment by the German High Command of Dr Clemen, a professor of Bonn University, as guardian of monuments in France and Belgium, and of Dr Otto von Falke, director of the Museum of Industrial Art in Berlin, as commissioner for art with the German civil administration in Belgium. They were not men of the same type as Denon and Neveu, but guardians of art, whose integrity could not be called in question and who had no thought of enriching their museum, their university or the state in any way.

During the winter of 1914–15, Clemen drew up a number of official reports on the condition of the monuments entrusted to his keeping and, in December 1914, he published a lengthy article, 'The protection of monuments and the War', in the *International Monthly Review of Science and the Arts*.

Extracts were published in the press and drew the attention of Albert Bartholomé, the well-known French sculptor, whom Clemen had introduced in 1902 to the German public in a highly appreciative article in *Die Kunst*. His comments were answered by Clemen in articles in the press and also in an open letter published in *Die Kunst*.

It must be regarded as something new that on both sides the need of some form of art protection was accepted as a matter of

216

course; the dispute was only whether or not everything possible was being done to ensure it. It was agreed that art should stand outside war, that it should in fact be less involved in the sufferings of war than human beings, even civilians. This principle was carried to such lengths from the French and Belgian side that no town hall or church tower was to be endangered even if soldiers or artillery were concealed in or behind it, irrespective of the cost in lives or military advantages.

In former times the conqueror had imposed his will on the conquered, and no complaint or objection or exchange of views had been possible. In these more recent days the press and the recognition of the neutrality of countries not involved, Holland, for example, and Switzerland, allowed a lively discussion to be conducted, not only about the destruction and looting of art, but also about measures for its preservation. Naturally, the sufferers, chiefly the French and Belgians, made numerous justifiable as well as exaggerated and unfounded complaints. More important, however, than these indignant accusations was the mere fact that the question was debated, and that Clemen's report on the 'Historic buildings in east Belgium', for example, should have been open to discussion.

The idea of art plunder of the traditional kind was once and once only canvassed in Germany, and this occurred shortly after the outbreak of war. A contributor to the review, *Die Kunst*, early in 1915 asked the question: 'Shall we take pictures from Belgium for German galleries?' The suggestion was made that now perhaps the opportunity had come to reassemble the Ghent altarpiece, which had been dismembered at the beginning of the nineteenth century, and to set it up as a whole again in some church on the left bank of the Rhine. But at once scholars, artists and keepers of museums rose in protest against the mere thought of plundering the art of any occupied or conquered country. French plunder of the Napoleonic era was recalled with lively horror and German hands were raised in unequivocal disapproval. Bode, still the mouthpiece of German museum directors, wrote, 'My conviction is that all civilized countries

P   217

should have their own artistic creations and all their lawful artistic possessions left them intact and that the same principles of protection should be exercised in enemy territory as at home.' Even the possibility of works of art being carried off from occupied countries to America by purchase was anticipated by legal enactment.

'A Friend of Art' who raised the question of 'Works of Art as War Indemnities' in 1915 was given equally short shrift. One argument used in his reproval shows with particular clearness how views had altered since earlier times; while the French earlier had demanded the removal of Italian art to Paris in recognition of the blood and sweat offered up by the victorious soldiers, G. Swarzenski maintained in an issue of *Die Kunst*: 'Popular sentiment will, indeed must, declare, "We have not sacrificed life and property in order to add to our artistic possessions. The damage done by the war, the values it destroys, are so great that we must not regard even a fraction of these spiritual values as an indemnity." ' This would mean that 'the purpose of war was not the insurance and strengthening of a country's own economic and political life, but the weakening and destruction of the enemy's spiritual and cultural existence. This aim, which would lead to the impoverishment of mankind, is not perhaps acceptable to any of the countries at war and certainly not to the German Empire.'

Bode, in a Turin newspaper, rebutted imputations made against him: ' . . . the assertion that I have drawn up a list of works of art as plunder is ridiculous to the point of being farcical . . .' The museum director, von Falke, mentioned above, declared in the name of the Imperial Government in Belgium that no work of art was to be removed from the country. In the summer of 1915, German military orders for the protection of historic and artistic monuments in Brussels were emphatic.

All this, however, could do little to prevent extensive destruction of buildings and of the contents of museums in the course of a war conducted with modern artillery. In the *Kunstchronik* of October 1914, we read: 'Implicit confidence may be placed in our Army Command, which will never forget its duty to civilization even in the heat of battle. Yet even these duties have their limits. All possible sacrifices must be made for the preservation of precious legacies of the past. But where the whole is at stake, their protection cannot be guaranteed.' The destruction of a large part of Louvain aroused the liveliest horror throughout the world, quite apart from the question of guilt; even in the days of Napoleon the destruction of Italian palaces and German castles had never been a war risk. But now war meant observation-posts and machine-gunners in church towers, and gun-emplacements and ammunition dumps in the cover of Gothic gateways and town-halls. At the beginning of the war military necessities and possibilities were still curbed by the idea that war was a matter of weapons, 'a duel between armies', so that the protection of historic and artistic monuments was 'possible in itself'. And in fact article 27 of the Hague Convention said:

'In sieges and bombardments all available precautions must be adopted to spare buildings devoted to divine worship, art, education or social welfare, also historical monuments, hospitals and assembly points for wounded and sick, provided that they are not being used at the same time for military purposes. It is the duty of the besieged to mark these buildings and assembly points with easily visible marks, which must be made known beforehand to the besieging army.'

The Convention was concluded in peace time. The war brought with it situations, dilemmas and contingencies of quite another sort and, from the time of the first battles in Belgium to those in northern and eastern France, the problem of protecting works of art was no longer capable of solution, from whichever side the shells came. When French bombers appeared above Kolmar, where Grünewald's Isenheim altar-piece had remained since the restoration of Alsace to Germany, there was an outburst of dismay in the press at this new danger to works of art. The hope was expressed that 'the Isenheim altar-piece had long since been removed to a place of safety, far from Kolmar and the whole region likely to be directly affected by the war.' It was learnt at this very time that the much-travelled horses of St Mark's, after remaining in their old position for just a century since 1815, had now been taken away in fear of Austrian air bombardment. Early in 1918 many other works of art were removed from Venice to Rome: the equestrian statue of Colleoni, the most celebrated in the world, and also the one of Gattamelata from Padua.

But there was something else that occurred in this war for the first time—art plunder by the Russians. It was reported in the autumn of 1914 that they had removed the most valuable treasures of art and literature from the Ossolinski Museum at Lemberg to St Petersburg; 1,034 pictures, among them some by Raphael and Tintoretto, 28,000 engravings, 17,000 coins, 4,300 medallions, 142,000 books and 5,000 manuscripts, Polish national relics and various valuable historical documents. Yet for the time it was open to doubt whether this was really an act of spoliation or a temporary measure of safety 'in case of reprisals by the enemy if they made a brief incursion over the Russian frontier', since there were other works of art in Galicia from public galleries and the private collections of Polish landowners which, at first under Russian protection, were later taken 'for safety' to St Petersburg. But news of Russian behaviour with regard to works of art was contradictory. In the German press there was an obvious tendency to attribute the worst to the Russian barbarian, and every report of the destruction of a picture as, for example, the *Deposition* by Corinth in Tapiau, or the shelling of a church, was taken as confirmation. Yet it often happened that the Russians went out of their way to spare not only churches but town-halls and other important buildings.

When the prospect of a dictated peace drew near, the Germans stated their claim for the return by Russia of the twenty-one pictures taken by the French in 1806–7, then given to Josephine and acquired after her death by the Czar, Alexander I. Here again the dispute about art and justice was drawn into the realm of politics and propaganda, and very soon accusations were made of 'French robbery' and Russian 'receivers'. The demand for the restitution of the pictures duly made its appearance in the draft of the Russo-German treaty, but the Bolshevik government, no less nationalistic in the face of such demands by 'the capitalist and imperialist foreigner' than the czarist régime at its most absolute, never surrendered them.

18

Agreement by Treaty

Napoleon's peace terms, as we saw, nearly always included an article or paragraph stipulating the surrender of works of art and even sometimes the payment of the costs of packing and transport to Paris. These exactions were always resented as being particularly insulting, mean and ruthless, and were defended only by the French. The nearer the prospect of an unfavourable conclusion of the First World War, the more lively were the fears in Germany of a repetition of these Napoleonic demands. To add to them, there appeared in the Paris paper *Lectures pour Tous* in the late summer of 1918 a list of all those works of art which German galleries would have to hand over to France as indemnity for a 'wantonly inflicted war'. They were grouped under two headings: those to be surrendered on historical grounds, and those to be surrendered because in spite of all their pedantry the Germans could not appreciate them. The first group contained nearly everything taken by Napoleon and restored in 1814–15, as well as all the trophies of war taken in 1870–1. In the second group were valuable pictures and pieces of sculpture, chiefly from Berlin and Munich, including all those by French masters, the most important works by Germans, many of Italian schools, the pictures from the royal palaces in Berlin, works by Rubens and those by Poussin and Claude Lorrain in Dresden; Cologne was to surrender medieval art in particular, and the list went a great deal further.

There had been no further mention for a long time of the suggestion of works of art as war indemnity made by Emil Schäffer in 1915—'the best pictures captured as booty in Belgium should be handed over to German galleries'—and this proposal, unique in its day, had only been published with editorial reservations, and it met with sharp reproof from all sides. The boot was now on the other foot: the Ghent altar-piece, the integration of which in Germany had been recommended and demanded, had now long since been claimed as a Belgian possession, including the parts in Berlin, and the question now was how this claim was to be rebutted.

Article XIX of the truce terms of 1918 gave a good idea of what the peace treaty was likely to contain. There was the clear indication that the French designed to recover all the loot they had acquired in such profusion after 1789. At one of the sittings of the truce commission the French gave a warning of the possible sale of works of art in the castles in Berlin and Potsdam. There was a rumour, they said, that the ex-Kaiser had accepted an offer from a group of dealers; and the sale would contravene the article mentioned above.

The Italians were not behindhand; they carried off valuable pictures and manuscripts from Vienna. And as they encountered little opposition the first time, they made a demand early in 1919, before the signing of peace, for a large number of ancient manuscripts, valuable armour from the Austrian Army Museum, and twenty-seven major works from the Vienna Gallery, particularly Italian masterpieces. The director of the Gallery, Dr E. Leisching, wrote on the occasion:

'It is hard to keep a cool head and yet give this affair its right name. A glance at the long list is enough to make the heart contract. Not one of the great collections in Vienna is left out; in many, large gaps, never again to be filled, will be left in the ranks of precious paintings, ornamented weapons and masterpieces of handicrafts, if the Italians succeed, or were to succeed in their design . . . What is at stake now is nothing less than the loss of works which are the spiritual possession of all those untold thousands who lay claim to a sense of beauty, to education, to culture, and to a feeling for

spiritual greatness and human dignity transcending all national boundaries. They are almost exclusively works of native origin, the loss of which would be deeply felt throughout the whole population, works which have found their way to the hearts and minds of the people; they are not only works of supreme merit which only professionals, research-students, artists and connoisseurs can appreciate. In a word, they want to take from us with a refinement of cruelty what would hurt us most, possessions imbued with the personality and spirit of our city in the highest degree and which express to all the world the fame, the charm and the very soul of Vienna.'

It was now known, too, what the terms of the treaty with Germany would be: reparation, namely, for the destruction of the library of Louvain by the surrender of manuscripts, old books, prints; surrender of the side panels of the Ghent altar-piece at present in Berlin, and also of the side panels of the *Last Supper* by Dirk Bouts, now in Munich, the centre panel of which was in Louvain. An article in the *Revue des Deux Mondes* early in 1919 also demanded the surrender of the *Bamberg Rider* and the founders' effigies from the cathedrals of Naumburg and Magdeburg, without making it clear whether this was in obedience to supernationalist prompting or just a ruse to test in advance what the reactions would be to this exploit in art plunder.

The Versailles Treaty finally laid down:

SPECIAL PROVISIONS

Article 245

Within six months of the coming into force of the present Treaty the German Government must restore to the French Government the trophies, archives, historical souvenirs or works of art carried away from France by the German authorities in the course of the war of 1870–1 and during this last war, in accordance with a list which will be communicated

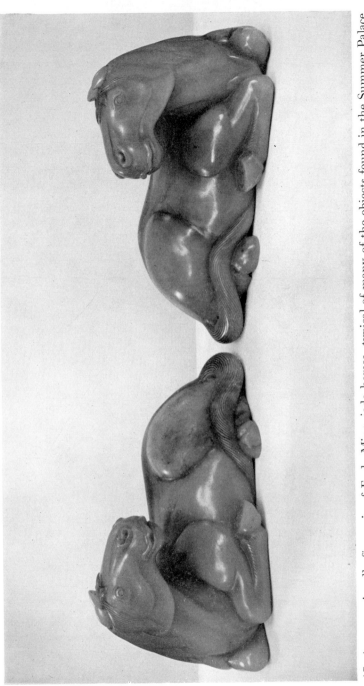

17. An exceptionally fine pair of Early Ming jade horses, typical of many of the objects found in the Summer Palace at Peking.

18. The LAST SUPPER by Dirk Bouts at Louvain.

to it by the French Government; particularly the French flags taken in the course of the war of 1870–1 and all the political papers taken by the German authorities on October 10, 1870, at the chateau of Cerçay, near Brunoy (Seine-et-Oise) belonging at the time to Mr Routher, formerly Minister of State.

Article 246

Within six months of the coming into force of the present treaty, Germany will restore to His Majesty the King of the Hedjaz the original Koran of the Caliph Othman, which was removed from Medina by the Turkish authorities and is stated to have been presented to the ex-Emperor William II.

Within the same period Germany will hand over to His Britannic Majesty's government the skull of the Sultan Mkwawa which was removed from the Protectorate of German East Africa and taken to Germany.

Article 247

Germany undertakes to furnish to the University of Louvain, within three months after a request made to it and transmitted through the intervention of the Reparation Commission, manuscripts, incunabula, printed books, maps and objects of collection corresponding in number and value to those destroyed by Germany in the burning of the Library of Louvain. All details regarding such replacement will be determined by the Reparation Commission.

Germany undertakes to deliver to Belgium, through the Reparation Commission, within six months of the coming into force of the present treaty, in order to enable Belgium to reconstitute two great artistic works:

(1) The leaves of the triptych of the *Mystic Lamb* painted by the van Eyck brothers, formerly in the Church of St Bavon at Ghent, now in the Berlin Museum;

(2) The leaves of the triptych of the *Last Supper*, painted by Dirk Bouts, formerly in the Church of St Peter at Lou-

vain, two of which are now in the Berlin Museum and two in the Old Pinakothek at Munich.

Since the end of the war brought with it the dismemberment of the Austro-Hungarian Monarchy, Austria was threatened with the distribution of its art possessions. The Treaty of St Germain, September 2, 1919, included these articles:

Article 196

With regard to all objects of artistic, archaeological, scientific or historical character forming part of the collections which formerly belonged to the Government or the Crown of the Austro-Hungarian Monarchy and are not otherwise provided for in this present treaty, Austria undertakes:

(a) To negotiate, when required, with the States concerned for an amicable arrangement whereby any portions thereof or any objects belonging thereto which ought to form part of the intellectual patrimony of the ceded districts may be returned to their districts of origin on terms of reciprocity, and

(b) For twenty years, unless a special arrangement is previously arrived at, not to alienate or disperse any of the said collections or to dispose of any of the above objects but at all times to ensure their safety and good condition and to make them available, together with inventories, catalogues and administrative documents relating to the said collections, at all reasonable times to students who are nationals of any of the Allied and Associated Powers.

The negotiations dragged on, but the Ministry of Education in Vienna, in whose charge the works of art were, still awaited the final onslaught. It came early in 1921 when a conference of all the succession states of the old monarchy assembled in Rome to decide on the execution of the treaty. The following report comes from one of the Austrians present at the meeting:

'Soon after our arrival we were summoned to attend a sitting of the commission, when we were handed the draft of an agreement reached by all the countries concerned, providing for the surrender of archives and the "sharing out of the museum". An international commission, we were told, had undertaken the apportionment of the contents of the museum among the different countries, allowing for the link between Hungary and Austria so that Austria might still have had to make good any deficiencies on the part of Hungary. The surroundings were in keeping with the substance of these proposals; there was still the atmosphere of St Germain; the sittings purposely took place in the former Austrian Embassy in the Palazzo Chigi. An eastern delegate presided over the meeting of this semi-juristic, semi-political committee, and instead of speaking of Austria he spoke of the country which had started the war; he would also preface his remarks with, "Whenever I come across pictures in some office in Vienna or Berlin which have been taken from Rumania . . ." In these circumstances any useful discussion was scarcely possible; nevertheless, Privy Councillor Redlich and our delegate, Professor Walker, succeeded in introducing an innocuous proposal for the archives on the basis of requisitions up to date. But this was at first impossible for the remaining possessions, from which, according to the treaty, each country was to be given its own intellectual heritage. We tried, in the first place, to come to an agreement with Hungary, which was in the same position as ourselves, but the attempt failed. Then we sought help and advice from the Western Powers. We got encouragement from that quarter; we were told not to be brow-beaten; we were not bound to more than friendly discussions. The phrase "intellectual heritage", they said, was purposely left elastic, so as to give us room for manoeuvre. The circumstances too were altered, and Casanova, the scrupulously correct head of the Italian archives, took the chair. The understanding between our opponents proved to be incomplete; one by one they began to lean towards separate talks with us and these in turn led to provisional arrangements . . .

'It may be asked how Austria ever got into the position of having such extensive claims made on her cultural possessions.

It was due in the first place to the attitude of the conqueror to the conquered and the wish to take from Austria what she valued most in what was left her, her cultural heritage. To this must be added the definite aim of the Succession States to outdo dethroned Vienna by enriching their own institutions, archives and museums, and to exalt their own national status by recovering whatever could be described as belonging to their own past. These destructive aims were energetically opposed by the great Western Powers . . .

'The conduct of the different succession states varied greatly. Italy did not wait for permission but took what it wanted; and when Austrian foreign policy aimed at an understanding with Italy, these requisitions had to be confirmed and added to, after which, certainly, Italy resigned further claims, and even promised its help in case of further exactions. Poland's conduct was praiseworthy; it took no advantage whatever of the rights conferred on it, and acquired by purchase a picture by Matejko which was of interest from the point of view of Polish history; it was therefore possible to make a suitable return at once. Czechoslovakia made exorbitant demands for the reparation of injustices suffered from the Hapsburgs and backed its long list of requisitions with a compendious indictment. The three-jurist-committee had the strength of mind to reject these demands *in toto* . . . It likewise threw out the Belgian plea for the treasure of the Order of the Golden Fleece and the Ildefonso altar-piece. We were advised to come to a compromise on side-issues affecting a few and less important pieces and we were able to do so at small sacrifice. Here too we had reason to thank the museum custodians for their thorough preparatory work and the lawyers to almost the same degree.

'Hungary's attitude was quite different from the very beginning. It was our toughest and most vigorous opponent. The whole public opinion of the country was behind its delegates—the press and the educated classes made themselves felt to such purpose that negotiations were severely prejudiced. The teaching of history in Hungary pays special attention even in the intermediate schools to its historic monuments and records; hence there is a widespread familiarity with the most important sources, such as the manuscript in the National Library in Vienna, known as Anonymous; hence the imprint on their bank notes of the reliefs of King Matthias and his wife now demanded of us; and hence the universal popular clamour for the surrender of other important objects besides the treasure of Attila and his sword . . .

'The Hungarian demands could only be resisted in quite a few cases and this left the largest and most important group of objects to be disputed. Of these may be mentioned above all many relics of the early Middle Ages, to which we could not allow that the Hungarians had any claim, many fine pieces from the collection of weapons, Corvinus manuscripts, the sword of Charlemagne, an insignia of the Holy Roman Empire, the claim to which we regarded as provocative and rejected with vigour . . .

'Another obstinately contested object was the crown of Prince Bocskay, sent him by the Sultan and left after his death to the Emperor Matthias. It was now in the Vienna treasure chamber. Hungary's claims were countered by equally vigorous ones on the part of Rumania. The crown was said to have been used at a coronation at Karlsburg as a symbol of Siebenbürgen, and this called forth even more vehement protests and claims on the part of Hungary. These conflicting claims of Hungary and Rumania were met by our own Austrian claim, all the more successfully because we saw in this crown the most outstanding monument of Austrian and German co-operation in overcoming the Hungarian nobles, who were ever ready to betray the cause of freeing Europe from the Turks.

'After negotiations lasting many months and the intervention of the arbitrator, the differences were so narrowed down at last that it was possible to draw up terms of agreement at Baden in September 1927 . . .

'This agreement with little alteration was signed by both sides in Venice on November 27, 1932. It cost Austria about 180 works, among them about eighteen of outstanding importance; the most painful of the losses were several weapons of the finest workmanship, a few outstanding Corvinus manuscripts, the splendid reliefs of Matthias and his consort, and finally the portrait of the Infanta Maria Theresa, ascribed to Careno. To these must be added six other pictures of not very great importance from the picture gallery, about twenty modern Hungarian paintings, four medallions and coins, and further losses of weapons, and a few sacrifices of pieces of sculpture. Austria had to put her collections at the disposal of Hungary on favourable terms, to agree to a veto on the sale of any object of interest to Hungary and, following the fashion of the times, to promise friendly treatment of Hungarian exhibitions . . . On the Hungarian side all further claims of any kind on Austrian cultural possessions were solemnly renounced, and, finally, Hungary contributed a number of not very important pieces to Austrian collections. Nobody could welcome an agreement costing us such sacrifices, but as they were imposed on us by force we must reconcile ourselves to them with a good conscience as the best result obtainable. We must not consider merely the painfulness of the sacrifices; we have to remember too the claim to joint-ownership, the great number of objects of the utmost importance demanded of us, the difficulty encountered by weak countries in repelling attacks which stronger ones might ignore, and that, whereas the Hungarian claims were widely supported by public opinion, our resistance was not . . .'

Thus, fourteen years after the end of the war and the dissolution of the Hapsburg monarchy the problem of art plunder in this region was solved in a manner which was clearly in accord with the political ideas of that day: by negotiated agreement. The attitude of the 'Western Powers', mentioned above, undoubtedly contributed to this result. All in all, the Treaty of

Versailles was more lenient than historical example and the demands of the French press might have suggested. Moreover the French, not to mention their allies, never, as the Italians did in Vienna, extorted works of art in advance of the peace terms or in excess of them. In the case of Austria the Western Powers went even further: once Austria-Hungary was laid low and the political and military goal had been achieved, they displayed their interest in maintaining Vienna as the nucleus of Austrian culture and the historic centre of all that part of Europe, which the French in particular wished to influence politically, economically and financially and to save from collapse.

19

Plunder on the Home Front
and Abroad

While this agreement between Austria and Hungary was being concluded, a man in Germany who was opposed to negotiated agreements of any sort, in art as well as in politics, was preparing to seize power.

The view of art represented by Hitler, a view compounded of the intoxication of power, lack of education and race-hatred, found its first and alarming expression in the closing of the modern section of the former Crown Prince's National Gallery in Berlin, the so-called Chamber of Horrors, by the Reichs Minister for Education on October 30, 1936—just after the departure from Berlin of the foreign visitors to the Olympic Games.

Two months before this, the National-Socialist director of the Folkwang Museum at Essen had thrown out a painting by Kandinsky as a public act of purification and sold it to a dealer for 9,000 marks. In a subsequent discussion, he went on to demand that specimens of degenerate art should not only be tracked down in museums but also in their private lurking-places, and confiscated, handed over, or destroyed on the spot on pain of punishment.

Attacks, distortions, misrepresentations followed at short intervals, from Hans Hinkel, head of the Reichs Art Department, later Special Commissioner of the Third Reich for the Jewish Problem among Artists and plenipotentiary of the Reichs Government for the total war effort of the all German Rundfunk, or from Adolf Ziegler, President of the Reichs Department of the Plastic Arts, and many another National-Socialist.

On June 30, 1937, Ziegler received through Goebbels, the Reichs Minister for Popular Enlightenment and Propaganda, Hitler's authorization 'to select and to take into safe custody for the purpose of exhibition the examples of German degenerate art to be found in German imperial, provincial or municipal possession'. By July 6, Ziegler, on the strength of this 'Führer's order', visited the Wallraf-Richartz Museum in Cologne to inspect its modern section, which he condemned to destruction in spite of all the museum staff could do to interpose a delay or to create a diversion; at one blow Cologne lost its whole collection of Post-Impressionist art—most of it for ever. Finally, on July 19, Ziegler's 'authorization' produced the Munich 'Exhibition of Depraved Art', which was later to be seen also in Berlin, Leipzig, Düsseldorf and other cities interested in art. Paul Ortwin Rave, author of a very impressive account of National-Socialist policy with respect to art, wrote in 1949:

'The show was opened by Ziegler with a speech which unfortunately was disseminated only by the Rundfunk and so is not on record for reference. But thousands were present on the day. Of all the subsequent exhibitions of depraved art it made the greatest sensation in and outside Germany and hence has been widely remembered. There were two reasons. It was not just a local matter, got up by the Nazis of the place, but an enterprise sanctioned and carried out by the highest authorities. Also it was not one gallery which had been pillaged for this miserable purpose; all the larger galleries, twenty-five in number, had been methodically plundered of their most valuable and best known works, now crowded together in the least suitable conditions. One or two rooms of the cast collection of the Archaeological Institute in the old buildings of the Hofgarten had been vacated for them. All the pictures selected and forwarded by Ziegler's committee were huddled together in these long, narrow galleries with the worst

Q 233

possible lighting, because the windows were partly obscured by the screens projecting in front of them in which there were gaps that dazzled the eyes. The pictures were hung as though by idiots or children just as they came, as close together as possible, obstructed by pieces of sculpture on stands or on the ground, and provided with provocative descriptions and obscene gibes . . .

'The painters of the Brücke bore the brunt of the attack. Nolde was represented by twenty-seven paintings, Schmidt-Rottluff and Kirchner with twenty-five each, Otto Müller with thirteen. There were nine or ten of Rohlfs, Beckmann and Kokoschka, seven or eight of Corinth, Hofer, Heckel and Feiniger, six each of Dix, Molzahn, Pechstein and Franz Marc, among them the *Turm der Blauen Pferde* and also Lehmbruck's *Grosse Kniende*. There were foreigners with anything up to five, Jankel Adler, Marc Chagall, Wassily Kandinsky, El Lissitzky, Jean Metzinger, Piet Mondrian. Works by Nauen, Purrmann, Werner Heuser, Caspar, Scharff and others were hung under the inscription, "Such until today were the instructors of German youth."

'Now followed the operation called by Hitler and his associates a "purification", which was in fact nothing else but the plundering of the German people in a manner never before known. In all the towns of Germany pictures and works of sculpture which Ziegler and his uneducated committee called depraved were swept up in a campaign of barefaced plunder—even Munch and van Gogh were numbered with the proscribed; Grünewald was not spared the reproach of having the psychosis of original sin and Rembrandt was called the artist of the ghetto.

'Twelve thousand drawings and 5,000 pictures and sculptures were removed on that occasion from 101 public collections. Hitler inspected them in a store in Berlin and said that on no account would any of them be given back; on the contrary, he had no scruples over deciding on confiscation without compensation . . .

'Works by Cézanne, Signac, van Gogh, Munch and Franz Marc, taken from public galleries, were sold in this way through Angerer. Of the three paintings by Marc one came from Halle and two from the National Gallery of Berlin, the *Drei Rehe* and *Der Turm der Blauen Pferde*. The four by Munch all came from Berlin, among them *Die Schnelschipper*, a present from the artist. It was only when this scandalous circumstance was pointed out that it was finally given back. The most valuable items were the paintings by van Gogh, the portrait of Dr Gachet from Frankfurt and three from the National Gallery, among them the famous Garden of Daubigny. Signac's landscape (*St Tropez*) also came from Berlin; the Cézanne was from the Folkwang Museum at Essen. Alarm and consternation spread among collectors and art lovers, and there was anxiety also for the museums since these high-handed doings might deprive them of the private support and legacies they so much relied on. When the art dealer, Karl Haberstock, armed with a special authorization proceeded to commandeer the lovely Tahiti painting by Gauguin from the Cologne Gallery, the "Friends of the National Gallery" decided to anticipate the blow and to get rid of pictures by Braque, Juan Gris and Picasso, which seemed to be in danger.

'Besides all that Göring diverted to his own uses and the selection touring the country as an exhibition, there were many thousands of works from the German museums, oil paintings, watercolours, pastels, drawings, pieces of sculpture and a great quantity of prints and engravings; all this was stored in a warehouse in Köpenicker Strasse in East Berlin. What was to be done with it all? Documents of the Reichs Propaganda Ministry have turned up to relieve our curiosity. On the instructions of Goebbels of May 1938, a committee was appointed with the task of disposing of "the confiscated works of depraved art". The chairman, Franz Hofmann, selected seven colleagues, Ziegler, Schweitzer, Heinrich Hoffmann, Robert Scholz, representing Rosenberg's Office, and three art dealers, Haberstock, Meder, and Taeuber of Munich. While these three were busy behind the scenes, four dealers who were familiar with modern art and had connections abroad were given the special task of arranging for the sale. They were allowed to pick out what they liked and to sell them for foreign currency, but they were expressly forbidden to let it be thought that these works were of any value in Germany itself. Owing to the distance there was no indication that they came from German public collections.

'Dr Rolf Hetsch, of the Reichs Propaganda Ministry, had meanwhile made a catalogue of the confiscated works in six volumes. From this it appears that 730 items (including many drawings) were exhibited in the exhibition of depraved art. Later the number for propaganda exhibition was put higher— at 1,265; it is possible that the Institute for Cultural and Economic Propaganda, which arranged the exhibitions, supplied a second enterprise of the same sort, *Der Ewige Jude*, from the same source. The warehouse in Köpenicker Strasse is said to have accommodated altogether 1,290 oil paintings, 160 pieces of sculpture, 7,350 watercolours, drawings and prints and 5,300 loose sheets in 230 portfolios, making a total of 12,890 items.

'Introduced by his business acquaintance, Haberstock, the art dealer, Theodor Fischer of Lucerne inspected the goods and gave it as his opinion in a letter to Hoffmann of October 8, 1938, that the best means of liquidating the assets would be an international auction, proposals for which he enclosed. £3,000 sterling was the estimated return. The committee agreed, but withdrew some of the works listed, among them Slevogt's *Sardanapalus* (Berlin) and pieces of sculpture by Renée Sintenis and Fiori.

'In a report to Goebbels dated November 28, 1936, Hoffmann had given warning that the warehouse would soon be required as a grain store and would have to be vacated. The warehouse was in fact cleared on March 20, 1939, and the supposedly unsaleable remnant was burned in the yard of the chief fire-station to the number of 1,004 oil paintings and pieces of sculpture and 3,825 watercolours and drawings.

'By this time many outstanding works had gone abroad never to return and consequently the full light of world publicity was no longer shunned. The contacts with Fischer in Lucerne already mentioned were now to be carried to a successful conclusion. A final selection of 125 works was agreed upon and a plentifully illustrated and well produced catalogue was published. The works were all of the first rank. There were fifteen by Corinth alone (all masterpieces of the Berlin National Gallery), only three, however, by Liebermann, eight each by Marc, Hofer and Kokoschka, seven by Barlach and four by Lehmbruck, seven by Nolde and many more besides by all the members of the Brücke School. Coming to the French, there were four by Matisse, three Picassos of the blue period, and examples of Braque, Derain, Chagall, Pascin, Marie Laurencin; also the National Gallery Modigliani, the Mannheim Ensor, even the Frankfurt Gauguin and the Munich self-portrait by van Gogh. The Galerie Fischer showed the collection first for ten days in May in the Guildhall in Zürich, then for the whole of June in the Grand Hôtel National in Lucerne, where the auction was to be held.

'The Galerie Fischer was criticized in many quarters, particularly by American art lovers, for contributing to German armaments through the proceeds of the sale. Fischer replied to this charge in a circular letter; he said the idea was ridiculous and unjustifiable. The proceeds would be used exclusively to buy paintings by German artists for the benefit of the galleries from which the auctioned pictures had come. In the event, the galleries never saw a single English pound, the currency in which the prices were reckoned, nor a single Swiss frank. On June 30, the day of the sale, Lucerne was crowded with dealers, collectors and custodians and journalists from Switzerland, France, Belgium, Holland, England and America, and the whole town, according to a Dutch correspondent, was *en fête* all day long. The German public collections, after leading the world in their zeal for contemporary

art, lost their place for ever on that shameful day, to the pity-
ing shrugs of the whole world.'

Meanwhile developments in Germany had progressed much
further than that. In the order relating to the '*Einsatz*' of
Jewish possessions of December 3, 1938, we find:

Article IV

Jewellery, Jewels and Works of art

14

(1) Jews are forbidden to acquire, to pawn or to sell on
their own account any object of gold, platinum or silver,
also precious stones and pearls. Such articles, with the exception
of the realization of a pledge already in the hands of a non-
Jewish mortgagee at the time of the coming into force of this
order, may only pass out of Jewish possession through the channel of official purchasers appointed by the Reich. The same
applies to other jewellery and works of art as long as the price
of each item exceeds 1,000 Reichs Mark.

This order comes into force on the day of promulgation.

In connection with the *Abschiebung*, or pushing out, of the
Jews, the Reichs Minister for Finance on November 4, 1941,
further ordered not only the seizure of Jewish possessions but as
follows:

'Works of art (pictures, sculpture, etc), which are not clearly
objects of no value, are not to be sold. They are to be stored
in a proper manner and reported to the local representative
of the Reichs Chamber of the graphic and plastic arts. He
will say within one month whether these objects have museum
value. In that case special instructions will be issued. The rest
can be sold.'

When Hitler started on his wars in 1939, a new phase of art
plunder set in with them. The Army was determined to resume

the policy of art protection carried out in the First World War. Offices were created whose staffs were entrusted with the task of making inventories of the artistic possessions of Poland, France, Holland, Belgium, later of Greece and Russia, of protecting them against damage, robbery, etc. and to take care that they did not suffer from the consequences of war.

In the First World War the state and the army formed a unity in so far as in both the same tradition and moral outlook prevailed, and men of the same kind and the same convictions were in control. In the Second World War, on the contrary, the state and the army were by no means identical, nor was their answer to the question how war booty was to be dealt with. The state was in the hands of the Party and was determined to carry further that policy of plunder which it had initiated with such marked success in the case of depraved art. The army, on the other hand, strove to keep clear of the dirty business, which in Göring's case took the form of thieving on his own account, or, if possible, to put a stop to it in the interests of the good repute of the German army and the German people.

For a start the Jews had, of course, to bear the brunt in the conquered countries. A secretary of the German Embassy in Paris reported to Ribbentrop's Foreign Office:

'In pursuance of an order received from RAM for the safeguarding of Jewish artistic property in France, the initial steps were promptly taken. The relative lists were drawn up. In this matter, too, difficulties from the side of the military administration had to be overcome, in particular there were the general orders of the Commander-in-chief in France relating to the protection of art by which any removal of any work of art in French possession was expressly forbidden. After conferring with the head of the home administration, the chief of the military administration, and Secretary of State Schmidt, I obtained permission for the employment of the Secret Field Police for the safeguarding of Jewish artistic property and for conveying it into the keeping of the German

Embassy. This operation, in which several experts of my commission are taking part, has begun today with the search of the house of the Jew, Mandel. It is proposed to send all the art property stored next door to the German Embassy to Berlin by rail and not by road. Herr Dr Schmidt is providing suitable accommodation in some of the rooms of the Castle in Berlin. The consent of the army will have to be obtained for the transport from Paris to Berlin . . .

Kuensberg.'

But a *'citissime'* telegram, with the same signature and despatched on the same day, proves that it was not only works of art in private hands which were to be 'safeguarded':

'For Dept. Germany and Dept. Protokoll.—In pursuance of instructions received from the Reichs Minister for Foreign Affairs on July 21, 1940, preparations were promptly set in motion for the safeguarding of publicly owned works of art in France. First the Château of Chambord was inspected and the results already communicated obtained. Conferences with the Chief of the Military Administration in France, General Streccius, and his deputy in matters of the protection of art, Count Metternich, made it clear that army commands would not be given orders to further our task. This is still the situation today and the opposition we have to overcome is as great as ever. Thus in order to preserve a united front in face of the French authorities, an agreement was made through the Ambassador that the required lists of the works of art carried off should be provided through Count Metternich's office. As I was no further on by August 24, I went with my staff to the administration of the national museums to demand the lists and obtained them. To complete them it was necessary to have the authentication of the officials concerned in the delivery of the articles. The examination of the several thousand pages by the professors of my committee has got so far that the completion of the task may be expected by Thursday evening . . . '

240

19. The Crown of Prince Bocskay in the Vienna Treasure Chamber.

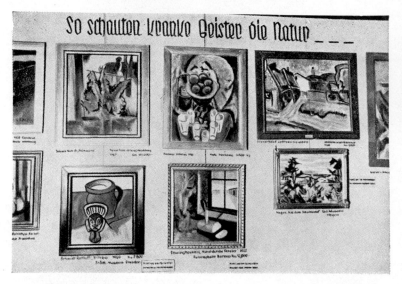

So schauten kranke Geister die Natur ___

20. The exhibition of 'Depraved Art' at Munich, 1937, with pictures by Schmidt-Rottluff, Kirchner, Davringhausen and Nagel.

21. Göring with the Mayor of Berlin, Lippert, and chief-secretary Körner choosing a picture for his own collection.

Count Wolff Metternich, mentioned in this report, later wrote an account of these events which leaves no doubt of the conflicting views of the Army and the *Einsatzstab Rosenberg* on the question of art plunder:

' . . . Early in August 1940, I received confidential information that a legation secretary, Freiherr von Kuensberg, had arrived in Paris, charged with a special commission to take possession of documents of the French Foreign Office in the war area. He said that he also had the task of confiscating a number of works of art, particularly such as were in the possession of Jews and other elements hostile to Germany. This was the first I had heard since taking over my duties of any attempt to misappropriate works of art either by official orders or on that pretence. It was also the first I had heard of the confiscation of the artistic property of Jews . . .

'I was convinced from the outset that von Kuensberg's activities were illegal and that he was merely a sort of modern freebooter, all the more because, as I was assured, he was set on going about his business without the knowledge of the art protection authorities. His arrival coincided with a push by Abetz, the Ambassador, which obviously had for its objective the withdrawal of movable works of art in France from the care of "Art Protection" and the manoeuvring of them into the power of the Embassy. It was clear to me that if the care of movable works of art was taken out of the hands of "Art Protection" and therefore of the Commander-in-chief, the door would be thrown wide open to depredation of every sort and that the protection of art would be reduced to a farce . . .

'I therefore reported the matter at once to the Commanding Officer, General Streccius, my superior officer. He in turn reported to Field-Marshal von Brauchitsch and received for answer that representatives of the Embassy or Foreign Office might be allowed to look at the lists of the works of art, but that none of the articles themselves might be moved.

Further, depots in the provinces were to be closely guarded. General Streccius had already had Chambord guarded on his own intiative. He made the same order for the other depots on September 1, 1940.

'A few days later I received a visit from Herr von Kuensberg and his staff. It was then I learned the full shamelessness of their plan. On the pretext of defective accommodation at Chambord, its contents (meaning important pictures) were to be taken to the Louvre, where a selection could be made at leisure and arrangements made for transport to Germany. In accordance with Field-Marshal Brauchitsch's decision, the representatives of the Embassy were to be allowed to see the lists of the works of art involved. The preparation of these naturally took some time, as they had in part to be compiled for the first time. Meanwhile members of Kuensberg's gang and the Embassy exerted pressure on the staffs of the French state museums in the most tactless and insupportable manner and finally extorted the lists from them by threat. With the permission of General Streccius, a visit to Chambord and other depots was arranged, in which, besides members of Kuensberg's lot, the expert adviser on Art Protection attached to the army in France, Dr Kuetgens, and other experts took part; as expected, it was found that the accommodation provided for the pictures was in all respects beyond criticism. With that, Kuensberg's plan was shown up and he and his commission returned to Berlin . . .

'The first mention of art and antiquities in Jewish possession was in the already quoted instruction from the head of the OKW of June 30 to the Commandant of Paris. Expropriation was not then the intention. At that time various works of art were taken to a house near the Embassy in the Rue de Lille by persons employed by the Embassy. They soon let it be known that they were members of a so-called *Einsatzstab Rosenberg*, the functions of which only became apparent by degrees. It was one of those numerous organizations which grew up beside the military administration in occupied countries and were responsible to some non-military authority in the Reich.

'There was a danger that the works already confiscated might be carried off, and also that they might deteriorate in the unsuitable conditions of the rooms in the Rue de Lille, and therefore by order of the Commanding Officer in Paris the Louvre was requested to give them accommodation. As nothing had been said up to now about their transport to Germany, it was hoped that they might be safe there.

'When the *Einsatzstab Rosenberg* began its operations it was another matter, because henceforward expropriation was carried out systematically and the intention of carrying off the spoil to Germany was openly declared.

'By the Führer's order, the *Einsatzstab* was to pursue its aims as a special command, responsible only to itself. This put the military administration, and with it "Art Protection", out of court. The OKW and the Commanding Officer accordingly refused to accept any responsibility for proceedings which they regarded as unlawful . . .

'The *Einsatzstab* made use of the rooms in the Louvre to start with; later they exchanged them for the exhibition rooms in the Jeu de Paume.

'Although it was clear even by the end of 1940 that the booty would be carried off to Germany and that Hitler and Göring intended to share it out between themselves and some of the German public collections, I decided to report to Göring when he came to Paris in February 1941 to inspect the spoil. I cherished the faint hope that it might be possible to say something of the objects and principles of Art Protection, and possibly to add a word or two about the scruples which might be felt over the treatment of Jewish artistic property. The risk was considerable, as I found when I was roughly cut short and dismissed.

'It was no secret from the autumn of 1940 onwards that elements in the Reich, supported by the NSDAP, were systematically and successfully robbing the military administration, set up by the Army, of one function after another. Thus the authority of this supreme OKH creation slowly crumbled away. I had to look on while "Art Protection", which was of course entirely dependent on the support of Military Administration and could under no circumstances submit to the influence of these alien elements, was slowly and surely undermined . . .'

Already on June 3, 1940, Field-Marshal Keitel had communicated an order to the Commander-in-chief of the army to the effect that Hitler had acceded to, and confirmed, a proposal of Reichs Führer Rosenberg that libraries and archives in occupied countries in Western Europe should be searched for documents of value to Germany, and that these documents should be taken possession of. The Secret State Police were to be entrusted with this operation, supported by archivists appointed by Reichs Führer Rosenberg. This order marked the beginning of the activities of the *Einsatzstab Rosenberg*, which later was busy also in Scandinavian countries—in the interests of the Party; it was responsible for the equipment of the so-called 'High School of the NSDAP', which was to come into being after the war. Rosenberg noted on September 6, 1940, in his *Political Diary*:

'I told the Führer of the find we had made in one of the Rothschild palaces in Paris: trap-door and concealed cellar with sixty-two cases of documents and books. There was also a small case containing porcelain buttons, which had belonged to Frederick the Great. On each one the uniform of a regiment was beautifully painted.'

Such finds left Rosenberg no peace. Ten days later he remarked:

'I told the Führer today that questions of law arose in connection with much of the stuff in the West . . .

'The French Government has outlawed some members of the Rothschild family and says that the Rothschild fortune has been forfeited to the state. Hence the German administra-

tion in France is in doubt whether it can any longer be regarded as enemy-Jewish property. I say yes, and all the more
because there are other members of the Rothschild family in
the south of France, who are still French citizens. The Rothschild family is an enemy-Jewish family and all machinations
whatsoever to rescue their possessions ought to leave us unmoved.

'The Führer agreed with me entirely, and said that this
was no case for scruples; we should carry off everything with
the least possible delay.

'I then brought up the Polish library. It had been taken to
France from Poland and put at the disposal of the French
Government for the purpose of research into Polish history.
Anti-German reconstructions of the history of Eastern Europe
had been fabricated out of this material time and time again.
In my view this library, too, ought to be removed to Germany
to serve the purposes of study we had in mind.

'The Führer emphatically endorsed my opinion and said
that even if the library had been Polish property, it would
automatically have become German property today.

'The Führer directed Colonel Schmundt to communicate
with the Commander-in-chief in France to that effect through
the OKW.

'Berlin, September 16, 1940.

(signed) A. Rosenberg.'

Hitler and Göring also had their own agents at work, who had
to pick out special plums from the great mass of booty and set
them aside for the Führer and the Reichs Marshal, and this in
such quantities that even Rosenberg became uneasy and insisted
on members of his staff obtaining receipts. The packing-cases
were marked H or AH, or G. At the Nuremberg Trials, however,
Rosenberg 'knew' that it was Göring's intention 'to leave his
collections to the German Reich and not as a private legacy'. A
Dr Bunjes of the Rosenberg staff gives more precise details in an
account of a meeting with Göring in Paris:

'I was ordered to report to the Reichs Marshal for the first time on February 4, 1941, at 18.30 in the Quai d'Orsay. Herr Feldführer von Behr of the *Einsatzstab Rosenberg* was also present. He wanted to know what was the actual situation with regard to the seizure of Jewish art property in occupied territory in the west. He took the opportunity to give Herr von Behr photographs of the objects the Führer wished to acquire for himself, and also of those he himself desired.

'As a matter of duty I informed the Reichs Marshal of the meeting to discuss the protest of the French Government about the "work of the *Einsatzstab Rosenberg*" which was held in the office of the Ministerial Director Dr Best. The Reichs Marshal said he would mention the matter to the Führer . . .

'Reichs Marshal Göring went on to ask news of the casting of the Diana of Fontainebleau. I handed him the contract concluded with Rudier for the taking of the cast. The Reichs Marshal was entirely satisfied with the contract and hoped soon to see the completed work . . .

'I then brought up the question of the collection of paintings on glass belonging to Reichsfreiherr von Stein. The Reichs Marshal is inclined to purchase the collection for his library at Karinhall, but thinks the price rather high and would like to have another word with the Führer first . . .

'On Wednesday, February 5, 1941, I was summoned by the Reichs Marshal to meet him in the Jeu de Paume, where he was inspecting the Jewish art treasures recently collected there.

'The Reichs Marshal inspected the exhibition, escorted by myself, and made a selection of the works to be sent to the Führer and those he wished to include in his own collection.

'I took the opportunity of being alone with the Reichs Marshal to draw his attention again to a note of protest of the French Government against the activity of the *Einsatzstab Rosenberg*, in which they referred to the clause in the Hague Convention recognized by Germany in the truce of Compiègne, and I pointed out that General Stulpnagel apparently took a view of the safeguarding of Jewish art treasures which was in contradiction with that entertained by the Reichs Marshal.

'The Reichs Marshal went into the matter thoroughly and directed as follows:

'(1) My orders are authoritative. You do exactly as I order. The works of art collected in the Jeu de Paume will be loaded at once in a special train and sent to Germany. Those items which are for the Führer and those which are for the Reichs Marshal will be loaded in separate wagons attached to the Reichs Marshal's special train and will accompany him on his return to Berlin at the beginning of next week. Herr Feld-führer von Behr will accompany the Reichs Marshal in his special train on his journey to Berlin.

'When I objected that the lawyers might be of another opinion and that the Commander-in-chief in France might make representations, the Reichs Marshal replied in these words: "Dear Bunjes, leave that to me. I am the highest lawyer in the State."

'The Reichs Marshal promised to send the written order for the removal of this Jewish property to Germany on Thursday, February 6, by courier from his headquarters to the chief of Military Administration, Paris . . .'

When the *Einsatzstab* made an interim report on its operations in 1943, it appeared that between September 17, 1940, and April 7, 1943, ten trains of ninety-two wagons, making a total of 2,765 packing-cases, had left for Germany, containing paintings, antique furniture, tapestries and other works of art. A special consignment of fifty-three articles had been despatched direct to the 'Führerbau' in Munich, and another with 594 pictures, pieces of sculpture, articles of furniture and textiles to Göring.

Originally Schloss Neuschwanstein was intended as the depot for all plundered or confiscated works of art, but when it was filled to overflowing, the administration responsible for Bavarian castles arranged for further space to be available in Schloss Herrenchiemsee. This, too, was soon filled, and the Reichs-statthalter 'created' further storage space in a Salesian monastery in Swabia and a castle on the upper Danube.

The *Einsatzstab* inventory up to April 1, 1943, gives 9,455 objects; among them:

    5,255 paintings
      297 sculptures
    1,572 pieces of old furniture
      307 textiles
    2,224 smaller objects including oriental works of art.

But, as mentioned above, this was only an interim report. Later, Rosenberg produced thirty-nine volumes with about 2,500 photographs of works of art 'seized' by his 'staff'. But by July 15, 1944, the 'seizures' had increased greatly. A list of those days includes 21,903 articles:

    5,281 paintings, pastels, watercolours and drawings
      684 miniatures, glass, enamel, books and manuscripts
      583 pieces of sculpture, terracottas, medallions and plaques
    2,477 pieces of furniture of historic and artistic value
      583 tapestries, carpets, embroideries, etc.
    5,825 articles of craftsmanship, such as porcelain, bronzes, faience, stone-ware, jewellery, coins, objects made from precious stones
    1,286 works of oriental art, bronzes, carvings, porcelain, pictures, screens, weapons
      259 objects of ancient art, sculpture, bronzes, vases, jewellery, dishes, cut gems, terracottas

In an introduction he says, 'The artistic and monetary value of these works is beyond computation.'

If all these objects had been photographed and the photographs bound up together, they would probably have required 300 or more portfolios. When Rosenberg produced the first volumes of his illustrated catalogue he wrote:

'The rest of this catalogue, now in preparation, will appear at suitable intervals. I will allow myself, in presenting the report you desired, to offer you, my Führer, twenty more of the portfolios in the hope that this brief concern with the beautiful creations of art, to which you are so deeply attached, may shed a ray of beauty and joy on the stern and exalted trials of your daily life.'

The pride which is audible in every word of this dedicatory letter was well justified. When prosecuting counsel at Nuremberg had some of the photographs thrown on the screen, the court saw paintings by Palma Vecchio, Velasquez, Joshua Reynolds, Watteau, Rubens, Rembrandt and Van Dyck, a piece of jewellery of the sixteenth century of gold, enamel and pearls, a piece of tapestry of the seventeenth century, a Japanese painting, Chinese porcelain, a cabinet with silver inlay of the time of Louis XIV, and a silver altar-piece of Spanish origin of the fifteenth or sixteenth century. 'I doubt,' counsel went on, 'whether any museum in the world, the Metropolitan in New York, the British Museum in London, the Louvre in Paris, or the Tretiakow Gallery in Moscow, could furnish such a list . . . Never in the history of the world was so great a collection assembled with so little scruple.'

20

Revolutionary Plunder
without Looting

If you look through the newspapers and periodicals of 1918 and 1919, you will find frequent references to the unexampled plundering by the Russian revolutionaries, 'the rabble of St Petersburg', the 'red insurrection' and so on. The most valuable treasures of the Hermitage, we were told, were no more; the eyes had been cut out of the pictures, and representations of the Madonna smeared. The Gallery of the Winter Palace in Petersburg had perished wholly or in part during the revolution, while at the same time Swedish newspapers reported that the famous collection of the Duke of Leuchtenberg had been safely transported to Sweden. The *Berliner Zeit* ended one of its reports about events in Riga with the words:

'All copper, brass, bronze, tin have been removed from the Cathedral and City museums; from the nine old bronze cannon of the Cathedral museum to the probably worthless medallions and plaques of the City museum [in terms of metal, that is to say] not to mention all objects of gold and silver, nothing is left. All the wonderful silver treasure of the Guild of the Schwarzen Haüpter, the most famous secular treasure of the north, with the long series of ceremonial services for the table and ornamented dishes dating from the beginning of the sixteenth century have been removed from the Scwarzhaüpterhaus and carried off to Moscow.'

Yet by October 1918, it was found that although the stories

250

of plunder and loot in Riga and other non-Russian places might be true, those concerning Russian towns, particularly St Petersburg, were mostly invented by people who were far from the scene, but wished to discredit the revolution. An eye-witness account says:

'Outwardly all is fairly quiet in St Petersburg and the news about street-fighting, incendiarism and other stirring events, is either sheer invention or gross exaggeration. On the other hand, the inward upheaval, the social deflation, etc, go farther and take more grotesque forms than anyone in Germany imagines. All that has been said about works of art, too, is sheer invention. The pictures in the Hermitage are nearly all accounted for and in good order. The re-opening of the gallery, the precious contents of which are still in Moscow, is to take place in November. The great private collections have been nationalized and only the Leuchtenberg (the best of which, however, was sold in England twelve years ago) was got out to Sweden for one and half million roubles. Sweden, all told, has bought a lot, but principally smaller pieces, and at very high prices, far higher than would be paid at German auctions for similar pictures. It is an unfounded rumour that great numbers of works have passed into American and English hands.'

The Soviet Government put an export ban on all works of artistic or historical value in September 1918. 'Many formerly rich and distinguished families were hard hit by this,' according to the December number of the German periodical *Der Kunsthandel*.

'Many of them tried to procure the means of existence by selling the old pictures, furniture, glass, porcelain which had been in their castles, country or town houses for centuries. Others may have attempted to get these possessions out of the country before they were totally destroyed by marauding peasants and workmen. Antiques by the shipload are said to have left St Petersburg for Sweden and Denmark during the last months. A strict prohibition of sales to foreigners is spoken of.'

Doubtless some of these shiploads were sent abroad to provide their émigré owners with a livelihood. The prohibition is identical with the measures adopted in France after 1789.

It was not until 1925 that really reliable accounts of the whole course of the revolution were available. A British member of Parliament, Martin Conway, went to Russia at the end of 1924 to see works of art there. 'And particularly those in public possession, or in the possession of the Czars before the revolution, also the private collections, the palaces and great houses, cathedrals, monasteries and their treasures, about all of which the British public, certainly, know nothing whatever.'

He was not concerned with the fact of the revolution itself; he was interested only in the effects of plunder, dispersal and destruction on the artistic inheritance of the Czars, the Church and the nobles. What chiefly overwhelmed him was not so much the Hermitage in Petersburg and the museums of Moscow as the bulk of unimaginable riches which had come down from the days of the Czars, 'the quantities of jewels, the profusion of silverware, more easily weighed by the ton than enumerated, the porcelain filling one gallery after another, not to mention the 75,000 pieces which there is no room to exhibit'. He mentions the large vases, tables and whole walls of lapis lazuli and malachite, about 20,000 ancient and modern statues and busts, enormous collections of drawings and sketches, endless accumulations of furniture, acres of hangings and carpets, thousands of ikons, antiques of all periods, among them 10,000 made of gold, state-coaches, arms and armour, dresses and robes stitched with pearls, books in gold bindings, goblets, crystal cups, gems, crowns, sceptres, historic costumes, whole libraries of illuminated manuscripts, early prints, etc.

The merest fraction of all this incredibly valuable artistic treasure was destroyed in the course of the revolution, or damaged or carried off, an astonishing thing when it is remembered that the Winter Palace was taken by storm and the rooms searched by the mob for its surviving defenders. The castle of Gatschina too was the scene of fighting and the Kremlin was shelled. Yet all accounts of looting and destruction in these buildings were proved to be false. Martin Conway was forced to contrast this with the events in France after 1789. There, possessions of the crown and church perished in vast quantities, but not in Russia. It is true the Russian revolutionaries stripped their opponents of all they had, but it might almost be said that they were guided by the Communist Manifesto, and while they murdered Czarists, reactionaries, imperialists and interventionists, they respected their property as the property of the people. And although the prohibition on the export of works of art was aimed first as a war measure against the 'ancient owners', even deeper went the desire not to lose these possessions to the foreigner, who was the enemy too.

The British visitor could not understand how the museums had survived the chaos of the revolution:

'Apparently the psychology of the Russian masses must be entirely different from that of the mob in the French Revolution. There were moments of the greatest danger, but all the museum staff and their employees down to the last charwoman were at one in the resolute defence of the public property committed to their charge. It must be emphasized that not a single theft took place, although the museums were at the mercy of their staff, who were not subject during those days to any sort of supervision; the custodians, mostly old soldiers, could have filled their pockets with small articles, the value of which they very well knew.'

The policy of confiscation, of appropriation to the socialist state, or, seen from the other side, the plundering by the revolutionaries, led naturally to a vast accumulation of treasures in the public museums. The 11,000 pictures of the Hermitage were increased by 4,000 from private collections, besides many thousands of ikons.

Conway was a convinced upholder of private property. He saw in these Russian confiscations on a huge scale nothing but the proof of how little the public gains from the sacrifices of innumerable individuals. But he could not help admiring the respect for art shown by the revolutionaries and their hangers-on and associates. How different the behaviour of these same Russians was to be a quarter of a century later on foreign soil!

The Vandals were souvenir-hunters, the perpetrators of the Sack of Rome and even the armies of Napoleon himself mere plunderers, eager for loot, compared with the Russians when they invaded Germany. It is not even possible to compare Stalin and his soldiers to Hitler and his 'paladins'. Hitler, Göring, the *Einsatzstab Rosenberg* and all the other plunderers, large or small, of the Third Reich acted in France and elsewhere on the principle that might was right and took what they wanted. The Führer was inspired also by Napoleon's idea that the leadership of Europe having passed, in this case, from France to Germany, museums, galleries, libraries and archives had to follow.

In the case of the Russians in 1945, the belief was that nothing could be in the right hands unless it was in the hands of the proletariat and owned by the communist state. It was a duty therefore to loot all private property of every sort. Further, since the National-Socialist state was a criminal state which had been conquered at the cost of tremendous exertions, all public collections were loot to be carried off, destroyed or scattered to the winds. Lastly, the troops were given the order on crossing the German frontier to take their revenge in all possible ways for the sufferings inflicted on the Russian people.

It is impossible to ascertain in any detail what the consequences were to the property of private persons.

Walter Gorlitz in his book on the *Junkers*, the inhabitants of eastern Germany whom the Bolsheviks so particularly detested, has given some examples. The 25,000 volumes of the library of the Arnim family at Boitzenburg were carried off to Moscow. Castles famous in history, like the great Hohenzollern palace in Berlin, the pride of their districts and the country, were burnt, blown up, reduced to building material, levelled to the ground, because they were monuments of Germany's past. On Russian orders Schloss Stolpe was plundered by the German populace; documents and library, to the value of millions of marks, were removed and a collection of rare vases trampled to fragments on the grass. The valuable collections of the Princes zu Eulenberg-Hertefeld in Schloss Liebenberg perished, as did all the works of art from public galleries stored for safety in the castles of the nobility. This happened to the pictures and other possessions of the Bremer Museum, which had been put for safety in Schloss Karnzow; the vast Eckardstein library perished in Protzel, where squatters in the castle burnt the last volumes to keep themselves warm; the same fate overtook the library of Frau von Friedland in Kunersdorf, a library of 93,000 volumes, including original manuscripts of Chamisso, and the Bethmann-Hollweg archives in Hohenfinow, with all the papers of the former chancellor, and much else.

There was no Denon at work here, no Neveu, and no *Einsatzstab Rosenberg* coming to 'safeguard', to catalogue and carry off, there was simply the free play of the baser instincts of an army deliberately relieved of discipline, and which had later to be restored to discipline by methods that knew no mercy.

In Saxony alone, 200 castles had been destroyed by 1946 lest any memory should remain of the great part played by the nobles in the country's past; and with them, in many cases, perished pictures, libraries, sculpture, porcelain, gold and silverware and precious stones.

Nor did the re-erected Polish state, which had been stripped by the Third Reich, spare artistic possessions in the territories it annexed and occupied. Innumerable works of art were destroyed, castles and houses pulled down to provide material for rebuilding Warsaw and other towns, and movables, in so far as they were not looted and stolen, often ended up in Poland's new or old public collections and became Polish works of art in defiance of their origin. Thus we read in a Polish report of 1946 on 'Making good, losses to Polish Museums':

255

'The severe losses suffered by our museums are in some measure balanced by the contents of private collections which fell to the state in consequence of measures of land-reform, and also of public collections in the territory added to Poland in the West. A quantitative comparison is not possible owing to lack of data, but it appears certain that these new acquisitions, coming as they do from outside, do not make up for our most grievous losses, which are those in the domain of Polish culture.'

This tells us, among other things, that practically the whole of Silesia's movable possessions in the way of art, in so far as it had not fallen a prey to plunder and destruction, had been removed to Poland, principally to Warsaw. The head of what was known as Polish 'Revindication' mentioned, in an account of his operations published in 1947, the despatch of 131 lorry loads and twenty-two railway wagon loads, chiefly of works of art.

The Berlin museums suffered the worst depredations. The Russians knew very well that thanks to Bode and his successors these were the richest collections in Germany; and they were in undisputed and unshared control of Berlin long enough to get to work in their own time.

In 1953 the former state Museums of Berlin published in memory of Wilhelm von Bode an account in one volume of *The Berlin Museums*, according to which their contents were for the most part evacuated shortly before the end of the war. They were discovered in mines in territory occupied by British and American troops. By order of the Army Commands they all had to be removed to the museum of Wiesbaden and the Schloss zu Celle. From 1948–9 all the Berlin works of art were handed over to the loyal keeping of the administrations of Hesse and Lower Saxony, and so came once more into German hands. The various museum departments, of which there were nineteen, made a cautious estimate of the losses incurred through Soviet military occupation. At the last moment many of their treasures were put into two large flak towers, where it was hoped they

would be safe. Yet nearly everything in the Flak Tower Friedrichshain was destroyed by fire, whether deliberately or by
accident has never been ascertained. In any case, the Russians
did nothing to put the fire out, or to let others do so, or to rescue
the works of art, and the fire burned for days. As to the fate of
other works of art removed for safety, here is the report of the
Egyptian Department, made with the express avoidance of
judgment or reproach:

'Then, in May 1945, the Russians set about the removal of
all the objects stored in the cellars of the Mint and the Zoo
Flak Tower, packing them, large and small, in cases. Then,
from December 1945 up to March 1946, followed very considerable consignments from the Museum cellars and the wrecked
galleries of the New Museum. Among these pieces sent eastwards, there were more than 300 of the largest size, many of
the smaller statues of all periods, and a large part of the most
precious small objects, and nearly all the papyri which had
been on view.'

The department of antiquities also suffered very severely. It
lost 18,000 pieces of sculpture, the large and the small frieze of
the Pergamum altar, about 100 pieces of sculpture from Pergamum, those from Magnesia, its whole display of movable
architectural features with the exception of three and the pick
of the works not on view, 8,000 of the miscellaneous objects,
7,000 vases, 9,000 gems, 2,000 pieces of paste, 6,500 terracottas,
among them exquisite Tanagra figures, 3,000 objects from diggings undertaken by the Museum in various places and a library.
Two hundred pictures, among them invaluable works of the
Italian schools and works by Rubens and Van Dyck, perished by
fire in the Flak Tower Friedrichshain. About 250 pictures were
taken from the Museum cellars, mostly of the second and third
rank, but also many of the first rank, the whole contents of the
Schinkel Museum, the whole collection of drawings, etc. The
copperplate engravings in the Zoo Flak Tower were 'carried off
by the Russians before the arrival of the English', and from

the museum itself the complete works of Piranesi in forty volumes. The Museum of Applied Art lost heavily; so did the Museum of Pre- and Early History: gold and silver objects, the *Treasure of Priam* dug up by Schliemann, precious statuettes and stones, old catalogues and 400 cases full of first-class works, 400 cases from Schönebeck on the Elbe, and some also from the Lebus research centre. The Russians carried off all of the Far Eastern Department which was in the Zoo Flak Tower before the arrival of their Western allies. The same occurred with the collection of arms and armour there. The numismatic department 'with its reference library, its German wood and stone moulds, plaster casts and paper money all went East'. They robbed the Museum library of 622 packing-cases of books, 'the main part of the library'.

Never before did a city, a whole nation, suffer such losses by plunder.

Our account of the history of art plunder may close at this point. But art plunder can never end as long as works of art exist and there are people, states and nations to whom art has any meaning. Some plunder because they desire to possess, to enjoy and to control the stock of art; others to humiliate the enemy or to deny him, once conquered and overthrown, the enjoyment and possession of it.

That is one side of the picture. The other, more pleasing and more worthy of imitation, is illustrated by the following episode. The Picture Gallery of Cassel was able in 1956 to issue a catalogue with the title: *Pictures of the Cassel Gallery Returned*, with a preface by the Austrian Minister for Education, in which he said:

'Thirty-six pictures from the Cassel Gallery were removed to Vienna for safety in 1942. They are now restored after having been on display in the Vienna Art History Museum.

258

'It is a matter of course to go to the aid of a neighbour in peril without waiting to ask the why and the wherefore.

'It is also a matter of course that these pictures, now that the danger has passed and that certain difficulties are over, the causes of which are certainly not to be laid at Austria's door, should be returned to their rightful owners. It should be the wish and the aim of all of us that such matters of course should be common form. Austria and Germany are for many reasons called upon to give an example in this case. The restoration of these pictures to Cassel and the friendly gesture of Cassel in permitting them to be previously exhibited in Austria are a contribution to and a proof of what Europe should regard as its common heritage—the ideals of European civilization which even catastrophes and devastation cannot destroy!'

May this prove to be the true answer to the question raised at the outset of this book!

INDEX

260

126, 140, 144, 146, 154, 157–8, 161–2, 167, 224, 252–3
Civil War in England, 100, 102
Clement VII, Pope, 59
Coins, 24–6, 52, 55–6, 77–9, 92, 109, 145, 149, 162, 166, 170, 172–3, 188–9, 207, 220, 230, 248, 258
Colleoni, statue of, 220, Pl.2
Constantinople, 19, 22, 32ff., 41ff., 68–9, 73–4, 93, 101, 112, 123–7, 129–31, 197 (*see also* Byzantium)
Correggio, 93, 96, 113
Craftsmen, removal of, 44–5
Cromwell, Oliver, 98, 100
Crown Jewels, of England, 57
Crusades, 32ff., 44, 68, 149, 197

Damascus, 33–5
Danton, Georges-Jacques, 143
David, Louis, 165, 193
'Decadent' art, 233ff., Pl.20
Denmark, 81, 112, 170, 251
Denon, Dominique Vivant, 85, 165–73, 176–7, 180, 186, 188–93, 195–6, 199, 216, 255, Pl.15
Dirk Bouts' *Last Supper*, 224, 225, Pl.18
Dürer, Albrecht, 90, 99, 102, 144
Dyck, Anthony Van, 97, 101–2, 104–7, 113, 249, 257

Egypt and Egyptian art, 13, 15, 39, 43–4, 112, 122–3, 128–9, 131, 153, 165, 257
Elgin, Thomas Bruce, 7th Earl of, 122–33, 159, 176, 180, 201, Pl.9
Elgin Marbles, 122–33, 176, 180, Pl.10
England and English art, 15, 20, 50, 93, 95ff., 103ff., 110–11, 112, 115, 118–19, 122–3, 128–34, 146–7, 153, 156–62, 166, 170, 173–6, 179–86, 188, 190, 194–5, 197–9, 201ff., 211, 213–14, 225, 237, 249, 251–4, 256–7
Engravings, 163–4, 166, 171–2, 176, 196, 220, 235, 257
Etchings, copper-plate, 116, 165
Etruscans, 24, 196
Eugene, Prince of Savoy, 107–8
Eyck, Brothers van, 146, 217, 223–5

Ferdinand, King of Spain, 184
Flanders and Flemish art, 97, 99, 102, 146, 173, 182
Forgeries, 111, 116, 171, 181
Fragonard's *Stolen Kiss*, 135, 138
France, 31, 60, 67, 70–1, 76, 80, 88, 94, 97, 104, 108–12, 118–19, 122–3, 125, 128, 131, 134, 136, 139–59, 143, 161–77, 179–80, 182ff., 209–20, 222–5, 231, 235, 237, 239–47, 249, 252–4
Franco-Prussian War, 209, 211, 224–5
Frederick the Great, King of Prussia, 113–15, 117–18, 151, 172, 194, 244
Frederick William III, King of Prussia, 187
Frederick-Augustus I, King of Poland, 112–14
Frederick-Augustus II, King of Poland, 115–16, 118, 134
French Revolution, 120–1, 136, 139–99, 162–3, 167–8, 170, 177–8, 180–3, 186–7, 252–3
Frescoes, 67, 178
Furniture, 47, 71, 77–8, 90–2, 98, 108–9, 112, 136–8, 172, 193, 203, 206, 247–9, 251–2

Genoa, 31, 42, 53, 64
Germany and German art, 16, 21, 59–60, 64, 66–9, 71, 75–6, 80–1, 83–90, 93–5, 102–5, 109–12, 117–20, 144–6, 157, 161–6, 168–72, 176, 180–3, 185, 190–1, 195, 200, 208–25, 229, 232–51, 254–6, 258–9
Giorgione, 112
Giotto, 198
Goths, 18–21, 64, 67–8
Grand Tour of Italy, 15, 110, 160–1, 182
Grandson, Battle of, 46–51, 54–7
Greece, 13, 15, 18–19, 33, 37, 73, 101, 122–33, 176, 180, 210, 239
Greeks, Ancient, 13–15, 18–19, 33, 37, 101, 122–33, 145, 159, 175, 179–80
Gregorovius, 21, 61–9
Grimm, Hermann, 31